E. Curran
1962

THE NATIONAL CONFERENCE
OF CATHOLIC CHARITIES

THE
NATIONAL CONFERENCE
OF
CATHOLIC CHARITIES
1910–1960

DONALD P. GAVIN

PROFESSOR OF HISTORY
JOHN CARROLL UNIVERSITY
CLEVELAND, OHIO

CATHOLIC LIFE PUBLICATIONS
BRUCE PRESS • MILWAUKEE

NIHIL OBSTAT:

Harry A. Echle

IMPRIMATUR:

✠ Patrick A. O'Boyle
Archbishop of Washington
February 12, 1962

Foreword

THE Catholic Charities movement in the United States has been blessed with a good sense of timing. It received its initial impetus at a time of significant social change in our country. The young and vigorous profession of social service was still in the process of its own formation when, in 1910, the National Conference of Catholic Charities was established at The Catholic University of America in Washington, D. C. As a result of this initial effort, the Catholic Charities movement was prepared to coordinate and to perfect the activity of individual and institutional efforts in the apostolate of charity in the Church, so that its distinct identity would never be lost in the wider development of the social-welfare field.

This historical review of the National Conference of Catholic Charities is equally well timed. Many significant changes are appearing on the horizon of social welfare in our day. There is, sad to say, a discernible diminution of interest in, and responsibility for, the personal welfare of our neighbors. There is a parallel development of grave concern which expresses itself in the growing tendency to entrust an ever greater measure of responsibility for social welfare into the hands of government. No thinking citizen will deny the responsibility of government for the welfare of all citizens, but voluntary effort and individual responsibility must not in any way be diminished because of the increased interest of government in the social-welfare field.

This historical review is a faithful chronicle of the efforts of many wonderful men and women possessed of dedication, knowledge, and vision, who formalized the structure of Catholic Charities in America and set forth clearly the function of the practice of

charity within the Church. Special commendation is due the leadership exercised by the Society of St. Vincent de Paul and by the
rector and faculty of The Catholic University of America. Catholic
Charities in the United States is indebted to all of them, but to
those of us who have known Catholic Charities so intimately over
the years, the figures of Monsignor William J. Kerby and Monsignor
John O'Grady stand out as the giants of Catholic Charities. Their
vision and their tireless dedication to the cause of charity have
been largely responsible for the stature of the National Conference
of Catholic Charities in our day.

This review restates with needed vigor the commitment of the
Church to the practice of charity through personal service in direct
assistance to those in need, through organized agency programs and
in institutional services of many kinds. From the beginning, this
Conference stressed that charity is an awareness of the bond that
unites man to God, and man to man; that our Catholic Charities
cannot isolate themselves from the life of the community; that
charity and social justice are interrelated; that Catholic Charities
must do more than relieve suffering: they must strive always for a
social order in which principles of social justice are basic and
supreme. This Conference has always had high aims, and has
labored unceasingly to fulfill them. It has sought to bring to the
noblest of causes — the Charity of Christ — the best of human
experience, the highest of motivation, the vision of the newest in
science, but keeping always in mind the intrepid spirit of the pioneer
champions of the poor, who for so long labored lovingly but silently
in ministering to every form of human need.

It is our earnest hope that this account of the National Conference of Catholic Charities will remind all of us in the apostolate of
Christ's Charity of our duty to keep at an ever higher level the
standards of our performance, of our need to improve and to refine
constantly our efforts to obey the commands of Christ to love our
neighbors as ourselves.

✝ Patrick A. O'Boyle
Archbishop of Washington

July 26, 1962

Preface

THE National Conference of Catholic Charities is the central organization for Catholic charities in the United States. In the words of a brochure published by the National Conference "it provides a national service to our Diocesan agencies; it interprets their work on a national scale; it represents the whole of Catholic Charities on national and local issues, and today, increasingly, in international matters since it is a member of the International Conference of Catholic Charities established in Rome on December 12, 1951."

This brief account of the first fifty years of the National Conference of Catholic Charities is an attempt to describe the conditions under which the idea for the conference was conceived, to recount its efforts to provide opportunities for an exchange of views among Catholics engaged in social work, to promote a literature of Catholic social work by encouraging research, to improve standards in the work of relief and prevention of social ills, and to assist diocesan organizations in the development of their programs. One of the more important chapters in this story is the effort of the National Conference to bring to bear on the various proposals in the field of social legislation the impact of Catholic social philosophy.

Throughout its history the National Conference of Catholic Charities has worked closely with the Society of St. Vincent de Paul, the Conference of Religious, the Diocesan Directors of Catholic Charities, and the National Catholic Welfare Conference. This history, however, is not a history of the cooperating organizations but rather of the National Conference itself and its problems in establishing its position and accomplishing its objectives. Nor is this a history of Catholic charitable institutions except in so far as they affect or are affected by the National Conference. Nor is the present study intended to be an exhaustive one of the National Conference; however, it is hoped that enough of the story has been presented to give an evaluation of the farsightedness of the founders of the National Conference and the significance of the accomplishments of the first half century of the Conference's existence.

The author wishes to express his appreciation to Miss Jane Gallagher of the National Conference office for her invaluable assistance in locating materials for the history, for her many helpful suggestions, for her innumerable courtesies on many occasions, and for her valuable criticism of the completed manuscript. Monsignor John O'Grady, secretary of the National Conference since 1920, and his successor, Monsignor Raymond J. Gallagher, must also be commended for their unselfish assistance in making the author's task just a bit easier. The following members of the history department at John Carroll University also leave the author greatly in their debt: Dr. Thomas E. Auge who gave unsparingly of his time to read and discuss the manuscript; Reverend Thomas P. Conry, S.J., who also read the manuscript and whose suggestions were particularly useful. A word of special thanks must go to the Most Reverend Leo C. Byrne, Coadjutor Bishop of Wichita, Kansas, for his frank and constructive criticism. Dr. George E. Grauel, Director of the Department of English at John Carroll University, was most gracious in making suggestions on the final draft. For the errors of commission and omission that remain the author must assume full responsibility.

Contents

THE NATIONAL CONFERENCE
OF CATHOLIC CHARITIES

CHAPTER I

Movement Toward Organized
Charity, 1880–1910

ADDRESSING the annual meeting of the National Conference of
Catholic Charities in 1925, Patrick Cardinal Hayes, Archbishop of
New York, declared that "organized Christian charity, at least in
America, must be recognized in our day as of stern necessity."[1]
This necessity arose from the rapid industrialization and urbanization
of the country in the last quarter of the nineteenth century. The
problem of caring for the less fortunate citizens of the community
had become a complicated and often frustrating one. In the less complex organization of rural society the knowledge of each member of
the community about each other made it much easier to assess the
merits of any case of need, and the cohesive force of the community
made it easier for men of good will to apply the remedy. The
anonymous relationship of the urban area made it difficult to know
the circumstances of the person in need and there was often suspicion on the part of the giver that the recipient might not have
been entirely honest in presenting his case. Even if all claims on
charity in the city were genuine, there was the further problem of
the ever increasing number of these claims, far beyond the individual's ability to cope with. It was the continued efforts of Catholics to carry on the traditional mission of charity in the Church
that prompted Cardinal Hayes to add that an "immense store of
holy energy quite dissipates itself in private charities to the neglect
of greater opportunities . . . with a resulting lack of spiritual exercise and growth in Christlike stature."[2] It was the hope of the
Cardinal that Catholics would come to realize "that organized
charity in no way affects the personal element in the mission of

1

mercy" but rather that it would develop a "sense of union in Christ, by increasing in the faithful lively sympathy for a larger number of God's unfortunates and by educating them to a realization of their power for service."[3]

A Catholic in 1875 would have considered his charitable activities confined to the parish level or, perhaps, to some private organization devoted to charitable activity. Although it was the Ordinary of the diocese who had the responsibility for the care of the poor, it was to the parish priest that the individual Catholic usually turned for guidance in fostering the works of charity. If the parishioner had strong national ties, however, he might turn to the particular society founded by his national group to care for their own immigrants. He might, under other circumstances, support one of the numerous religious communities established to care for neglected children of Catholic families. In any case, he was generally not cognizant of any charitable activity beyond his own local circle. He was usually not aware that problems were arising which were beyond the means of the parish or even the diocese to cope with. Contrary to the traditions of his Church, he was parochial or provincial in his outlook in the field of charity. That Cardinal Hayes should find it necessary as late as 1925 to encourage organized Catholic charities indicates to some extent the difficulty with which Catholics in general accepted the broader horizons of charity.

Reluctance to adopt a wider outlook on charitable activities was not the only cause of opposition by Catholics to the reappraisal of the traditional methods of philanthropy forced by the industrialization and urbanization of society at the turn of the century. Much criticism was directed against the "scientific" approach of the new concepts of social work which displayed a greater tendency to look into the causes of social evils and to try to remove them. Relief was now considered only part of the problem. One result was the great emphasis placed on case work and record files. The fear of many Catholics was that the techniques would destroy the spirit of Christian charity and make it an impersonal thing.

For the most part, however, it would appear that Catholic principles of social reform as enunciated in Pope Leo XIII's Encyclical

Rerum Novarum in 1891 were falling on deaf ears. There was a defensive attitude on the part of many Catholics toward the developments in the field of charity. Some objected to the humanitarian approach of the 1890's, others to the growing professional approach of social work. Much of this opposition was probably colored by previous differences of opinion with the nonsectarian agencies, which were largely Protestant in origin. A particularly bitter controversy had developed with the New York Children's Aid Society in the 1870's and carried through to 1900. The controversy, which we shall treat shortly, involved the relative merits of institutional as against foster home care for children as well as the charge made by Catholics that children were placed in homes by the Society without any regard for the religious faith of the children. The *Proceedings of the National Conference of Social Work* for the last quarter of the nineteenth century reflects some of the bitterness involved.

During this period there was by Catholics an occasional venture outside of local interests when it was realized that an orphanage set up in a parish had grown too large to manage. The orphanage was then turned over to the diocese, where the burden of management often fell on the religious community which staffed it because the bishop found it difficult to enlist diocesan support for such an institution. The parish was content to take care of its own poor and to leave the rest to the bishop.

The organization of charitable activities outside of the Catholic Church proceeded, however, and the new methods continued to gain acceptance despite what some Catholics thought about them. In the early 1870's there had been attempts at organization of boards of public charities on a national basis. The National Conference of Charities and Corrections in 1879 was the outgrowth of these meetings. The Conference continued under this name until 1917, when the name was changed to The National Conference of Social Work. On the local level there were successful attempts to gather together the charity organizations of a single city into a unit. The first Charity Organization Society, as this grouping came to be known, was established in Buffalo in 1877, where the evils of overlapping relief giving were quite noticeable. Other cities soon followed the example of Buffalo, and by 1910, the Charity Organization Society movement had affected nearly every major city. This movement not only was responsible for the spread of the casework technique but also gave birth to a great many private social agencies. The interest was not primarily in relief but rather in eliminating the conditions which made relief necessary. One of the principal interests of the Charity Organization Societies was housing conditions. Improve the environment and you will eliminate many of the causes of poverty, it was argued. The prevention of tuberculosis and efforts to establish juvenile courts were also among the interests of the movement. The whole concept of family social work appears to have developed from these societies.

The social settlement movement, which grew out of the same background as that of the Charity Organization Society, was aimed at providing special programs to teach American customs to immigrants, as well as at giving the more fortunate an opportunity to share their lives with the less fortunate by living in the settlement. Jane Addams, who founded Hull House in Chicago in 1899, and Lillian Wald, who founded Henry Street Settlement in New York City in 1893, are two examples of leaders in the settlement movement. Boys' and girls' clubs to combat juvenile delinquency, work projects, and day nurseries for children of working mothers were among the activities of those interested in the settlement. The movement as a whole, however, did not make any direct contribution to professional social work. It represented a development in which there was not a particular concern for study and research but rather one in which the chief interest was in getting to know one's fellowman and in making his life as comfortable as possible.

By 1908 the "social gospel," having steadily gained in acceptance since the 1880's, had received endorsement from the Federal Council of Churches of Christ in America, which was organized in that year; and in 1909 President Roosevelt called a White House Conference to discuss a program for the care of dependent children. The rising tide of social protest of the last quarter of the nineteenth century had undoubtedly produced results. There was growing conviction that poverty and crime were caused by social conditions and that it was the duty of the social worker to discover the cause and awaken society to its obligations.

During this formative period of organized social work, Catholic charitable agencies had almost no contact with each other. Each did its work in its own way and operated as if there were nothing to be learned from agency contacts with each other. There was little contact with public and other private institutions. Consequently, problems involving the care of children, which was Catholic charities chief interest, were frequently arising. Foster home placement of children, which begins with the efforts of Charles Loring Brace and the New York Children's Aid Society in 1853, caused all kinds of difficulty because of the charge that these children were being placed in homes without any regard to their religious faith. Mr. Brace devoted most of his life to taking children from the streets of New York City and sending them to homes in the Western United States. The New York Catholic Protectory was established in 1863 to care for dependent Catholic children. There was no opposition to the idea of foster homes per se, but there were few Catholic homes available in New York City for these children. Most of the Catholics were relatively recent immigrants and had not established themselves sufficiently to comply with either residence or economic requirements of foster homes. The beginning of systematic child placing for Catholics comes with the establishment of the Catholic Home Bureau of New York in 1898 by the Society of St. Vincent de Paul. A similar bureau was established in Newark, New Jersey, in 1903 by the Reverend Francis Foy. This was further recognition of the foster home trend and the necessity of developing some kind of a program. The Diocese of Boston in 1903, Hartford in 1904, and San Francisco in 1907 also established bureaus to care for dependent children and place them in foster homes.

The organization of public and nonsectarian agencies made many of those interested in Catholic charity realize that, unless similar organization was effected by the Church, problems even greater than those arising out of child-care institutions might well develop. In 1910, with the exception of the Society of St. Vincent de Paul, there were no organized Catholic charities in the United States. The

Society, whose beginnings in the United States date from 1845, had been organized on a national level since 1864 and had held ten national meetings by 1910. There had also been one international meeting in 1904. This accomplishment in organization is all the more remarkable when it is realized that it was achieved despite extremely strong local and diocesan traditions of provincialism in the United States. These traditions, stemming largely from immigrant backgrounds, gave local charity organizations a national rather than a religious outlook.

The Society, with an estimated membership of 12,000 in the United States in 1910, was dissatisfied with the parochial outlook on charity.[4] In Baltimore in 1907 the Vincentians had organized a Central Bureau of the Society devoted to a city-wide program of family work. The bureau employed full-time workers who supplemented the efforts of the parish conferences of the Society. This was an attempt to do for family programs of social work what the New York City Vincentians had done for child placing in 1898. The Bureau was a significant advance in the direction of coordinated Catholic charities in the United States.

One of the most outstanding members of the Society of St. Vincent de Paul at the turn of the century was Thomas M. Mulry. He had become a member of the Society in New York City at the age of twenty-two. He remained active in all of the Society's projects until his death in 1916 at the age of sixty-one. This "Ozanam of America" had not confined his work to the Vincentians but had joined the Charity Organization Society and mounted platforms to speak at local, state, and national meetings to lend his support to the new social movement. He was largely instrumental in founding the St. Vincent de Paul *Quarterly*; he served as a member of the Board of Managers of the New York Catholic Protectory, and served also as President of the National Conference of Social Work in 1907 and 1908. He was the first Catholic layman to be so honored. He was president of the Superior Council of the Society of St. Vincent de Paul of New York City in 1905 and first secretary of the Superior Council of the United States in 1915. He was one of the chief organizers of the National Conference of Catholic Charities in 1910. His business interests did not prevent him from devoting most of his time to the works of charity. His unique contribution is that, in an age when Catholicism in the United States had a strong parochial outlook, he was a national figure spearheading a movement for the national coordination of Catholic Charities.

Edmond J. Butler, a contemporary of Mr. Mulry, was another Vincentian who played an extremely important role in the development of organized Catholic Charities. Born in 1855, he was one of the pioneers of the organization of the Society on a national basis. In 1915 he became secretary of the Superior Council, a position which he held at his death in 1937. He was actively engaged in charitable activities and social work all of his adult life. He had served as a Tenement House Commissioner of New York City and as a member of the New York State Probation Commission. He was also business manager of the St. Vincent de Paul *Quarterly* for many years. Like Mr. Mulry, he was convinced that while the spirit of Catholic charities must remain forever the same, the methods and techniques can change with the times. He, too, was a strong advocate of the National Conference of Catholic Charities.

Although not as prominent on the national scene as either Mr. Mulry or Mr. Butler, Robert Biggs of Baltimore, Maryland, was another Vincentian who played a major role in improving the efficiency of Catholic charitable activities. As president of the Baltimore Particular Council of the Society of St. Vincent de Paul in 1907 he had paved the way for the establishment of Society's Central Bureau in that year in Baltimore. He was a strong advocate of the necessity of paid social workers and mapped out the Baltimore program of child care, family relief, and protective care which became the basis for programs of Catholic charities in other cities.[5] He also was one of the founders of the National Conference of Catholic Charities.

The continued contacts of these and other Vincentians with local Charity Organization Societies prior to 1910 convinced them of the need for cooperation in the field of charity. The chaotic condition of charities in a large city in those years was such that a person in need of relief could be shunted from agency to agency looking for the relief that was all the time waiting for him.[6] Considerations of race, nationality, need, type of relief, and so on, presented such a bewildering array of societies for each type that a person in need of relief needed a directory to show him where he might go. It is little wonder, then, that the Vincentians, acquainted with the advantages of organization and coordination, should have desired to apply what they had learned to Catholic charities. They realized the value of a central bureau and were willing to recognize that full-time workers were needed to make the volunteer "truly effective."[7]

Mr. Mulry's great regret was that more Catholics had not taken advantage of the opportunity to attend the meetings of the non-sectarian conferences and share the experiences of the Vincentians. The importance of these meetings, as Mr. Mulry saw them, was that they helped form "public opinion which in turn influences legislatures to enact laws to carry out the ideas originally ventilated at such conferences."[8] The National Conference of Charities and Correction meeting in New York City in 1898 demonstrated what could be done. This conference, Mr. Mulry felt, "was one of the most successful ever held in the twenty-five years of the life of the National Conference" for it was the "first time that Catholics were largely represented, and one of the few times that Catholic ideas were brought forward, and not only were tolerated, but met with approval."[9] Archbishop Michael A. Corrigan of New York addressed the opening evening meeting and was convinced that "the good resulting from these conferences should encourage us to take a more active interest in them for the future. Intelligent, educated Catholic men and women should identify themselves with all such movements."[10]

While men like Mulry, Butler, and Biggs might supply leadership, it was no easy matter to enlist from among the mass of Catholics followers who apppeared to have appreciation of the issues involved. This apathy on the part of Catholics was charged to a lack of any sense of group responsibility by Monsignor William J. Kerby, a professor of sociology at Catholic University, in an article submitted to Reverend John J. Burke, C.S.P., editor of the *Catholic*

World in 1906. After reading the article, Father Burke wrote to Monsignor Kerby that he was struck by the "seeming injustice done the Catholic laity of this country for their lack of group consciousness and group enthusiasm."[11] The explanation for the lack, Father Burke thought, was "(to speak frankly) due, not so much to the lay Catholics themselves, as to the manner in which ecclesiastical authority has prevented them from sharing that which is a fundemental [sic] necessity for group consciousness, namely, an active, personal part in the organization."[12]

Whatever the cause, Catholic lethargy had to give way to action if the demands of the times were to be met. As Monsignor D. J. McMahon of New York City put it, "United Catholic charity, up to the present, in this state, [New York] is scarcely anything else than representation from the St. Vincent de Paul Society. It is, indeed, to your credit and to your honor, but it is not enough for the Catholic cause."[13] Monsignor McMahon stressed the need for more thorough investigation of cases, greater cooperation among existing agencies, and a binding together of all of these engaged in the relief of the distressed. He was convinced that, "Charity must be regarded in our times not alone as a religious question but, because of the aid given by the State, as a public question also."[14]

The growing national sentiment against children's institutions made it imperative that Catholics, whatever their feelings about organization and social work, be represented in conferences dealing with children's problems. Since Catholics by this time had the largest number of children's institutions, failure to make the proper defense of them could be disastrous. While it was true that some were opposed to these institutions because they were Catholic, it was also true that there were many who simply felt that any institution did not provide the benefits a good foster home could.

The National Conference of Charities held in Washington, D. C., in 1901 demonstrated what could happen if Catholics failed to attend and remained inactive. Catholics received at that time little or no recognition in the makeup of the various committees. Mr. Mulry had objected that, while as Catholics no special consideration was due them, yet, as representatives of some of the most important charitable institutions in the country, some recognition should have been given.[15] Since the bulletin for the National Conference issued a strong statement against aid to private charities, the action in leaving Catholics off the committees became all the more significant. Mr. Mulry's protest carried sufficient weight, however, and the meeting held in Milwaukee in 1902 found the Catholic leaders better represented on the committees.[16] In his address to the New York State Conference of Charities and Corrections in November, 1901, Archbishop Corrigan had noted that among the benefits of cooperation of Catholics with the nonsectarian enterprises would be the removal of prejudices and misunderstandings and the opportunity to "accentuate earnest and honest efforts for good."[17] Another great advantage that the Archbishop saw was that such meetings did not legislate or commit anyone blindly to untried theories in the suggested trial of new methods.[18] The 1902 meeting gave ample opportunity to demonstrate these advantages.

With Vincentians playing such an important role in cooperative efforts on a local scale, it is not surprising that their national meetings provided the opportunities necessary to broaden the scope of their activities. The Vincentian leaders had the foresight to envision local problems as national problems and sought some means by which the experience of each local society might be made available to all. Discussion of the problem of national organizations was particularly in evidence at the national meeting of the Society of St. Vincent de Paul in Louisville, Kentucky, in 1897. The practicality of a national conference seemed so evident to many of the leaders that another meeting was held at Cliff Haven, New York, August, 1898, at the invitation of the officers of the Catholic Summer School of America. There was hope expressed that at least a New York State organization could be established as a preliminary to a national one.[19] Such suggestions were apparently premature since no tangible results came from these meetings.

Although there was then a temporary cessation of direct activities toward the establishment of a national organization, the idea of cooperation on a national scale by no means died. With the approval of Archbishop John Farley of New York and the cooperation of The Catholic University, a comprehensive exhibit of Catholic Charities in the United States was set up at the St. Louis Exposition in 1903. The exhibit consisted of photographs of the various types of institutions and their work. Brief accounts of the institutions together with summaries of their accomplishments accompanied the pictures. Maps showing the location of the institutions and charts indicating growth beginning with 1850 were also included. The exhibit received the Grand Prize and two gold medals — which later turned out to be bronze according to Monsignor Kerby, who considered this exhibit the first real attempt to convey any impression of Catholic charities in a national way.[20]

The Richmond, Virginia, meeting of the Vincentians in 1908 is of special significance in the efforts made at that meeting to create a national organization of Catholic charities. By this time there had been a widening of interest in the movement. Monsignor William J. White, who had been appointed Director of Catholic Charities in Brooklyn, New York, in 1899 and had organized a Women's Auxiliary of the Society of St. Vincent de Paul by 1903, became a very active participant in this meeting. Monsignor White was particularly interested in the immigrant and the working man and believed that more should be done for prevention rather than relief. He had organized a program of recreational and other activities that was later consolidated into the Catholic Settlement Association in 1908. Monsignor Denis J. McMahon supervisor of Catholic charities in New York City, was a prime mover at the meeting of an attempt to organize a national association of women's organizations engaged in Catholic charities. The organization, known as St. Elizabeth's Union, was established during the Richmond meeting and was clearly modeled after the Society of St. Vincent de Paul. Mrs. Joseph J. O'Donohue of New York City became its president and Monsignor William J. Kerby its moderator. Although this organization was to be short-lived, the spirit behind it was not. The Richmond meeting marked the joining of forces of both laymen and ecclesiastics interested in the works of Charity. It was apparent from his action at the meeting that Mr. Mulry thought it was time that the combined counsel of all those interested in the movement should be sought and some form of national organization effected. Monsignor McMahon likewise agreed that the moment was opportune and in collaboration with Mr. Mulry assembled all the representatives of the various Catholic organizations represented at Richmond to examine the possibilities of a national organization.

It is significant that these men are virtually the same ones who responded to Bishop Thomas Shahan's call in 1910 to come to Catholic University for the founding of the National Conference of Catholic Charities. For this reason one may consider this Richmond meeting the real foundation of the National Conference of Catholic Charities. Certainly there is considerable truth in the statement of Monsignor John O'Grady that, "the meetings of the Society of St. Vincent de Paul and of Catholic Women's organizations held in Richmond laid the foundation of a National Conference of Catholic Charities, although the participants did not realize that they were preparing the way for a National Conference of Catholic Charities."[21]

The pioneer efforts of the Society of St. Vincent de Paul in creating a national outlook for Catholic charities cannot be underestimated. The Society was the only organization in the Church devoted to the service of the poor which held national and even international meetings. It was at these meetings that members became painfully aware of the isolation of Catholic agencies from each other. Each institution went its own way, published few or no reports, developed no theoretical discussions of the problems, held no conferences for a comparison of results or sharing of common problems, and in general had little or no personal contact with others engaged in similar work. The Catholic lay leaders developed through the Society of St. Vincent de Paul were keenly aware that the times called for concerted action. Catholic cooperation was complicated too often by nationality problems, an unwillingness to cooperate with institutions not connected with the Church, a refusal to recognize the growth of social work. It was to the credit of the Vincentians that they were able to rise above petty jealousies and have the vision to see the future clearly. These leaders saw the importance of a thorough grounding in the principles of his own faith for the Catholic social worker thrust into contact with those who had no appreciation of Catholic values. They were also certain that little progress could be made without a literature which would command the respect of their fellow workers in public and non-sectarian work. The determination of men like Mulry and Butler was to bear fruit finally in the response to the call of Bishop J. Shahan, rector of The Catholic University of America, in 1910 to come to the university and set the machinery in motion for the founding of the National Conference of Catholic Charities.

Notes — Chapter I

1. The National Conference of Catholic Charities *Proceedings* (Washington, 1925), pp. xix–xx. Hereafter this material will be cited as N.C.C.C. *Proceedings*.
2. *Ibid.*
3. *Ibid.*
4. John Marron, "Organized Catholic Charities," N.C.C.C. *Proceedings*, 1910, p. 396. Mr Marron, a Pittsburgh lawyer and a Vincentian, had been asked to make a study of Catholic Charity organizations for the first National Conference of Catholic Charities meeting.
5. Monsignor John O'Grady, *Catholic Charities in the United States* (Washington, 1930), p. 437.
6. A. G. Warner, S. A. Queen, E. B. Harper, *American Charities and Social Work* (New York, 1942), p. 203.
7. O'Grady, *Catholic Charities*, p. 257.
8. Thomas M. Mulry, "Catholics and Charity Conferences, A Plea and a Protest," St. Vincent de Paul *Quarterly*, Vol. VI, No. 3, Aug., 1901, p. 175.
9. *Ibid.*, p. 176.
10. *Ibid.*, p. 177.
11. Reverend John J. Burke, C.S.P., to Reverend William J. Kerby, November 7, 1906, in The Catholic University Archives.
12. *Ibid.*
13. Monsignor D. J. McMahon, "United Charities — A Plea for Cooperation in Benevolent Work," St. Vincent de Paul *Quarterly*, Nov., 1901, Vol. VI, No. 4, p. 257.
14. *Ibid.*, p. 265.
15. Mulry, "Catholics and Charity Conferences," p. 177.
16. *Ibid.*
17. St. Vincent de Paul *Quarterly*, Feb., 1902, Vol. VII, No. 1, p. 6.
18. *Ibid.*
19. *Ibid.*, Vol. III, pp. 31–32.
20. N.C.C.C. *Proceedings*, 1928, p. 11.
21. O'Grady, *Catholic Charities*, p. 265.

CHAPTER II

Establishing the National Conference
of Catholic Charities

PERHAPS no better criticism of the condition of Catholic charities in 1910 can be found than the comments of Monsignor Kerby to the effect that,

> Every unpleasant effect of provincialism was in evidence. Relations between our relief work and civic movements were usually remote and without distinction. The units of our Catholic Charities displayed a spirit of offishness that made them to some degree socially ineffective. A defensive attitude on the part of our charitable agencies made criticism unwelcome and they were satisfied at times with ineffective or futile work. In 1910 outside of religious communities for which I do not now speak, I know of no courses of formal instruction in aims and methods in Catholic Charities. They were totally without academic impulse. We had no literature except the 21 volumes of the St. Vincent de Paul Quarterly.[1]

Bishop Shahan was equally critical of the years before 1910, which he called "a period of mutual isolation, a time of general unpreparedness for the vast and growing social changes which were everywhere asserting themselves."[2] Still worse, according to the Bishop, was that the lack of trained social workers, the absence of a literature of social work, and the failure of leaders of Catholic charitable activities to have personal contact with each other were only vaguely realized.[3] "This," the Bishop continued, "emphasized not the lack of Catholic charitable work and endeavor, but the absence of a far-reaching charitable organization for the lack of which the incredible latency of Catholic charitable effort was not being developed to its fullest capacity."[4]

The general lack of contact of Catholic institutions and leaders with the movement outside of the Church in the field of social service was also lamented by Bishop Shahan. He did not deny the value of the limited contacts of men like Mulry and Butler but, while the "outside movement had gone ahead attracting great ability, producing highly important literature, interpreting social experiences, formulating standards affecting public opinion and legislation and building up a tremendous and impressive tradition," the Catholic leaders who were in touch with this movement lacked the "channel by which to convey their impressions to our numerous but un-organized units."[5]

Born in 1857, Bishop Shahan had grown up with the problems confronting the Church in attempting to create bonds of union among the various immigrant groups. His experience as chancellor in the Diocese of Hartford from 1883 to 1888 had shown him how difficult it was to overcome these and other centrifugal tendencies in the Church. He was, therefore, most sympathetic toward all movements that tended to develop a national outlook for Catholic social work in the United States. He hoped to see the influence of The Catholic University spread to the Catholic charities movement by training its leaders and contributing to its research.

It was fortunate that a man of Bishop Shahan's caliber and influence was receptive to the suggestion to use The Catholic University leadership in creating the necessary media for organizing Catholic charities efforts on a national basis. Monsignor Kerby was of the opinion that while some kind of a National Conference of Catholic Charities would have been created, that it came in 1910 was to be attributed to the "openmindedness, courage, scholarship and insight of Bishop Shahan,"[6] who took the step at a time "when approval was none too generous and there was a rather widespread indifference as to its purpose."[7] For this reason Monsignor Kerby felt that, so far as the origin and growth of the National Conference of Catholic Charities was concerned, "no element in its success can be freed from debt to Bishop Shahan."[8] So great has been the general appreciation of the role of Bishop Shahan that Edmund B. Butler, president of the National Conference of Catholic Charities in 1950, felt that "the real founder of the Conference was the Right

Reverend Monsignor Shahan, Rector of The Catholic University."[9]

The origin of the National Conference of Catholic Charities, however, must be attributed to a combination of circumstances rather than to the exclusive efforts of any one person. To a great degree the idea of a permanent organization was the outcome of a deep-seated feeling among the many Catholic men and women engaged in charitable enterprise who had become convinced that only the collective forces of the Church were capable of meeting the challenge of the times. The national meetings of the Society of St. Vincent de Paul tended only to further the desire for some means of coping with the increasingly complex problems affecting both the material and spiritual welfare of the poor. "The great variety of policies met by Catholic Charities in dealing with the States, with philanthropic organizations, and with one another, seemed to make necessary some effort to discover the underlying instincts and appreciations which animate the Charities of the Church."[10] These were the principal motives behind the first meeting of the National Conference of Catholic Charities in 1910.

At the 1909 meeting of the National Conference of Social Work the Catholics in attendance discussed at length the desirability of a Catholic Conference on a national basis. Brother Barnabas, who had organized a Placing Bureau for dependent children at the New York Catholic Protectory where he was in charge, was asked to approach Bishop Shahan in an effort to get The Catholic University to sponsor a national conference.[11] Brother Barnabas, who had entered the Brothers of the Christian Schools in 1885 at the age of twenty, had long been engaged in the service of youth. In many ways his years cover the transitional period from older ways to newer methods in social work. In an age when many Catholics were completely satisfied with institutional care of children he was insistent on the policy of placing them in foster homes. He was also an effective writer and a fluent and persuasive speaker. Brother Barnabas had been associated for years with Thomas Mulry and had discussed with him the advantages of getting Catholic charity workers together at least annually. The Richmond meeting of Vincentians in 1908 found this sentiment worthy of translation into action, but it took the added encouragement of the discussions in 1909 to produce results.

"The master stroke that ushered in a new era in Catholic social work," according to Bishop Shahan, was supplied by Brother Barnabas' letter to the Bishop in November, 1909.[12] In this letter, which has since disappeared, Brother Barnabas insisted, according to the Bishop who received it, that The Catholic University had a duty to take action which would bring about a national conference of some kind "which would quicken the forces of life in us and enable us to take advantage of everything wholesome in modern progressive thought and action for the service and welfare of the poor and suffering."[13] Brother Barnabas was convinced that "since all coming development in social work must be educational, the alliance of the proposed conference with the University was natural and full of promise."[14]

Bishop Shahan immediately conferred with Monsignor Kerby, and the result was the calling of a meeting at The Catholic University in February of 1910 whose purpose according to the "minutes" was to "discuss the feasibility and advisability of inaugurating an annual Conference of Catholic Charities."[15] It would also be the purpose of the proposed conference to make an exchange of views possible so as to "bring the most progressive in touch with the least progressive," and to assist in the formation of a general Catholic position on some of the problems of social work in order to bring about a "sense of solidarity among those engaged in the work."[16] Twenty-six of those most active in Catholic social work were invited to attend this organizational meeting. All but four attended. Brother Barnabas was one of those unable to attend. The representation was mostly from the cities of Washington, Baltimore, New York, Brooklyn, Philadelphia, and Boston; Chicago, Cincinnati, and New Orleans also had representation.[17]

Bishop Shahan announced to those assembled for the meeting on February 19, 1910, that His Eminence, Cardinal Gibbons, had given his approval for the meeting and its purposes. For three days this group of leaders of Catholic charities deliberated on the ways and means of implementing their proposals. A committee on the organization under the chairmanship of Robert Biggs and composed of Monsignor Kerby, Doctor McKenna, Judge DeLacy, Richard Crane, Frank Johann, Timothy Hurley, and David Tilley recommended that a National Conference of Catholic Charities be organized and that the invitation of The Catholic University to hold the first meeting be accepted.[18] The Conference would offer "an open forum for discussion" and membership should consist of representatives of all lay and religious associations engaged in Catholic charities in the United States.[19] A provisional executive committee was selected to organize the conference for the September meeting. Bishop Thomas J. Shahan was president of this committee, Thomas Mulry, vice-president, Monsignor Kerby, secretary, Judge DeLacy, treasurer. Other members of the committee were Thomas Rapier, Bishop Anderson of Boston, Mrs. Thomas Carter from Montana, and James F. Kennedy from Chicago.

Six months of preparation for the first meeting followed. The entire United States was canvassed by means of questionnaires designed to give a true picture of the condition of Catholic charities. The questionnaire directed to the dioceses asked such questions as the number of organizations of Catholic men and women engaged in strictly charitable works; number of members active in each organization, whether the organizations were parochial, diocesan, or national; what cooperation with other Catholic agencies existed; what records were kept; what relations with public agencies prevailed; what provisions for the study of local situations were made. The questionnaire sent to the states sought information on the State Board of Charities, the conduct and policies of state institutions, and the relations of state institutions to Catholic institutions. All reports on these questionnaires were to be filed before the opening of the Conference, and digests of them were to be presented to those attending the Conference.

On September 25, 1910, four hundred delegates from twenty-four states and thirty-eight cities assembled at The Catholic University of America in Washington, D. C., to attend the first meeting of the National Conference of Catholic Charities. The sessions opened with a Solemn High Mass on Sunday, September 25, in McMahon

Hall. After the Mass the Apostolic Delegate, the Most Reverend Diomede Falconio, later Cardinal Falconio, and Bishop Shahan held a reception in the lobby and the University was host to the entire group for luncheon.

In the evening a public meeting in the National Theater was presided over by His Eminence, Cardinal Gibbons, who in a few brief remarks, expressed the hope that the National Conference would "realize more than the earnest hopes of its friends."[20] A short address was then given by Bishop Shahan on "The Practical Mission of the Conference," in which he made a special plea for "preventive charity," observing that, "It is very well to care for the wounded who have fallen at a very dangerous pass on the mountain side, but is it not much better to construct a solid safeguard at the pass itself, where such accidents occur so frequently?"[21] Bishop Shahan then outlined the four day program which was to devote one day to a discussion of the statistics compiled from answers to the questionnaires on the state of Catholic charities in the country. Other topics for the remaining days concerned the protection of young girls in large cities, the dependent family, social reform, delinquency, and the matter of permanent organization of the National Conference of Catholic Charities.

The statistical report on the condition of Catholic charities in the United States given on the second day of the meeting revealed a number of significant things. The recurring statement in the reports that no systematic records were kept by the various organizations was explained by asserting that the intimate knowledge which the worker in Catholic charity had of his clients served the same purpose as a written record.[22] The reports concerned only the field of lay charities and not the whole field of Catholic Action; the absence of reference to participation in social movements did not mean, however, that no one was engaged in this work. Perhaps one of the most notable features of the reports was the fact that special mention was so frequently made of the fair treatment given to Catholic agencies by public and private non-Catholic bodies. A small number of isolated instances to the contrary were reported, but the general picture was favorable enough to cause the St.

Vincent de Paul *Quarterly* to observe that "the spirit of cooperation seems to be extending more and more every day and, to those who fear that the organization of the National Conference of Catholic Charities might interfere with the National Conference of Charities and Corrections representing all denominations, we can only state that the former will bring the Catholic people in even closer touch than ever with the work of these latter conferences."[23]

Among the conclusions drawn by the Honorable Charles A. DeCourcy, Judge of the Superior Court of Massachusetts, who was asked to summarize the reports, was that at the moment no real necessity existed for the organization of state conferences of Catholic charities. According to the Judge the unit of organization should be the diocese, with an executive committee of active men and women and an annual conference in the diocese. Efficient organization and progressive methods were absolutely essential because of the complexity of the situation; and "participation in the work of Public Boards, state conferences, associated charities and the like" were, as Judge DeCourcy put it, "nothing less than a public duty."[24] The judge urged the adoption of a standard "not less catholic and charitable than our neighbor; the standard of cooperation."[25]

The four days of the conference produced a clearer understanding among the delegates of the principles of Catholic action in the social field and better realization of some of the problems to be met. The most tangible immediate result was the firm establishment of the National Conference of Catholic charities as a permanent organization, a clearinghouse for further exchange of ideas and mutual aid. Bishop Shahan was elected president and Monsignor Kerby, secretary. The desire of the delegates to get together and know one another is most evident from the pages of the records of the meeting, which was to be held every two years. In particular, there was an insistent demand for a federation of the various women's organizations and a closer relationship between the works of the organization of both men and the women engaged in charitable activity.[26]

Among the resolutions adopted at the conclusion of the meeting was one of "hearty thanks" to Bishop Shahan and Monsignor Kerby "for their prompt acceptance of the suggestion of Reverend Brother

Barnabas that a National Conference of Catholic Charities be called."[27] Then followed the concluding ceremonies, which were held in the White House, where "a handshake, a few felicitous words of greeting, a generous bestowal of the typical Taft style . . . were the salient features of a reception tendered to the delegates to the Conference of Catholic Charities."[28] The delegates could indeed depart for their homes satisfied that in Catholic charity circles a "drift into the shallow conviction that we cannot learn anything new," had been halted.[29] These men urged that Catholic philosophy, doctrine, and supernatural motivation and inspiration be maintained and supplemented by progress in method.[30] One of the most important tasks of the Conference in the future would be, it was hoped, "effective instruction in the facts of poverty" and an awakening of a social conscience.[31]

The widespread publicity which the conference received from the newspapers resulted in at least one person's overestimating what kind of work was intended. It seems that one lady who had read about the formation of the conference drew her own conclusions as to what its immediate value would be. She wrote to Bishop Shahan concerning her sister, whom she described as "very old, very irritable and in all ways difficult" and asked that the National Conference take her and provide for her.[32] Monsignor Kerby said he was instructed by Bishop Shahan to reply that the Conference "intended only to talk about charity and not to do it."[33]

Monsignor Kerby's more serious duties, as Secretary of the Conference however, were devoted to an extended analysis of the results of the first meeting of the National Conference. He wanted "to catch the collective tone of the gathering; to find out what the delegates discovered; what new purposes were formed; what larger outlooks were suggested."[34] The most obvious thing that impressed Monsignor Kerby was the evident desire of the delegates to cooperate. He had no doubts that one of the reasons the permanent organization was effected was that everyone wanted it. He praised the delegates for their willingness to do as much as possible in pointing out what should be done without defining things so sharply as to hamper progress. The fact that the Conference would not vote on any questions and that the views expressed in the sessions were to be accepted only as the personal opinions of the authors was evidence of this good judgment. Monsignor Kerby was also well pleased with the up-to-date views of the various delegates and thought that the Conference was "nearly as progressive as Leo XIII or Pius X."[35] Therefore, without invading the autonomy of any existing organization, Monsignor Kerby saw the National Conference as a sounding board "creating opportunity through which the national consciousness of our Catholic charities may come to expression."[36]

If the progressive spirit among the leaders of Catholic charities was to have its proper influence, such a national organization was an absolute necessity in Monsignor Kerby's mind. That the hierarchy and the clergy who had spoken and written on behalf of social reform seemed reluctant to appear before congressional committees discussing these problems was further evidence of the need of a means through which the Church's views could be expressed. Moreover, talent and experience among Catholic lay leaders were being drained off to civic and nonreligious movements because the Church lacked an organization in which they could express themselves. The result was that the conservative tendencies in Catholic charities tended to predominate by default and "the enthusiasm, the faith in humanity, the impulse to service, that have scattered these Catholics among many movements would have served as well to bring them into one mighty organization, focusing their scattered energies into strength. The feeling was pronounced among the delegates that the Conference would render this great service to our charities as a whole."[37]

Since the delegates included so many who were members of boards of directors in schools of philanthropy, members of state boards of charity, members of associated charities, and members of various committees engaged in preventive and relief work, it is not surprising that they were very much in favor of cooperation with public and with other private charities. In their deliberations in this first meeting they urged participation in these other charities up to the point where philosophy or principle was involved. It was probably this background that induced the delegates to refrain from placing any emphasis in their discussions on "abuses or infringements of Catholic interests."[38] Monsignor Kerby praised "this sense of the organic relation of charity to religious consciousness," which he felt "amounted really to an instinct."[39] From whatever point he viewed the Conference, he saw only the good that it could accomplish. It reaffirmed the convictions of the delegates in their ability to accomplish the tremendous amount of work to be done.

To attribute the founding of the National Conference of Catholic Charities and the success of the first meeting to any one person would not be fair to the others who shared in the venture. Monsignor Kerby, or Doctor Kerby, as he was better known, must, however, be given credit as the principal organizer of the Conference. As a youth he had been an active member of the Society of St. Vincent de Paul. As practically the only general organization of Catholic men in the United States devoted primarily to charity, the Society produced the men who were to point the new way. Doctor Kerby was quick to appreciate the fact that when the National Conference was proposed those who would be most enthusiastic in its support and willing to provide leadership would come from the ranks of the Society. Casting his lot with the Vincentians, Doctor Kerby had played a major role in the early attempts at national organization and admitted readily that the National Conference could not have been founded without the "vision and generous cooperation of the Society of St. Vincent de Paul."[40]

Doctor Kerby, however, was always giving the credit to others. In his own writings he constantly placed the contributions of Thomas Mulry, Brother Barnabas, and Bishop Shahan far above his own. He himself avoided any conspicuous role. Yet those who knew him well were quick to recognize that he was the organizer of the Conference. When raised to the rank of Domestic Prelate in 1934, he was described as the "guiding and directing hand" of the National Conference from its founding to 1920, when he resigned as its Secretary.[41] In 1936, upon the occasion of the death of Monsignor Kerby, the editor of the *Ecclesiastical Review* noted that, "Through his labor it [The National Conference] was launched:

through his perseverence and his guidance, and trust that the authorities of the Church had in him, it continued and grew."[42]

In 1916, at the death of Thomas Mulry, Monsignor Kerby had paid a similar tribute to the Vincentian for whom, according to the Monsignor, the work of helping create and guide the National Conference "was the last new endeavor of his career in this great field."[43] Monsignor Kerby felt that "while the Conference is still too young to be an honor to him, too immature to express his vision which it has caught, it has no hope more honorable than that the tradition of his name and the inspiration of his example may help it serve the great purpose to which he consecrated his life."[44] There can be no question that, without the contributions of Monsignor Kerby, Thomas Mulry, and their co-workers among the Vincentians, the National Conference would have had a much later birth. While Brother Barnabas might still have had the quick response of Bishop Shahan to his timely suggestion, both men would have lacked the human resources necessary for the realization of their dreams.

The National Conference of Catholic Charities thus came into being as a very practical response to the needs of the times. Brother Barnabas probably best represents the practical approach while Bishop Shahan and Monsignor Kerby represent the more academic or philosophical approach. The merger of these two points of view produced an experiment that promised to fill the need of some centralization of effort in the field of charity. This first conference was composed chiefly of lay volunteers and professional social workers. The St. Vincent de Paul Quarterly observed that "it was certainly very gratifying to find the clergy so well represented at all the meetings and to notice the very friendly spirit which existed between them and the laity, thus indicating that they are working shoulder to shoulder in the good cause."[45]

One may well agree with Bishop Shahan who, in a letter to Thomas Mulry shortly after the closing of the first Conference meeting, stated that the success of the meeting was due to the preparations and guidance of the "good men who for so many years have patiently and modestly toiled in the ranks of the St. Vincent de Paul Society."[46] As the Bishop so correctly put it, "the Conference may truly be called the flower of the Society's works for fifty years."[47]

Notes — Chapter II

1. Address of Monsignor William J. Kerby at the Conference Dinner October 2. N.C.C.C. *Proceedings*, 1935, p. 64.
2. *Ibid.*, pp. 7–8.
3. *Ibid.*, p. 8.
4. *Ibid.*
5. *Ibid.*
6. Monsignor William J. Kerby, "Bishop Shahan and Our Catholic Charities" (no date), MS, p. 1.
7. *Ibid.*
8. *Ibid.*
9. Presidential address of Edmond B. Butler, N.C.C.C. *Proceedings*, 1950, p. 6.
10. *Ibid.*, 1910, p. 11.
11. O'Grady, *Catholic Charities*, p. 430.
12. Bishop Thomas J. Shahan, "The Conference and Catholic Social Work," N.C.C.C. *Proceedings*, 1925, p. 8.
13. *Ibid.*, pp. 8–9.
14. *Ibid.*, p. 9.
15. N.C.C.C. *Proceedings*, 1910, p. 12, "Minutes of the Preliminary Meeting," February 19, 20, 1910.
16. *Ibid.*
17. "Minutes" of the February 19, 1910 meeting in N.C.C.C. *Proceedings*, 1910. Those invited were Brother Barnabas from Lincolndale, N. Y.; Robert Biggs, Joseph W. Brooks, P. J. McEvoy, and Reverend Hugh Monaghan from Baltimore, Edmond J. Butler, Monsignor Dennis J. McMahon, Doctor Charles F. McKenna, and Thomas M. Mulry from New York City; Monsignor William J. White from Brooklyn; Richard Crane from Cincinnati; Honorable William H. DeLacy, William F. Downey, Monsignor William J. Kerby, Doctor Charles P. Neill (U. S. Commissioner of Labor) and Monsignor Thomas J. Shahan from Washington; Michael F. Doyle, Monsignor N. F. Fisher, Frank J. Johann, and John Rea from Philadelphia; Reverend Francis Foy, Nutley, N. J.; Timothy D. Hurley and James F. Kennedy from Chicago, Thomas G. Rapier from New Orleans, David F. Tilley from Boston. The four who did not attend the meeting were Brother Barnabas, Monsignor Fisher, Dr. Neill, and Thomas Rapier. The vast majority of those invited were Vincentians.
18. *Ibid.*, p. 13.
19. *Ibid.*
20. N.C.C.C. *Proceedings*, 1910, p. 34.
21. *Ibid.*, p. 37.
22. *Ibid.*, p. 50.
23. St. Vincent de Paul *Quarterly*, Vol. XV, No. 4, p. 331.
24. N.C.C.C. *Proceedings*, 1910, p. 70.
25. *Ibid.*

26. *Ibid.*, pp. 418–419.
27. *Ibid.*, p. 234.
28. Washington *Herald*, Sept. 29, 1910.
29. Monsignor William J. Kerby, "Problems in Charity," N.C.C.C. *Proceedings*, 1910, p. 405.
30. *Ibid.*, p. 406.
31. *Ibid.*, p. 408.
32. *Ibid.*, 1935, p. 63.
33. *Ibid.*
34. *Ibid.*, 1910, pp. 411–412.
35. *Ibid.*, p. 414.
36. *Ibid.*, p. 412.
37. *Ibid.*, p. 416.
38. *Ibid.*
39. *Ibid.*, p. 417.
40. *MS* Rev. William J. Kerby, "Frederic Ozanam," 1933.
41. *MS* Sermon of Rev. Ignatius Smith, O.O., Apr. 19, 1934.
42. *Ecclesiastical Review*, Sept., 1936, Vol. XCV, No. 3, pp. 230–231.
43. *MS* Rev. Dr. William J. Kerby, "Tribute to Thomas Maurice Mulry, 1855–1916."
44. *Ibid.*
45. St. Vincent de Paul *Quarterly*, Vol. XV, No. 4, p. 331.
46. Bishop Thomas J. Shahan to Thomas Mulry, Oct. 7, 1910.
47. *Ibid.*

CHAPTER III

Building a National Outlook in Catholic Charities, 1910–1925

THE great need for a national organization of workers in Catholic charities was partially fulfilled by the creation of the National Conference of Catholic Charities in 1910. Since, however, this conference was the result of the action of but a small and advanced segment of those engaged in the work, it would be necessary to sell the idea of a national organization to the others. The good that a National Conference could accomplish would be limited by the degree of acceptance of its position in charity activity, and for this reason Monsignor Kerby took great care to emphasize that the National Conference "will invade no field now occupied; it will displace no organization, and will in no way enter the field of actual relief."[1]

The real role of the Conference was to "explore conditions, renew the inspiration of old ideals, guide wisely in the larger relations of the work, and thus serve in no mean way to make our methods equal to our problems, our aims worthy of our ideals, and our achievements worthy of our faith and its noble traditions of charity."[2] The Conference, therefore, was to bring the workers in Catholic charities into closer contact with each other in order to facilitate an exchange of views so that sound policies might be given more general expression. In order to aid in the accomplishment of this objective, the collecting of information concerning charity organizations and their problems as well as the encouragement of the development of a literature of catholic social work were to be among the functions of the Conference.

The difficulties in the way of the accomplishment of the Conference's objectives were numerous. Differences of opinion on major issues even among those in favor of the Conference idea were numerous and sharp. The *Proceedings* of the various national meetings contain some evidence of these clashes, but it is probably only part of the story since it has been asserted that "the gentle secretary [Monsignor Kerby] eliminated many of the records of the conflicts that took place."[3] The criticism of traditional methods, such as institutional care of dependent children, was one of the issues. It would be difficult to list all of the others since it was generally true as Monsignor Kerby stated, that "all fundamentals in charity work are questioned nowadays."[4] The nature of poverty and its causes, whether prevention should be stressed along with relief, the role of the state in charity, the place of the volunteer, and the relations of the organizations to each other certainly stand out among the most frequently discussed issues.

Common to many of these issues was the question of standards. The problem was not so much one of the inadequacy of Catholic institutions but rather an unwillingness to look upon new methods and ideas without suspicion. Monsignor Kerby said that Catholics should be more "open-minded toward every problem of charity. Let us," he added, "hold to our philosophy, to our doctrine, to our supernatural motive and inspiration. Then let us seek progress in method and practical aim from friend and from critic, from conservative and radical, from new and old."[5] Robert Biggs, now a member of the Executive Committee of the National Conference, felt that Catholic agencies could probably do the work in a manner in keeping with the best standards were it not for certain features of rules of religious communities limiting activities to certan hours or to certain methods. Mr. Biggs singled out lack of training and experience as additional factors and warned that "Catholics cannot much longer with credit to themselves or with credit to the Church leave the burden of properly caring for our poor fall upon the shoulders of the non-Catholic or purely philanthropic agencies."[6]

Nationalism, still strong among Catholic immigrants, served also to make the task of the National Conference more difficult. Each national group had no objection to caring for its own unfortunates.

To contribute to the care of those of other national groups, however, seemed to be asking too much. Thus the financial reason tended to strengthen and reinforce national lines and, in many instances, practically rule out cooperation on the local level.

More basic than any of the problems just mentioned, however, was a Catholic conservative temperament and the general apathy toward social problems. Here was one problem that persisted at least through this early period and tended to operate as a damper on many projects. Monsignor Kerby had little patience with the Catholic worker who mistook his temperament for Catholic doctrine and tended to "convert his limitations into Catholic principles."[7] The Secretary warned those whose temperament was conservative, and whose conservatism represented "no thinking whatever," against resisting all changes "by alleging that they are opposed to Catholic doctrine."[8] Referring to those organizations that refused to keep records, Monsignor Kerby said that it was common to find them arguing against keeping records only because they were incapable or unwilling to keep adequate ones. He further criticized the conservative's "sense of superiority" which prevents him from recognizing the role of training and the need of knowledge in dealing with social change. The Monsignor saw two basic assumptions underlying this conservative temperament: the volunteer is superior to the paid worker; bigotry is the inspiration of all non-Catholic organizations.[9]

There were others who felt that plain apathy rather than a conservative temperament was the basic reason for Catholic charities not progressing as rapidly as it should have. Reverend Joseph McSorley, C.S.P. said that an examination of conscience was in order for many Catholics. "Confess!" he exclaimed, "it is not impossibility or inexpedience that has retarded us so much as the lack of interest and of knowledge."[10] In Washington, D. C., in 1912, with a Catholic population of about 70,000, or 20 per cent of the population, there were only two Catholics in the Citizens Relief Association.[11] In St. Louis, May, 1912, an attempt to get Catholics to attend sessions of a city-wide conference failed to bring them out in any appreciable numbers. It was pointed out that the letters sent to pastors announcing the meeting were obviously not taken very seriously, and

it was quite probable that many of them were never even read.[12]
The simple fact seemed to be that there was little sympathy with
the movement. Curiously enough a call to a similar meeting in 1914
resulted in a packed hall. A charge of twenty-five cents admission
was made at this time. A nominal charge had increased the importance of attendance.

Despite the climate of conservatism and apathy, it was hoped that
the National Conference of Catholic Charities would be the instrument to change the situation. Monsignor William J. White, Diocesan Director of Catholic Charities in Brooklyn, voiced the sentiments of the progressive element when he expressed the hope that
"this Conference ought to mark the beginning of a Catholic Social
Reform Movement on national lines."[13] Before action could result,
however, he felt that a program of study was necessary. Dr. Charles
P. Neill, U. S. Commissioner of Labor in 1910, agreed that "if this
National Conference of Charities will form its beginning interest
itself in the social and industrial causes of poverty and will prepare
its members to take the attitude which Christianity and social
sympathy and common sense suggest, the Conference will honor the
Church and give noble service to the cause of humanity."[14]

Monsignor White was of the opinion that the course of action
that should be charted was between the extremes of those maintaining that the Church had no business in engaging in a social
program and those who thought that the Church should be a social
reform club. Objections to experts in social problems would dis-
appear if advocates of each of these extremes realized that experts
are means and not ends. The idea, as Monsignor White saw it,
was to eliminate the demoralizing effects of poverty and destitution
so that victims of these conditions would be in a better position
to listen to the Church's voice. In this way the Brooklyn Catholic
Charities Director felt that Catholic charity workers could meet
with those of secular organizations in a common war on social and
economic evils.[15]

Many of the leaders of the National Conference were convinced
that Catholics could no longer remain aloof from the great developments in social work in the world outside of the Church. The

problem was to move Catholic thinking off dead center. As
Monsignor Kerby put it, "the new is not always wrong. The old
is not always the last expression of wisdom. The adjustment of the
old and the new is a challenge to our zeal, intelligence and faith."[16]
The contribution of the generation of that day was thought by
him to lie in the development of a scholarly literature, the recognition of the role of the trained worker, and an arousing of the
public conscience to the point where it would demand the necessary
reforms.

If the problem of arousing this new spirit among the laity was
complicated by the lethargy already described, this condition seemed
no less true of the clergy. The mere thought of attending meetings
for any purpose was strangely abhorrent even for an age that had
not as yet become committee conscious. The Reverend John F.
Fenelon, S.S., writing in the St. Vincent de Paul *Quarterly* was
convinced after observing his fellow clergy, that many of them
considered such meetings to be "pretentious but useless gatherings,
where the talkers talk forever, while the workers work at home."[17]
This idea, which could be attributed to impatience and prejudice
as well as inertia, had to be dispelled before the biennial meeting
of the National Conference of Catholic Charities could become
an effective instrument. It is a tribute to the quality of these meetings that erosion of these antagonistic ideas ultimately resulted in
shaping a new attitude of mind. While the number of delegates
at the biennial meeting showed only about a 10–20 per cent increase
by 1918, the number of cities represented more than doubled —
evidence the leaven was having its effect.[18]

Two objectives of these early meetings were to insist on the duty
of the clergy to be informed on the facts of social work and to
develop a sense of responsibility in the priests for the encouragement of social work. For this reason the topics dealt with at these
meetings generally dealt with new standards and policies in Catholic
social work that had met with approval, and a criticism of mistaken
standards which affected Catholic interest.

An incident which Monsignor Kerby related in a letter to the Reverend George O'Connor of the Catholic Charities Bureau in Boston

recalled in 1925 shows that the clergy were not always appreciative of these efforts in their behalf. One of Monsignor Kerby's many duties was the giving of clergy retreats. Invariably he was requested by the bishop who had invited him to devote at least one or two of the conferences to diocesan charities and welfare. These bishops attributed the general lack of interest in social affairs to the fact that the older priests had had no experience in these matters, while the younger ones had no one to guide them. Often a bishop felt that there was too great a tendency on the part of the priest to transfer his duty of looking after the poor in the parish to the various charitable organizations of the diocese.[19] Monsignor Kerby soon found out that when he was scheduled to give a retreat the clergy looked forward, and not always with joyous anticipation, to a large dose of sociology. At a retreat he once gave in Baltimore he felt that he would limit himself to only one conference on social work. In that one conference he gave an interpretation of the work of the Juvenile Court on the last day of the retreat. Leaving the chapel after the talk, Monsignor Kerby overheard one of the priests remark, "That dang fellow gave this whole retreat in order to put that talk over on us."[20]

The clergy were not the only ones needing instruction in the field of social work. The calling of the National Conference of Catholic Charities was only part of a movement that recognized also the need for Catholic schools of social work where future leaders both lay and clerical could be trained. The four schools in existence in 1910 at New York City, Boston, Chicago, and St. Louis were all under nonsectarian control. The Catholic University was a logical choice to become a leader in the field of social work. It already had a department of sociology under the guidance of Monsignor Kerby which could provide a basis for this important area of study. Loyola University of Chicago began instruction in social work in 1912, and a systematic course offering was established in 1913 and 1914. It is not surprising, therefore, that an important place on the program of the meeting of the National Conference of Catholic Charities in 1914 was reserved for discussion of such training courses.

Assuming that the real problem in Catholic charities in 1910 was isolation and perhaps also a large measure of inertia, the leaders of the National Conference felt that what was needed was the pooling of their individual experiences into a common fund from which all might draw. Hence the biennial meeting, the schools of social study, and other means of contact with people and a good literature of social work would be important aids in attaining the goal of coordination. They soon discovered that these things were but a beginning. Definite planning and perhaps a complete overhauling of the structure of Catholic charities appeared necessary to accomplish the original aims of the Conference.

City conferences of the type inaugurated in Pittsburgh in 1910 were one evidence of recognition of the broader problem and of the attempt to try new methods of planning. All Catholic organizations of the city joined to form a permanent organization which was to become an official medium of communication between pastors, relief societies, and institutions. Information, statistics, emergency relief, employment, and general direction of the charitable activities of the diocese became its program. The pattern had been set by an even more extensive effort of this sort by the Vincentians in Baltimore in 1906. Distinct advantages were immediately apparent where these conferences were organized. In St. Louis, where previous efforts of the various Catholic charitable organizations to get on the endorsed list of charities in the city had failed, all of the charities listed by the 1913 city conference were endorsed.[21] The trouble previously had been that each organization in its own isolated way had failed to report in the prescribed manner. Delegates to the National Conference soon discovered that the city conference contacts enabled them to come to the biennial meeting with a better understanding of the problems they faced. On their return the delegates were in a better position to apply the general principles of the National Conference to the local situations.

By 1916 it was apparent that the effort to build a national outlook in Catholic charities was making some progress. Bishop Shahan could report to the second General Session of the 1916 Conference that a national outlook had been achieved. The National Conference had, he asserted, "enabled us to begin the organization of our thinking . . . coordination of effort, which cannot fail to promote efficiency, to clarify our understanding of problems of poverty and relief."[22] The national office now had a daily schedule of work, was sending out information, and was in contact with all Catholic relief agencies. Since, as the bishop pointed out, "narrow outlooks produce no greatness, arouse no collective enthusiasm, produce no prophets in any work, and establish no traditions which uplift the race," he could only hope that the National Conference of Catholic Charities had "definitely closed the old parochial epoch of isolation."[23] Mrs. Samuel K. Wilson, president of the Catholic Women's League of Chicago, speaking at the same meeting pointed out how the information and inspiration received by the delegates at the 1910 meeting resulted in the establishment of Protectory for Friendless Girls as a section of the Women's League in Chicago. Some eleven hundred girls had been cared for in the first year and in 1915 the number was four thousand.[24] Here was one instance of the impact of the national organization on a local situation.

There was little question in the minds of those closest to the National Conference of Catholic Charities that by 1916 there were many things that remained to be accomplished despite satisfactory progress. Discussion of the advisability of meeting only every two years had been frequent. The general sentiment seemed to favor the continuation of the initial practice. There were those, like the Reverend H. G. Monaghan of Baltimore, who felt that yearly meetings would be too much work for Monsignor Kerby along with his other duties. In response to the claim that annual meetings would infuse more life into the Conference, Father Monaghan observed that "more life than has been shown would be unnatural and dangerous."[25] Others, like Judge DeLacy, feared that annual meetings might interfere with the delegates' local duties. The Conference voted in 1912 to continue the biennial meeting and resisted efforts to change the place of meeting from Catholic University.[26]

Although "a certain ignorance, a certain apathy, a certain old-fashioned traditionalism" had been overcome in the harmony of these early meetings, "here and there a little distrust and a little weakness and a little coldness, fed perhaps by the novelty of any new enterprise" still remained as obstacles.[27] For this as well as for many other reasons the program for the future envisioned more specific research work. The "silent propaganda" of Conference reports needed amplification and reinforcement. Bishop Shahan in particular was anxious to see the Conference develop this area in such a way as to increase the number and quality of research papers and to encourage a taste for research among the social workers. The right kind of research would tend to fulfill the role of the Conference as a laboratory in which the quality of Catholic social work could be tested. Bishop Shahan felt that in this manner the extremes of conservatism and radicalism could be corrected so that delegates would continue to find "correction no less than instruction" through the services of the National Conference.[28]

While the biennial meetings of the National Conference of Catholic Charities were providing the opportunities for the formation of a common viewpoint on significant issues, the problem of operation on the local level remained unsolved. The need for local boards to prevent duplication of effort, to prevent the waste of funds, to encourage coordination of activities, and to cooperate with the Charity Organization Movement, was readily apparent. The few priests like Monsignor McMahon, Monsignor White, and Father Maurice O'Connor of Boston, who had taken charge of activities in their respective areas, were not in an executive position where they could direct activities particularly of the religious communities which had been conspicuously absent from the early National Conference meetings. The impact of the National Conference, however, through its returning delegates, helped in the creation of the Central Bureau of Diocesan Charities. Bishop Shahan felt that this was one rather immediate tangible result of the National Conference.[29]

Not everyone was convinced, however, that diocesan organization was the answer to the problem. There were those who felt that the national approach was sufficient, while others were reluctant to think of any organization beyond the parish level.[30] The need for trained workers, the demands for standards and progressive methods as well as the desire for cooperation with other agencies, all tended to make it apparent that diocesan organization was the most logical approach. Again it was Monsignor Kerby and the Vincentians who showed the way. As early as 1913 Monsignor Kerby pointed out that "the primary aim of effective charity is to give the relief that is needed, when and where it is needed."[31] Coordination was, therefore, essential because of the large number of organizations working in the same field. Since an organization made up entirely of volunteers might not find such work so simple, some authority had to be established and respected. The "particular aversion" in Catholic circles to the "card catalog" also had to be overcome. As Monsignor Kerby observed, "the original card catalog in human history is memory. Writing and recording are simply mechanical aids to it."[32] The central office with paid workers was considered a necessity. Parishes working alone could hardly be expected to provide the proper base for the necessary services. Nor could the dioceses operate in isolation.

Fears that the central organization would become an independent agency competing with those it pretended to serve were frequently voiced.[33] As one man expressed it, "the only harmonious policy of most of the charities consists in their concerted efforts in attacking and undermining the associated charities."[34] Other objections to coordination of diocesan charitable activities were an outgrowth of provincialism or tradition. Against those who stood their ground against change, Reverend Michael J. Scanlon, Diocesan Director of Catholic Charities, of Boston, argued that "there is no sense and much less reason in assuming that a rule or method adopted generations, if not centuries ago, to meet such practical problems as the care of the sick, of the orphans, of the wayward, or of the dependent, should remain as unchanged as the eternal verities."[35]

A practical consideration, however, tended to aid the movement toward centralization on the local level. The Community Chest movement pioneered by the Cleveland Chamber of Commerce, and charity endorsement committees raised important questions for the Catholic organizations. The civic drive to prevent waste of funds and overlapping agency functions had progressed to a point where failure of the agency to get proper endorsement could lead to a serious loss of revenue. On the other hand a central agency for

Catholic institutions could be of inestimable value in coordinating efforts and providing better contact with the directors of the Community Chest.

Bitter controversy developed over the use of this method of acquiring funds. Catholics in cities like Baltimore and St. Louis felt they had a sufficiently firm foundation and could do without help from the Community Chests. Other places like Cincinnati, St. Paul, Omaha, or Rochester saw advantages in the new movement. Some like Judge William H. DeLacy, treasurer of the National Conference, who subscribed to the movement in principle objected to any need for endorsement for Catholic charities on the ground that "besides control, the committee might also take credit for the work."[36] Fear was expressed that some of these organizations could be destroyed if they failed to receive approval because of their weak financial condition. Reverend Frederic Siedenburg, S.J., then dean of the Loyola School of Social Service in Chicago, took the position that where a Catholic agency received its support solely from Catholics it should not seek endorsement. Where the agency appealed to the general public for support then the public was entitled to know what it was supporting. Father Siedenburg had no fear of investigation because he believed that "if any of our Catholic charities are inferior, we, too, want to know it and have them brought up to standard."[37] Then there were also those who like Michael Weller contended that, "we have too many professionals . . . may the Lord protect us against the professional sociologist! That is to say, the individual who embraces that laudable career for the revenue only."[38] In the long run, however, the advantages of community fund raising contributed to the necessity of a central coordinating agency for Catholic charities in many cities.

The most important step toward realization of the idea of centralization on the local level was the action taken at the 1916 National Conference meeting by the fourteen diocesan directors of Catholic charities present at the meeting. With the hope of establishing a permanent national committee, these directors met and voted to request that such a committee be added to the list of committees already authorized under the National Conference of Catholic Charities.[39] This action, which was approved, represented the beginnings of the close relationship of the diocesan directors and the National Conference of Catholic Charities.

While we will examine later the operations and accomplishments of this Committee it should be noted here that its creation tended to take the leadership of the National Conference from the hands of laymen, Vincentians and others, and place it in the hands of the clergy. Discussion of the wisdom of this action created overtones that found their way into discussions on policies for some time. The necessity of the move, however, can hardly be questioned. Many of the laity, "earnest neophytes in charity work," accustomed to look to the clergy for direction and leadership, were unable to understand the "cold reception" which they often received in the parish rectory.[40] The clash of the "old" and the "new" in Catholic charity could only be resolved by the wholehearted cooperation of the parish clergy. The support and sympathy of the older organizations that had borne the burden of Catholic charities for the past generation had to be enlisted if the goals of the National Conference were to be achieved. Only if a diocesan bureau could be organized to enlist the aid of the clergy and these organizations, could the aims be achieved. It was unlikely that lay leadership alone could accomplish this.

The work of organization on the diocesan level was slow but progress was being made, and the National Conference had an important share in the developments. By 1922 some thirty-five Central Bureaus of Catholic Charities had been formed. A few of these exercised supervision over all the charities in the diocese while others confined their direction to the charities of individual cities within the diocese. Many new activities were created and older ones expanded.

The appointment of a diocesan director of Catholic charities was undoubtedly a progressive step toward coordination of activities which in many dioceses had been organized as individual corporations with the bishop as president of the corporation. The director's success in getting cooperation from these organizations, some of which owed further allegiance to a national or even international body, was not always immediate. The pressures of the federations of public and other private charities within the cities were, in the long run, to heighten the need for Catholic organization along similar lines and provide the diocesan director with one of his best arguments. The lack of organization in many places was finding the Catholic agency unprepared to meet new emergencies in the field of charity. In some areas the problem of the professional vagrant who had made a fair living presenting his case to each agency in turn, had convinced some of the need for coordination. Since most of these agencies did not even keep records, the vagrant's activities had been extensive.

By 1920 many were urging that the National Conference hold annual instead of biennial meetings and that they be held in cities other than Washington. The idea was that the stimulus to the local organization would be a tremendous advantage in its efforts to coordinate local activities. Since the management of the National Conference had been largely in the hands of The Catholic University personnel, and these men were too busy to undertake preparations for annual meetings, the biennial meeting idea had prevailed. Limited Conference funds were also a factor preventing the change to an annual meeting.

At the 1920 meeting, however, it was decided that the national meeting should be held annually and that cities other than Washington should be selected. The 1921 meeting was held in Milwaukee, and the success of the move was surprising. The attendance almost doubled, and the result was an effort to increase the membership so as to afford a broader base for the increased expenses. It was necessary also to increase the office force of the national office in order to "release the Secretary of the Conference from the tyranny of detail."[41] The practical result of the holding of the annual meeting in various cities was to bring the message of National Conference of Catholic Charities to all of the neighboring cities and thus sow the seeds of the future bureaus of charity. The goal was a well-directed bureau in every diocese under the supervision of the appointed directors of charity.

From the origin of the National Conference in 1910 to 1920 much of the work had fallen on the shoulders of its secretary,

Monsignor Kerby. The increasing burden of the work had forced him to resign in 1920 and the office of secretary was given to Monsignor John O'Grady, whose abilities and energy were immediately evident in the organization of both the 1920 and 1921 annual meetings.

One of the real problems demanding solution before the ideals of the National Conference could be even remotely realized was the spirit of aloofness prevailing among the religious communities engaged in charitable activities. The first half of the nineteenth century had seen many of these communities become established at a time when "the institutions of Catholic Charities became largely the expression of the interest of the different ethnic groups in their own children."[42] The debate in the 1880's and 1890's over the relative merits of the institution vs. the foster home had left its mark on these child-care institutions and they seemed to react by withdrawing further from the public scene. One large community, according to Monsignor Kerby, even forbade its members from attending or taking part in any public meetings. They made little or no effort to coordinate affairs even among themselves. A search made in 1910 to discover any evidence of such cooperation failed to disclose a single instance.[43] Yet over seventy-five per cent of the charitable work was being done by these religious communities. The approach of the sisterhoods to the problems of charity was to deal in a practical way with a particular problem as it appeared in the day-to-day activity and to leave theory to those who had the time and inclination to discuss it.

In 1919, Monsignor O'Grady, then assistant secretary of the National Conference, had in his travels become impressed with the magnitude of the problem and the necessity of doing something about it. What appeared to convince Monsignor O'Grady of the possibility of solving this problem was his experience in finding religious superiors deaf to his suggestions until they were told of some other institution which had found the particular method in question quite useful. The sparse attendance of the religious at the National Conference meetings from 1910 and 1920 when general

attendance had increased from 350 to 1000 was something that had
to be remedied. If the two thousand religious could be brought into
communication with each other through the instrumentality of the
National Conference a large step forward toward coordination of
all charitable efforts would have been taken.

While superiors might listen to Monsignor O'Grady's suggestions
and information on occasion, the greater problem of how to reconcile
the semicloistered atmosphere of most of the communities with
contact with the outside world remained. Fear that the religious
life of the sisters would be interrupted, that it was not advisable for
them to mingle with layfolk, that Sisters should not speak in public,
all these and many other obstacles were overcome sufficiently to
permit the establishment of the Conference of Religious in 1920
at the National Conference meeting of that year at Catholic
University.

One hundred thirty-nine sisters representing twenty-three communities attended a "Special Conference of Religious engaged in
Social and Charitable Work."[44] They participated in special sessions
from which lay persons were practically excluded. They met in a
separate university building set aside for their exclusive use. This
was the first opportunity that the religious had had of learning how
other communities approached problems that all had in common.
So successful was this venture that it was agreed that just as the
diocesan directors of charities had organized their own committee
to plan their own programs within the framework of the National
Conference, so the Religious might do the same. Accordingly, an
Organization Committee was set up and at the end of the Conference Sister Miriam Regina, S.C., Superior of St. Joseph's Female
Orphan Asylum in Brooklyn, was elected chairman, Sister M.
Celestine, O.S.F., of St. Joseph's Home, Peekskill, New York,
secretary.

The continued existence of the Conference of Religious was both
a difficult and important undertaking. Many of the original obstacles
such as transportation, housing, and reluctance to participate in
public meetings, remained to offer resistance to the effort to bring
the practices of the religious and the theories of social work in

closer contact. Monsignor Kerby put his finger on one of the basic problems when he observed in 1919 that,

> The Sisterhoods and Brotherhoods are the most conservative elements in Catholic Charity. Their work, their reverence for traditions, and the circumstances in which their social service is performed slow down the action of the elements which make for change . . . the danger of making a mistake by changing too slowly and by misunderstanding innovation is always present.[45]

The combined efforts of Monsignor O'Grady and Mother Miriam Regina, C.S., until her death in 1935 were indispensable factors in the successful growth of the Conference of Religious in minimizing these obstacles. It was the firm conviction of Monsignor O'Grady that the Conference would be one of the most important factors in making the institutional work of the Sisters better known, and thus offsetting the tendency to publicize only the weak points of the institutions. His view was that "we have nothing to hide from the world, and we owe it to ourselves, to our Superiors, to all Catholic people to let the world know what we are doing."[46] That the Conference was able to do just that was due largely to the determination and cooperation of its founders.

The relation of the Conference of Religious to the National Conference of Catholic Charities was not an organic one at the time of its establishment. Before 1920 very few members of religious communities were members of the National Conference. Within the next twenty years a large proportion of the National Conference membership came to be drawn from the religious. The problem then was whether to bring the Conference of Religious into closer relationship with the National Conference. This matter was brought up before the Executive Committee of the National Conference in September, 1942. The basic question was whether the National Conference could serve the religious more effectively. The Sisters themselves had not raised any question but the members of the Executive Committee thought that perhaps the Sisters ought to be included in district meetings of the Conference, that the *Catholic Charities Review* could be made more attractive to religious, and that a *de jure* relationship between the two groups would be mutually beneficial. No action was taken, however, and the discussion concluded with the observation that the current arrangement was satisfactory.[47]

Perhaps, one of the great strong points of the leaders of these early years was their willingness to engage in constructive self-criticism. Despite many recognized gains since the formation of the National Conference of Catholic Charities in 1910, it was still obvious by the early 1920's that a great deal of misunderstanding and lack of coordination existed among Catholic charitable agencies. Lack of sufficient funds to cover existing agencies was part of the problem of the efforts of the Central Diocesan Bureau to extend help to new areas.

Other problems could be seen in the frequently somewhat touchy relations between lay and religious workers. Lay persons who had figured largely in the founding of the National Conference were beginning to feel the impact of the shift from lay leadership through the establishment of the Diocesan Directors Committee and the Conference of Religious. One lay worker analyzed the problem as chiefly a psychological one due, in fact, to a great difference in the point of view upon life,

> The religious, a person vowed to obedience, when in authority, often expects from the lay worker a docility similar to that required in his own rule of life. It may be that independence of action for the lay person is necessary to efficiency, submission has not become a virtue; and it may eliminate the initiative required to bring success. . . . It should be realized that a group of lay workers cannot be disciplined as though they were members of a religious community.[48]

On the whole, however, the years down to 1925 witnessed tremendous gains. Monsignor Kerby described the period as "an orderly revolution which brings the best in newer methods and scholarship into intimate relation with the spiritual quality of Charity as the Church conceives it."[49] Isolation of Catholic agencies was breaking down and giving way to a national approach. No longer could an agency excuse its failure to keep in touch with the Catholic movement. There could be no question that the National Conference of Catholic Charities through its progressive leadership had played a major role in their development. Nor could The Catholic University be denied its share of credit in assisting in this work.

Monsignor Kerby, however, was of the opinion that the price the University paid for its participation was a bit too high. In a letter to Archbishop Curley in 1923, in which he lamented the failure of its graduates to continue research, Monsignor Kerby went on to say that,

> The University has been forced to take on a rather practical character that is distinct from technical research although of very great value in the life of the Church. The University was asked in 1909 to take steps toward the organization of the National Conference of Catholic Charities. It did so in 1910. In order to do this the National Conference absorbed over half of my time and nearly all of my vacations for ten years. It is now taking the time, energy, and vacations of Dr. O'Grady. The up-building of a national outlook in Catholic Charities, the beginning of a worthy permanent literature, the foundation of the Catholic Charities Review by Dr. Ryan, and the defense and discriminating, support of worthy standards in charity must be credited to the University. All of this has been of real service to National Catholic life. But it is a service largely distinct from research.[50]

Notes — Chapter III

1. Monsignor William J. Kerby, "Problems in Charity," N.C.C.C. *Proceedings,* 1910, p. 410.
2. *Ibid.*
3. Monsignor O'Grady, in *Catholic Charities Review,* Sept., 1936, Vol. 20, No. 7, p. 226.
4. Monsignor William J. Kerby, "Problems in Charity," N.C.C.C. *Proceedings,* 1910, p. 402.
5. *Ibid.,* pp. 405–406.
6. Robert Biggs, "The Problems of Dependency," N.C.C.C. *Proceedings,* 1910, pp. 96–97.
7. Monsignor William J. Kerby, "The New and Old in Catholic Charity," *Catholic Charities Review,* Jan., 1919, Vol. 3, No. 1, pp. 8–9.
8. *Ibid.*
9. *Ibid.,* p. 10.
10. Reverend Joseph McSorley, C.S.P., "The Catholic Layman and Social Reform," N.C.C.C. *Proceedings,* 1910, p. 184.
11. *Ibid.,* 1912, p. 128.
12. N.C.C.C. *Proceedings,* 1914, p. 95, Report of Monsignor J. J. Butler.
13. Monsignor William J. White, "The Reform Problems which the Church should meet," N.C.C.C. *Proceedings,* 1910, p. 176.

14. Dr. Charles P. Neill to Dr. Kerby, Aug. 8, 1910, in N.C.C.C. *Proceedings*, 1910, p. 178.
15. St. Vincent de Paul *Quarterly*, May, 1910, Vol. 15, No. 2, p. 207.
16. *Catholic Charities Review*, Jan., 1919, Vol. 3, No. 1, p. 8.
17. St. Vincent de Paul *Quarterly*, May, 1915, Vol. 20, No. 2, p. 89.
18. *Catholic Charities Review*, Sept., 1920, Vol. 4, No. 7, p. 213.
19. Bishop John Cantrell to Monsignor Kerby, Jan. 7, 1926.
20. Monsignor Kerby to Reverend George P. O'Connor, Oct. 30, 1925.
21. Monsignor John J. Butler, "The Conference of Catholic Charities of the City of St. Louis," N.C.C.C. *Proceedings*, 1914, p. 96.
22. N.C.C.C. *Proceedings*, 1916, p. 59.
23. *Ibid.*
24. *Ibid.*, p. 28.
25. N.C.C.C. *Proceedings*, 1912, p. 356.
26. *Ibid.*, p. 354.
27. Bishop Shahan's opening remarks at 1914 meetings; N.C.C.C. *Proceedings*, 1914, p. 32.
28. N.C.C.C. *Proceedings*, 1916, pp. 59–60.
29. N.C.C.C. *Proceedings*, 1922, p. 11.
30. *Catholic Charities Review*, Jan., 1922, Vol. 6, No. 1, p. 7.
31. St. Vincent de Paul *Quarterly*, Nov., 1913, Vol. 18, No. 4, p. 263.
32. *Ibid.*, p. 266.
33. N.C.C.C. *Proceedings*, 1912, p. 94. Dr. James E. Hagerty, "Cooperation Among All Charities."
34. *Ibid.*
35. *Catholic Charities Review*, Jan., 1922, Vol. 6, No. 1, p. 7.
36. N.C.C.C. *Proceedings*, 1914, p. 45.
37. *Ibid.*, p. 46.
38. *Ibid.*, p. 53.
39. N.C.C.C. *Proceedings*, 1916, p. 397.
40. Margaret Tucker, "Cross Currents in Catholic Charities," *Catholic Charities Review*, Mar., 1922, Vol. 6, No. 3, p. 76.
41. *Catholic Charities Review*, Oct., 1921, Vol. 5, No. 8, p. 262.
42. O'Grady, *Catholic Charities in the U. S.*, p. 32.
43. N.C.C.C. *Proceedings*, 1935, p. 64.
44. "Proceedings of the Special Conference of Religious Engaged in Social and Charitable Work" (Washington, D. C., 1920).
45. Monsignor Kerby, "The New and Old in Catholic Charities," *Catholic Charities Review*, Jan., 1919, Vol. 3, No. 1, p. 11.
46. "Proceedings of Special Conference of Religious," p. 73.
47. "Executive Committee of the National Conference of Catholic Charities, Minutes," Sept. 26, 1942, p. 1.
48. Margaret Tucker, "Cross Currents in Catholic Charities," *Catholic Charities Review*, Mar., 1922, Vol. 6, No. 3, p. 77.
49. Monsignor Kerby, "Bishop Shahan and Our Catholic Charities," p. 2.
50. Monsignor Kerby to Archbishop Curley, Jan. 19, 1923.

CHAPTER IV

Developing Social Work Standards

ONE of the great concerns of the early leadership of the National Conference of Catholic Charities was the lack of a vigorous technical literature of Catholic social work. Monsignor Kerby explained this deficiency as being due in great measure to the fact that most of the charity workers were men and women who were devoting their leisure to charity.[1] This leisure, subject to "prior claims of personal interest,"[2] left little time for the necessary reflection and analysis required to produce the desired literature. Moreover, most of these workers had never developed the habit of written expression of their views. They were content to do the necessary tasks as quickly and quietly as possible. Since as Monsignor Kerby observed "instinct for privacy is very strong in Catholic charity, notably so in our religious communities,"[3] it is not surprising that the religious too engaged in this "conspiracy" of silence. In Monsignor Kerby's view these people had been trained in the school of life rather than schooled by special training for the work they were doing. He applauded the new movement to develop a more scientific approach to charity as "undoubtedly wise,"[4] since the institutional reports that were available gave little evidence of insight into methods and concern for standards.[5]

The most valuable literature of Catholic charity in existence was in the St. Vincent de Paul *Quarterly*. Published between 1895 and 1916, this magazine contained the papers and addresses given at the various meetings of the Society. Again the leadership of the Vincentians was to be found in the efforts to keep the Church in touch with the developments in the field of social work. In November, 1895, Thomas Mulry had argued that it was time for

46

the Vincentians in the United States to have their own bulletin. The *Irish Bulletin* of the Society had circulated successfully in the United States up to that time, but Mr. Mulry felt that there were some six to seven thousand members who did not read it.[6] These he wanted to reach. The only objection he encountered from his fellow Vincentians was the fear that an American Bulletin would be unwelcome competition for the *Irish Bulletin*. Mr. Mulry assured the members of the Society that the need for a bulletin primarily committed to the publication of the American news of the Society was paramount, and the *Quarterly* was launched in November, 1895. It was the purpose of the magazine to "demonstrate to the Catholics of America that our organization is something more than a mere relief agency, and that our aims extend far beyond the mere food and clothing we give."[7]

So successful was the new *Quarterly* that four years after its founding there was a demand that it be made a monthly. Nothing came of this demand and it was not until the Richmond meeting of the Society in 1908 that the issue was again raised. On that occasion a committee was appointed to study the question but there appears to be no record of its report. About the same time Monsignor Kerby entered into correspondence with Monsignor John A. Ryan, then a priest in the Diocese of St. Paul, who replied that he was interested in a "weekly paper devoted to the social and industrial questions from the side of Christian principles."[8] Monsignor Ryan hoped to be transferred to New York City to manage such a venture. Again nothing materialized.

One year later Monsignor Ryan revived the idea of a Vincentian monthly in a letter to Monsignor Kerby in which he said that such a magazine was "badly needed" but rejected the idea that he manage such a venture as not "sufficiently close" to his plans.[9] Monsignor Ryan still had hopes of getting into publishing on the social question without any ties with the Vincentians. As he told Monsignor Kerby, "if I ever get into the field that I have in mind I should want to be master of the enterprise myself. . . . The work that I have in mind must be done thoroughly and independently from the beginning, or it is not worth anything."[10]

The Vincentians, meanwhile, had been facing the problems of the inevitable development of the paid charity worker. The earlier attitude that charity was a service given without any material return was slowly giving way to the view that a lay worker could devote his entire life to the service of charity, and that he would thereby be forced to depend on the returns of his labor for the livelihood of himself and his family. This problem of full-time service had to be faced sooner or later, and the Vincentians began to feel an even greater necessity for literature and advice to guide the social worker in this new approach.

The 1890's had seen the peak of middle class humanitarianism which consisted of a "variety of activities carried on by the charitably-minded members of the well-to-do class on behalf of the unfortunate members of the 'lower classes.' "[11] The rapidly developing professional approach was having its influence on the Vincentians even though they worked from a more Christian motive. The duplication of effort and the too frequent attempts to provide only material relief concerned the Vincentians greatly. By 1907 the advisability of full-time paid service in connection with child-care activities of the Society was readily admitted. The establishment of a central office in Baltimore for the Society with a paid staff was looked upon as a necessary development. The limitations of volunteer service were recognized.

Robert Biggs of Baltimore felt so strongly that the concept of relief only should give way to relief plus rehabilitation and prevention, that he warned anyone who had no other conception of charity than relief to "stay out of the work or learn the new methods in it."[12] Emphasizing the great changes that had come in social work he asserted that "we have reached the point where the problem of caring for our poor is too large for individual effort and too complex for the men and women who have not had the opportunity to give them special study."[13]

With this experience in mind it is not surprising that when the National Conference of Catholic Charities was established in 1910 these same men again revived the idea of a monthly review to keep the members up-to-date on developments in the field of social work.

The Conference voted in favor of establishing a national periodical at its 1910 meeting. The man behind the revived efforts was again Monsignor Kerby. It was at his suggestion that a joint committee of the Conference and the Society was appointed to study the possibility of a Catholic Charities monthly. What the Monsignor had in mind was to use the *St. Vincent Quarterly* as the basis of the new review. He explained his plans to Monsignor Ryan once again.

This time Monsignor Ryan was inclined to view the possibility of editing the new review with a little more interest. Although still cherishing his hope of editing a social and economic review in New York City, Monsignor Ryan wrote to Monsignor Kerby that while he was reluctant to give a definite answer,

> the publication as changed according to your plan would afford a vehicle for many views that I should like to exploit; on the other hand, it would not be nearly as satisfactory as a journal devoted specifically to social reform in the usual sense of that phrase. More-over, there is the question as to whether those in control of the Vincent de Paul publication would give me the degree of control that would be essential to satisfactory work. Yet it may be that a new publication of the kind that I have in mind will not materialize for years to come.[14]

However, Monsignor Ryan felt compelled to get into publishing and so he gave a qualified acceptance to the plans of Monsignor Kerby pending "satisfactory arrangements . . . as to remuneration, freedom of writing," and the consent of his Archbishop.[15] Yet, no further action was taken at the time.

In 1914 another vote was taken at the biennial meeting of the National Conference in favor of establishing a monthly review. The Society of St. Vincent de Paul at its meeting voted unanimously in favor of "changing the *St. Vincent de Paul Quarterly* into a monthly publication devoted to theoretical and practical aspects of Catholic Charity."[16] The step was to be taken in conjunction with a committee from the National Conference so that the interests of both groups would be taken care of. In November, 1915, the Superior Council of the Society of St. Vincent de Paul decided that in any change the new review should replace the *Quarterly*. At the meeting of the National Conference of Catholic Charities in September, 1916, the *Catholic Charities Review* was formally established and Monsignor Ryan became its editor. The *Quarterly*, which had given a continuous record of Catholic charities activities for twenty-one years, ceased publication and merged its interests with the new review whose first issue came out in January, 1917.

The decision to launch the *Catholic Charities Review* met with enthusiastic support from the members of the National Conference. Dr. Charles P. Neill noted the challenge to traditional methods, the need for trained workers, and the necessity for an exchange of views among the workers. The Reverend John J. Burke, C.S.P., wondered "that this wise step had been so long delayed."[17] The Reverend John T. McNicholas, O.P., later Archbishop of Cincinnati, rejoiced that the "spirit and action of this meeting make it memorable. Not one of us would have dared to predict that the establishment of the *Catholic Charities Review* could have been effected, accompanied by the extraordinary enthusiasm and determination we have just witnessed."[18] He predicted that the *Review* had "every promise of enduring service."[19] Bishop Shahan called the establishment of the review a direct result of the National Conference's desire to create an organ of its own. He claimed that the appearance of the *Review* would be "welcomed by all in the country who are interested in relief work."[20]

The *Catholic Charities Review* was designed to promote the objectives of the National Conference of Catholic Charities to "exchange views, to collect and publish information, to develop and express a general policy towards distinctive modern problems, methods and tendencies; and to create a literature of Catholic Charity."[21] The monthly journal was intended to supplement and extend the opportunities for discussion brought about by the biennial and later annual meetings of the National Conference. It was Monsignor Ryan's hope that modern problems and tendencies in relief and prevention would be treated in such a way as to "accelerate this movement and make it more solid and definite."[22] The published proceedings of the Conference meetings marked a step forward toward a literature of Catholic charity but since the circulation of these was somewhat limited it was hoped that the new *Review* would be able to reach a much greater number of people.

The *Catholic Charities Review* began as a thirty-two page magazine published monthy except during July and August. The contents were divided among seven departments. There was an editorial section, a section devoted to the reports of societies and institutions the greater part of which was devoted to the Society of St. Vincent de Paul, one on doctrinal principles underlying charity, another on social movements, one on general news, a section devoted to questions, and one to book reviews. Most of the early issues were devoted to prospects for state aid, the controversy over institutional vs. home care for children, social reform, birth control, and social philosophy. One gets the impression that there was a minimum of analysis in these articles and that the emphasis was more on "preaching."

The financial health of the publication in its early years left something to be desired. Monsignor Ryan, in 1918, felt that the number of subscriptions should have been close to 10,000 whereas the number was about 3600.[23] The latter number he felt was not "a sufficiently large number from any point of view"[24] and the venture was operating at a slight loss.[25]

Monsignor Ryan was no more satisfied with the lack of progress in another phase of the operation of the *Review*. He regretted the lack of assistance he had thus far received by way of contributions of articles regarding the achievements of Catholic charities in the various fields of endeavor.[26] If the journal was to provide the information and inspiration intended, then persons in the various institutions would have to take the time to write up their experiences and submit them for publication. Thus far there had been few such contributions from people qualified to speak. Monsignor Ryan felt that the problems created by World War I were things about which those qualified should have something to say. He warned that things were not going to return to the good old days.[27]

By 1919 Monsignor Kerby joined in the criticism of those who were not alert to the newer developments of "industrial democracy." He found it necessary to emphasize the great value of investigation studies which would measure the extent of the problem of poverty as "the first step in any intelligent effort to deal with it."[28] Too much time had been devoted to what Monsignor Kerby called the "literature of inspiration" which he considered adequate enough since it was largely an interpretation of the Gospel.[29] Despite the fact that specialists were being developed, and that schools of social work had been established there was still a great lack of factual material about how well the Catholics were taking care of their own poor. Monsignor Kerby called attention to the fact that despite the claim that everything was being done for the poor and the unfortunate, it was clear that in many of the cities this was simply not so. Monsignor Kerby was of the opinion that not only was the job not being done but there was evidence that it was becoming too big a job to be done by the Catholics alone even for their own poor.[30] For this reason investigation of the facts and publication of the results was very necessary. Without the facts there could be no sound interpretation of the problem. It was here that the *Catholic Charities Review* could provide the medium through which the hopes of the founders of the National Conference could be realized. In the ensuing years some progress was made along these lines. By 1926 Monsignor Kerby described the contribution of the *Review* to this progress as "beyond measurement."[31] By that time the *Review* had a circulation of 6000, still considerably short of Monsignor Ryan's expectations.

In the early 1940's a question as to the contents of the *Catholic Charities Review* arose. The problem appeared to be one of too much emphasis on technical material. At a meeting of the Executive Committee of the National Conference of Catholic Charities in Houston, Texas, in October, 1941 some suggestions were made for changes in the *Review*. Monsignor O'Grady commented on some basic principles which he felt should be observed before any change was contemplated. For one thing the *Review* must be considered a joint project of the National Conference and the Society of St. Vincent de Paul and any contemplated change should be discussed with the Vincentians. In any event, the responsibility of securing and editing technical materials should be retained by the National Conference office. Because the *Review* was the official organ of

Executive Committee of the First National Conference of Catholic Charities

Frank J. Johann   James F. Kennedy
T. D. Hurley   Robert Biggs   Richard Crane
Wm. F. Downey   Dr. Charles F. McKenna
Rev. H. G. Monaghan
P. J. McEvoy   Rev. Francis Foy   David F. Tilley   Rev. Dr. Wm. J. Kerby   Michael F. Doyle   Joseph W. Brooks
Rev. Dr. M. J. O'Connor   Edmond J. Butler
John Rea   Hon. Wm. H. DeLacy   Thomas M. Mulry   Monsignor Shahan   Monsignor McMahon   Monsignor White

Delegates to the First National Conference of Catholic Charities, Catholic University of America, September 25–28, 1910

Catholic social work these technical articles must be published, or else one would assume that the Review was "a popular magazine for volunteers."[32]

In March, 1942, the Executive Committee came to the conclusion that no fundamental change was to be made in the method of publishing the Review.[33] A contemplated agreement with the Denver Register had not met with approval. It was further decided to improve the quality and character of the Review, by adding a new department containing a digest of local, national, and foreign news in the field of social work as well as brief reports submitted by Diocesan Bureaus. Included also were to be reports on National Conference activities and general information on Catholic institutions and agencies. There was to be some experimentation in style and makeup of the Review. There was also a recommendation to add to the staff of the publication so that one member could give full time to the magazine. The suggestion that additional revenue might be gained from advertising was rejected as not feasible. In general it was agreed that the readers of the magazine comprised four groups: clergy, religious, professional workers, and volunteers, and that all groups should have their interests served in the Review.

About a year later, however, a question was raised about the possibility of a separate periodical for professional workers. Monsignor O'Grady had questioned whether the publication of materials on practices in Catholic social work really belonged within the framework of the Catholic Charities Review. It was estimated that to publish another journal for these materials would cost about $5,000 a year.[34] For this and other reasons the publication of the material in monograph form seemed to be a better solution. While it was still thought that there was a great deficiency of material illustrating the integration of Catholic philosophy with casework practice the Catholic Charities Review was considered to be the periodical in which this relationship should be treated.

To accomplish in one periodical an approach that would do justice to both philosophy and practice seemed to be the most desirable plan of action, but there were those who felt that to do this would require more contributions from the religious. A suggestion was made to the Executive Committee by Sister Agnita Miriam, S.C., Chairman of Conference of Religious that the sisters might pool their material for this purpose.[35] Sister Miriam noted that unless there is a training course for the sisters in their novitiate to prepare them for social work they were not likely to have as good an understanding of the problems of both institutional and foster care. She also recommended measures to insure the religious' greater insight into family life. The *Review* could be of great assistance in these matters despite the fact that there seemed to be a tendency on the part of the volunteers and religious especially to read more frequently in the leaflets and publications of their own organizations than in the *Review*.[36]

In December, 1956, the *Catholic Charities Review* made an evaluation of its contribution as the organ of the National Conference. Several points were emphasized, among them attention of the *Review* to the basic problems of the American community particularly in recent years. The journal has "emphasized a work program in preference to a purely relief program" and it has "favored benefits based on rights rather than relief."[37] Moreover, it "has constantly stressed the need for social research as the basis of all community programs" — to a point where its influence is making some headway.[38] The *Review* has worked for closer relationship between social work and the social sciences. It has further emphasized the role of the voluntary agency operating on a religious basis and stressed the great potentiality of individual self-help. Above all it has "emphasized the importance of close working relationship between Catholics and other religious groups in dealing with common problems confronting them in the American community."[39]

In the evaluation of the role of the *Catholic Charities Review*, it should be noted that the omnipresent problem of the relationship of the trained social worker and the volunteer was never denied full treatment in its pages. Intended as a medium of exchange of views for the trained worker, the *Review* did not hesitate to give space to the volunteer or the critics of professional social work. If the *Review* frequently received criticism from both the volunteer and the professional it was perhaps because it was attempting to serve too many masters.

The first meeting of the National Conference in 1910 witnessed the opening round of the discussion of the relative merits of the volunteer and the paid worker. Robert Biggs, the Baltimore Vincentian who had had considerable experience with paid social service made a vigorous defense of the professional worker. It was Biggs' opinion that the idea of trained workers was basically what Pere Bailey, first president of the St. Vincent de Paul Society had in mind in 1833 when he advised Vincentians to place "your education, your intelligence and your knowledge of life at the disposal of the poor."[40] This ideal had been lost by the Catholic worker, so Biggs claimed, had been picked up by the trained social worker, and now was looked on with suspicion by the Catholic social worker. The Catholic social worker, Biggs observed, was perhaps more concerned with "looking at the spiritual benefit flowing back to himself rather than to the amount of practical benefit he confers upon the dependent."[41] The trained worker, on the other hand has "in mind, always, as his first consideration the dependent" and he consequently finds it much easier to cooperate with other agencies necessary to accomplish the best possible solution for the dependent.[42] The trained worker is conscious of the need for coordination of resources and the usefulness of study.

Mr. Biggs, however, did not draw a distinction which left the volunteer in the class of the untrained worker. He urged that each city have a corps of trained workers, "volunteers if possible — paid if necessary" but able to cooperate with existing agencies so that "the work for the family may be placed beyond the contingencies of . . . business engagements and beyond the reach of failures resulting from . . . lack of knowledge, lack of experience, or lack of time."[43]

In the discussion which followed Mr. Biggs' talk there could be observed all of the crosscurrents of opinion with which the National Conference of Catholic Charities had to deal in promoting professional standards for Catholic social work. It is true that Mr.

Biggs had stanch support for his views from many quarters but this was chiefly the support of those who were already convinced of the necessity of the trained worker. Quite common among the remarks of the volunteers was the impression that the Society of St. Vincent de Paul had been attacked and needed defense. Some felt that the Vincentians were fully capable of doing the work, apparently missing the full impact of Biggs' talk. Others preferred the "sympathetic way" of the members of the Society who go about their work "more quietly."[44] It was apparently difficult for many volunteers to go beyond the concept of relief to remedial work. These people were not in agreement with the views of Reverend Peter J. O'Callaghan, C.S.P., of Chicago who held that "brains can do more than dollars,"[45] or Richard M. Reilly of Lancaster, Pennsylvania, who felt that "there is everything to gain and nothing to lose" in cooperation with secular agencies.[46]

The tendency of the Catholic to shrink from thoughts of trained charity workers, organization, records, and business methods in general in connection with charity was one of the major obstacles to be overcome at the local level by the National Conference. In 1912, Mr. Biggs attempted again to bring home to the second meeting of the National Conference of Catholic Charities the necessity of being concerned with more than relief in the treatment of social problems. Convinced that a large percentage of the poverty and misery of the day was preventable, he argued that Catholic social work could not be "carried on along the broad, progressive lines" intended by the National Conference within the framework of existing organizations without the establishment of "in every large city a central bureau in charge of a trained worker."[47] He even advocated trained workers in the parishes according to local needs. One of the commentators on Biggs' second talk in 1912 thought that perhaps the title "paid workers" was the cause of the mental block against the new movement. His answer was that "if it be pagan, Christianize it."[48]

One of the basic difficulties in the controversy over the trained worker and the volunteer appeared to arise from the failure of a majority to realize the preventive aspects of charity. Many could not see why relief, which had seemed adequate to them up to now, was not a sufficient solution to the social problems of the early twentieth century. At the 1914 meeting of the National Conference Dr. Charles P. Neill, former Federal Commissioner of Labor, and now Director of Welfare with the American Smelting and Refining Company, tried to impress upon the assembled delegates that what was needed was trained lay workers who would give their lives to "certain outside lines of work, just as our religious do to their traditional lines of work."[49] Such a worker would frequently have a more difficult task than that of the doctor and both needed training for their duties.

Dr. Neill could not understand why it was that the field of social work seemed to be the one area in which there was a feeling that no training was needed. He attributed the attitude, at least in part, to the fact that until recently no college had provided an adequate study program for this type of work. He looked forward to the day when special schools of social work would send out graduates "equipped to do the exacting work of social service, with skill that shows understanding and practical mastery, and with consecration that shows divine grace and social sympathy united in this noble work."[50] Dr. Neill was convinced that zeal alone was no more a sufficient reason for turning anyone loose on a social case than it was for sending someone with devotion alone to the sick to cure a disease. "The unintelligent, untrained charity worker can, in spite of disinterested zeal, often cause as much moral havoc as a result of his or her ministrations as an untrained practitioner of medicine could cause of a physical sort," warned Dr. Neill.[51]

There is one incident occurring during early 1913 that points up the extent to which feelings on this subject had spread. It seems that Monsignor Kerby was addressing a Sunday evening meeting of the "Ladies of Charity" and he was introduced by Agnes Repplier, chairman of the meeting, who in her opening remarks said: " 'We are about to hear from a priest who occupies the Chair of Sociology at the Catholic University, where almsgiving has become scientific. We expect to find curiosity (called investigate) substituted for charity and a system of records for alms.' "[52] Monsignor

Kerby smiled in returning the chairman's greeting and launched into a talk on the needs of society which had been created by urbanization. Among these were the need for records and some kind of system. He pointed out, too, that many social cases did not require investigation but only help. He received a standing ovation at the end of what a member of the audience considered one of Monsignor Kerby's "most effective addresses."[53]

During the early years of the National Conference's history this problem of the role of the trained worker always remained prominent in the discussions at the biennial meeting. The pages of the *Catholic Charities Review* reflect the great interest in this matter. The 1918 meeting of the National Conference gave special emphasis to the question. The April, 1919, issue of the *Catholic Charities Review* carried an article by Reverend J. Elliot Ross, C.S.P., analyzing at some length the special advantages of the professional social worker. He drew a parallel between social work and hospital work suggesting that a person would normally think twice before supporting a hospital staffed exclusively by volunteer workers who gave only part-time service. The charge against the hospital staffed by professionally trained people that the "money paid in salaries and record keeping ought to buy food for the poor patients would not appeal."[54] He condemned the attitude that held that "for a charity worker to inquire into the cause of one's poverty is to violate the sacred secrecy that should surround the poor," for "we can only know why people are poor by investigating."[55] Furthermore, he said, records were necessary to prevent fraud and duplication.

Father Ross had little patience with those who could not see that a scientific approach to poverty was as necessary as it was toward disease. He pointed out that the real distinction between a volunteer and a professional social worker "is not in the monetary compensation, but in the strictness and permanency of the bond uniting them to the work."[56] It was for this reason that he considered the religious communities as the "high water mark of professionalism."[57]

One of the results of the tendency to downgrade the professional social worker was the difficulty of enlisting these people in the service of Catholic agencies even where their help was actively sought by the more enlightened leaders. Two factors had already intervened to cause a decline of lay influence in Catholic charities: the creation of the Diocesan Directors Committee in 1916 and the establishment of the Conference of Religious in 1920. A third factor could be found in the uphill fight of the professional worker to establish a rightful place for himself in Catholic Charities.

Comments like the following from a "Conservative" of New York City to the editor of the *Catholic Charities Review* were not infrequent. It is understandable, therefore, that the Catholic social worker when confronted with this attitude frequently sought employment in public or in other private agencies. "Conservative New York" wanted the poor boxes in the church to read "For Social Service" instead of "For the Poor."[58] The writer continued his attack saying that he was sure that this would be a "much more progressive" way of doing things.

> It is very good to be sanguine, optimistic and progressive, and I am glad to see that you follow in the wake of Dr. Devine, though naturally from distance in training, a long way behind. It is somewhat of a shock for Catholic young men and women to take up the work of Charity as a profession, accustomed as they are, indeed taught as they are, to regard a work of charity purely as a voluntary task to be performed for their spiritual welfare, but of course it is possible in time to accustom them to regard it as a money making business first and as a spiritual affair afterwards.[59]

Mr. "Conservative" unleashed his full fury in finishing his letter by referring to the "theories of loud mouthed inexperienced social workers" whom he characterized in this manner "because the professional charity worker is never caught without his voice."[60]

The Catholic social worker, therefore, had many incentives to remain in other than Catholic agencies where he made up a fairly large portion of the workers. He had gone into this field as his only alternative to joining a religious community if he was inclined to work in the field of charity. Despite the efforts of the National Conference of Catholic Charities, he was still not accepted in Catholic circles where it was contended that the "vulgar phrase, social work" had been substituted for charity.[61] It was a strange situation in which the Catholic social worker tended to remain where he was, and have greater opportunity "to accomplish good work because of organization, and also because of sympathetic understanding between workers and executives."[62]

If the criticism of social work by Catholics had sprung from dissent resting on adequate information the tensions might not have been so great. However, much of it seemed to come from a conservative drift among Catholics coupled with a large share of misunderstanding of the purposes that inspired the movement for higher standards. Monsignor Kerby saw another reason for the criticism in the assumption that a systematic approach to social service was "cold blooded, erroneous in philosophy and a menace to faith."[63] Another source of misunderstanding could be found in the assumption that the volunteer was to be completely replaced by the full-time paid worker. With a certain prophetic analysis of the problem, Monsignor Kerby made it clear that while he and those who worked with him "were all of one mind in recognizing the need of training," and that it would not be long before all would recognize the need of "an increasing number of trained workers who may be paid adequate salaries in order that they may give themselves up entirely to the service of the poor."[64] Yet, there would always be, he contended, the need for many times more volunteers than paid workers.

The Reverend Frederic Siedenburg, S.J., then dean of the School of Social Service of Loyola University in Chicago, at the 1929 meeting of the National Conference of Catholic Charities attributed the lack of recognition of social work as a profession to the fact that social workers as a group had as yet not clearly defined their work.[65] Noting that it was only recently that nursing had come into its own, he looked forward to the day when social work as a professional field would also be so recognized. Because the social worker had not clearly defined his tasks, he was unable to interpret them clearly to the public. "As a result," said Father Siedenburg, "The average 'man on the street' thinks of social workers either as sentimental 'sob-sisters' or . . . as hatchet-faced, flat-heeled, brief-case carrying women, who go about poking their long noses into other people's business — never with the interest of the client at heart."[66]

By 1930 professional social work had begun to acquire some recognition. While it was true, as Father Siedenburg had pointed out, that the profession still lacked clear definition, it was equally true that the atmosphere in which discussions now took place was becoming more sympathetic toward the trained worker. Dr. Neill addressed the 1930 National Conference meeting on the subject and rejoiced that his earlier speech in defense of professional social work which had been blue-penciled by Monsignor Kerby, Mr. Mulry, and Mr. Butler, because it was "too strong [and] the Conference wouldn't stand it," now saw his deleted remarks being spoken by others and receiving applause in the Conference meetings.[67] Since the Conference, as he saw it, had been organized "to make a place for the trained worker in Catholic circles," he looked upon this change of spirit as evidence of the effectiveness of the first twenty years of the life of the Conference.

After the 1930's much of the discussion of the status of social work centered around the type of training the prospective worker should receive and the efforts to insure the social worker's Christian motives. Great concern was expressed over developing the proper attitude. Dr. Neill sounded the keynote here when he declared that,

> if social service is merely another field or "job," if it is merely a way of making a living, then we made a mistake in starting this organization. But if its purpose was, and its purpose is, to have work done as efficiently as training and ability can make it, and beyond this, to preserve the attitude that the work itself is Christlike, that it is done for the sake of Christ, then let us not sneer at attitudes.[68]

Fears that the trained Catholic social worker would be too greatly influenced by the secular environment of recent trends in social work training were often expressed. The failure of the social worker frequently to recognize the place of the confessional in Catholic life was cited as evidence of this materialistic approach.[69] The cause of this development was the "psychiatrical trend which has become the basis of all teaching in Protestant social work schools."[70] The real difficulty, according to the *Catholic Charities Review*, was that "we have no historical perspective. We have been nurtured on Protestant traditions. The literature we have been fed has been a broadened edition of the Protestantism of Tuckerman, of Harley, and Bruce."[71] The *Review* raised the question, "How long will it be before Catholic social work in America has the courage to develop its own culture and traditions?"[72]

Bishop James H. Ryan of Omaha observed some progress in this direction in 1935 noting that the opposition of universities to include training for the social worker was breaking down. The establishment of a School of Social Work at The Catholic University was a step in the right direction. "Social work is doomed," the Bishop stated, "if it looks for the training of its workers outside the university and according to standards which the university cannot and will not accept."[73] The Catholic University School of Social Work, as Bishop Ryan saw it, was the realization of the "ambition of the leaders of the National Conference of Catholic Charities over a period of 25 years. It is the special pride of the diocesan directors under the chairmanship of Monsignor Keegan."[74] A school such as this could go a long way in counteracting the secular approach to social work by supplying trained leaders for public as well as Catholic social work and trained priests for the diocese.

If, by 1935, "the well-meant but misleading couplet written by John Boyle O'Reilly was quoted with approval much more frequently a decade or two ago than it is today:

> 'Organized charity scrimped and iced
> In the name of a cautious and statistical Christ,' "[75]

it was due to the new respect which had been developed for professional social work. Much of the credit for this change would have to go to Monsignor Kerby who in the classroom and out had fostered a Catholic approach to social work training. If one were to think that the Catholic Church is "fossilized, reactionary, or insensible to advancing methods in social science and service, this Conference [National Conference of Catholic Charities] supplied the answer in its just appraisal and adoption of all truly progressive methods."[76] This accomplishment was a testimony to the quiet effectiveness of Monsignor Kerby's work.

Although great progress had been made by 1940 there was still much misunderstanding of the role of social work among Catholics. The increasing necessity of the social worker to study and analyze the economic problems of the 1930's had given rise to a new charge against the professional of excessive intellectualism just at the time his status was being recognized. The danger was admitted, and fears that this intellectualism could be carried too far often expressed. This new charge together with the older ones of "lack of sympathy and understanding, 'red tape' and statistics" did not make the lot of the social worker an easy one.[77] What appeared to be most needed in Catholic social service was the "recognition that modern social service is nothing but age-old Christian charity adapted to modern needs and conditions, and particularly a recognition by our Catholic schools of social service that the saints have been the world's best social workers."[78]

With the coming of World War II new problems beset the Catholic social work field. The draft, expansion of the Red Cross, and the tax drain on private funds created serious shortages of personnel in Catholic agencies. It was not surprising that many workers thought their only security was in the public welfare field. The problem of training the Catholic social worker also presented new difficulties. Reverend Walter McGuinn, S.J., dean of Boston College School of Social Work, in 1942 described the basic problem as one of "reconciling two seemingly irreconcilable bodies of knowledge, the principles of Catholic Doctrine and the techniques of a de-Christianized social work."[79]

In 1956 at the Buffalo meeting of the National Conference of Catholic Charities, Monsignor Fischer observed that while there had been marked progress in the "art of training new workers"[80] there was a lack of an equivalent progress in developing the "spiritual component of social work."[81] The chief defect as he saw it was that, "there seems to be no broad and general recognition that the Catholic social work program has something unique about it, something intrinsically valuable to the service itself and to the client recipients. Perhaps this fault is mostly our own."[82]

Notes — Chapter IV

1. Monsignor William J. Kerby, "An Interpretation," N.C.C.C. Proceedings, 1910, pp. 417–418.
2. Ibid.
3. Ibid.
4. Ibid.
5. O'Grady, Catholic Charities, p. 265.
6. St. Vincent de Paul Quarterly, Vol. 1, No. 1, Nov., 1895.
7. Ibid., p. 4.
8. Monsignor Ryan to Monsignor Kerby, Mar. 18, 1908.
9. Monsignor Ryan to Monsignor Kerby, Mar. 15, 1909.
10. Ibid.
11. A. G. Warner, S. A. Queen, E. B. Harper, American Charities and Social Work (New York, 1942), p. 25.
12. Robert Biggs, "The Problem of Dependency," N.C.C.C. Proceedings, 1910, p. 94.
13. Ibid., p. 95
14. Monsignor Ryan to Monsignor Kirby, Feb. 14, 1910.
15. Ibid.
16. N.C.C.C. Proceedings, 1914, p. 32.
17. N.C.C.C. Proceedings, 1916, p. 72.
18. Ibid., p. 74.
19. Ibid.
20. Bishop Thomas J. Shahan, Chairman's Address at the Second General Session, N.C.C.C. Proceedings, 1916, p. 61.
21. Monsignor John A. Ryan, "The Catholic Charities Review and the Future of the Conference," N.C.C.C. Proceedings, 1916, p. 65.
22. Ibid.
23. Monsignor John A. Ryan, "The Present and Future Mission of The Catholic Charities Review," N.C.C.C. Proceedings, 1918, p. 54.
24. Ibid.
25. Ibid.
26. Ibid., p. 55.
27. Ibid.
28. Monsignor William J. Kerby, "The New and the Old in Catholic Charities," Catholic Charities Review, Jan., 1919, Vol. 3, No. 1, p. 10.
29. Ibid., p. 11.
30. Ibid.
31. Monsignor William J. Kerby, "Trends in Social Work," N.C.C.C. Proceedings, 1926, p. 13.
32. "Minutes of the Executive Committee of the N.C.C.C.," Oct. 18, 1941, p. 5.
33. "Minutes of the Executive Committee of the N.C.C.C.," Mar. 20, 1942.
34. "Minutes of the Executive Committee of the N.C.C.C.," Apr. 28, 1943, p. 4.
35. Ibid., p. 10.
36. Ibid.
37. Catholic Charities Review, Dec., 1956, Vol. 40, No. 10, p. 1.
38. Ibid.
39. Ibid.
40. Robert Biggs, "The Problem of Dependency," N.C.C.C. Proceedings, 1910, p. 94.

41. *Ibid.*, p. 92.
42. *Ibid.*, p. 93.
43. *Ibid.*, p. 96.
44. *Ibid.*, p. 101.
45. *Ibid.*, p. 103.
46. *Ibid.*, p. 108.
47. N.C.C.C. *Proceedings*, 1912, p. 110.
48. *Ibid.*, p. 111.
49. Dr. Charles P. Neill, "Training for Social Work," N.C.C.C. *Proceedings*, 1914, p. 57.
50. *Ibid.*, p. 60.
51. *Ibid.*, p. 58.
52. MS., Sara E. Laughlin, Feb. 11, 1949, a member of the audience listening to the talk.
53. *Ibid.*
54. *Catholic Charities Review*, Apr., 1919, Vol. 3, No. 4, p. 106.
55. *Ibid.*
56. *Ibid.*
57. *Ibid.*
58. *Ibid.*, Sept., 1919, Vol. 3, No. 7, p. 203.
59. *Ibid.*
60. *Ibid.*, p. 204.
61. *Ibid.*, Mar., 1922, Vol. 6, No. 3, p. 75.
62. *Ibid.*, p. 76.
63. Monsignor William J. Kerby, "Resistance in Social Work," N.C.C.C. *Proceedings*, 1925, p. 59.
64. *Ibid.*, p. 60.
65. Reverend Frederic Siedenburg, S.J., "The Catholic College and Trained Social Workers," N.C.C.C. *Proceedings*, 1929, p. 101.
66. *Ibid.*
67. Dr. Charles P. Neill, "The Volunteer in the New Age," N.C.C.C. *Proceedings*, 1930, p. 34.
68. *Ibid.*, p. 39.
69. *Catholic Charities Review*, May, 1931, Vol. 15, No. 5, p. 147.
70. *Ibid.*
71. *Ibid.*
72. *Ibid.*
73. Bishop James A. Ryan, "A Training Program for Catholic Social Work," N.C.C.C. *Proceedings*, 1935, p. 47.
74. *Ibid.*, p. 51.
75. *Catholic Charities Review*, Sept., 1936, Vol. 20, No. 7, p. 229.
76. Bishop Joseph F. Rummel, "Why Catholic Charities?" N.C.C.C. *Proceedings*, 1932, p. 56.
77. Sister Victoria Francis, "The Responsibility of Religious for Interpretation of Social Work to Members of the Community," N.C.C.C. *Proceedings*, 1937, p. 147.
78. *Ibid.*, p. 150.
79. Rev. Walter McQuin, S.J., "Training in Case Work Skills," N.C.C.C. *Proceedings*, 1942, p. 50.
80. Monsignor Floyd F. Fischer, "Catholic Charities Service," N.C.C.C. *Proceedings*, 1956, p. 72.
81. *Ibid.*, p. 74.
82. *Ibid.*

CHAPTER V

Changing Status of the Volunteer

IT IS perhaps somewhat paradoxical that it was the volunteer who set in motion the development of organized social work and then found himself a victim of the movement he had fostered. The founders of the National Conference of Catholic Charities included many volunteers who, like Thomas Mulry, had "pointed the way to lay participation in the general field of social work."[1] These men were prepared to use the newer techniques and adapt them to a Christian philosophy. It was quite true as Monsignor O'Grady observed in 1925 that "some of the best developments in Catholic work have been inspired by volunteers," and that, "all our pioneer lay teachers were products of volunteer service" and a "powerful influence for good in their communities."[2]

The demands for full-time service brought on by increasing industrialization and urbanization of society were placing the volunteer at a serious disadvantage when placed alongside of the full-time professional social worker. It was not so much that the volunteer lacked training, for often he did not. The real difficulty was that "if the volunteer is in every sense a volunteer he will almost invariably have other claims that are paramount — family responsibilities, professional or business duties."[3] As a result, the continuity of service which was essential could rarely be given by the volunteer. As the work became more specialized the volunteer's lack of training would often add other difficulties, particularly when the courts sought to use him in certain types of cases.

Limitations of the volunteer were the subject of much discussion at the meetings of the National Conference of Catholic Charities. Robert Biggs frequently repeated his plea for a "thoroughly trained staff of educated and intelligent workers who will be city-wide in their field of activity."[4] In this manner the agency would permit neither "necessity nor urgent need to await too long the pleasure of the unobligated almoner."[5] The limitations of the volunteer were apparent from the beginning of the century in the field of child care. The criticism of institutional care common around the 1890's forced the development of Catholic child-placing agencies. The part-time volunteer was not well equipped to handle these cases.

By 1921 James Fitzgerald, Executive Secretary of the Society of St. Vincent de Paul in Detroit, was convinced that the "volunteer question has long enough been befogging issues" at National Conference meetings.[6] He thought it was time the issue was cleared up. Consequently, he attacked the generally accepted distinction between volunteer and professional workers which divided them into the unpaid and the paid workers. "This distinction," he asserted, "does not go to the essence of the matter. . . . Let us, then, stop sense-lessly dividing our social workers into 'paid' and 'unpaid' and try to lay the foundation for a united professional group fitted by training and experience for their work."[7] As Mr. Fitzgerald saw it, some Catholic workers were better trained than others. He proposed training for all.

Mr. Fitzgerald's views found a warm reception in many quarters. Most people now agreed that training was essential for the volunteer as well as for the professional. Moreover, the need for volunteers had not been diminished by the organization of charitable works. In fact, the increased volume of work made it quite clear that the volunteer would have to be an integral part of the system. The point of view of the volunteer and the individual personnel service which he could give were a part of the "precious heirloom of Christian civilization" which the National Conference of Catholic Charities was "bound to cherish and develop."[8] This was a contribution that the professional worker could not afford to ignore, nor could he avoid a large share of the blame for the lack of training of the volunteer.[9]

It was the recommendation of Mr. Fitzgerald at the National Conference meeting in 1921 that a training program for volunteers be set up in the Catholic agencies aimed at raising "the whole tone and standard and efficiency of our great Catholic charity work."[10] This program emphasized the "*training through organizations* and *not* through individuals."[11] It was the hope of the sponsors of this program that the trained volunteer would eliminate the possibility of volunteers working at cross-purposes with each other, sometimes in the same agency.

This development of trained volunteers was to be considered an essential part of the educational mission of the National Conference of Catholic Charities since every volunteer would then become a "missionary for broadcasting the message of organized Catholic Charities. Every volunteer is a step in recalling to the minds of our people that great and fundamental truth of their religion that personal service is one of their great obligations."[12]

By the mid 1920's hopeful signs of improvement in the development of the volunteer's role were apparent. Monsignor O'Grady, Secretary of the National Conference of Catholic Charities, observed that in his travels it was clear that the "best volunteer groups are no longer satisfied with the mere doling out of relief. They no longer base their judgment of a family on a casual visit to the home and on general neighborhood information."[13] This improvement was especially noticeable in the cities where central bureaus had been organized, proving that "without the leadership of a well organized case-working agency manned by a staff of well-trained workers, it is practically impossible to bring the work of volunteers up to a high standard."[14] Monsignor O'Grady noted that "the truth of this position has long since been recognized in Protestant work, and it is high time that more of our people come to recognize it."[15]

This influence of the trained worker on the volunteer, when properly developed, would have the effect of more properly defining the role of the volunteer. Much of the confusion as to the actual work of the volunteer was attributed to the "failure to study the work of volunteer groups in relation to modern case work standards."[16] Formerly it had been a common practice of volunteers to distribute large sums of money in relief but with little or no thought of working out a budget for the families concerned. The trained worker not only demonstrated a broader approach but usually increased the volume and variety of the work. The realization of the complexity of particular problems gave the volunteer an incentive to cooperate with the trained worker and convinced himself of his own need for training. The results could be seen in the improvement of records and the growing tendency to use the information from the areas of psychology, industry, medicine, public health, and public administration in the work of prevention as well as relief. Monsignor Kerby did not believe that by 1926, "the rate and quality of this progress are uniform throughout all of the ramifications of our Catholic work. But they are thoroughly established, easily recognized and rapidly growing. One could scarcely ask for more than this."[17]

One of the hoped-for advantages from all of this was the increase in numbers of both lay and religious social workers so that Catholic thought and practice could receive adequate representation at all kinds of conferences of social work. In providing the volunteer's share of this increase it had been discovered that the mass appeal for volunteers was not an appropriate means. Yet Monsignor O'Grady argued against abandoning these appeals since "sometimes they produce results in the most mysterious way."[18] The method of personal contact seemed to be the most productive with the active pastor having a great advantage in this regard.

One of the great tasks of the newly developing diocesan bureaus in the 1920's was to train and enlist the services of the volunteer. One of the major obstacles to be overcome in this relationship between the volunteer and the central bureau was the habit of the untrained volunteer to think almost exclusively in terms of relief. Frequently boasting that one hundred per cent of his funds were spent in relief, the volunteer often had difficulty in appreciating the work of any central organization of Catholic charities. An understanding of casework was difficult for the volunteer who considered his work in the past successful without this type of approach. Much of the responsibility for this lack of understanding of social service on the part of the volunteer could be attributed to defects in methods and policies of the central bureau.[19] If after a number of years, said Monsignor O'Grady, the central bureau is still misunderstood, then "the bureau is not doing good case work or it has failed to bring its work to the attention of the volunteers. . . . It cannot be repeated too frequently that good case work is the best advertising medium any social agency can have."[20]

In the opinion of Monsignor O'Grady there was not enough discussion of case problems in parish conferences.[21] Too little thought appeared to be given to the preparation of a definite program for these meetings. As a result many opportunities were lost in presenting the elements of family casework to volunteers, "and of bringing to their attention the concrete difficulties which the central office faces in dealing with parish conferences."[22]

For these and other reasons the general experience of directors of Catholic charities in the early days with volunteers appeared to be rather unsatisfactory despite efforts to bring the volunteer more fully into the newer aspects of social service. The chief problem seemed to be that the social work of the volunteer was so frequently interrupted by family and other responsibilities. This was not a new problem but it seemed accentuated as an issue at a time when the full-time worker of necessity had to plan his schedule on the assumption that volunteer help would be available. The complaint against the volunteer was that he felt "perfectly free at all times to disappoint at the last moment."[23]

The directors of diocesan bureaus were not discouraged, however, when they took a long range view of the situation. In the short run the effort expended in training the volunteer seemed like a waste of time, but the development of volunteers was a necessary part of the educational work of the central bureau and was encouraged by the National Conference. The great hope was to enlist the volunteer's interest in the broader aspects of community-wide movements as well as in the more immediate tasks of Catholic social work. If the conditions which gave rise to insufficient wages, irregular employment, insufficient health facilities, poor housing, neglected education, and a host of other social ills were to be remedied, such improvement would come about only through community action. Here the volunteer could be of inestimable service.

Apathy was, perhaps, one of the obstacles to growth along this line. Monsignor Kerby was particularly concerned with this aspect of the problem and felt that not enough had been done to awaken the interest of the prospective volunteer. Sometimes, he thought, this apathy took the form of "resistance honestly conceived and forcefully expressed . . . directed against standards of service, against alleged rigidities of system, against increasing expenses of administration or against an imaginary danger to the spiritual motive."[24] An intelligent opposition Monsignor Kerby did not mind. Nor did he object to "differences of judgment as to facts and results."[25] These he considered "inevitable and hardly to be regretted," because they "hinder premature conclusions, and, when rightly understood, keep us open-minded and watchful against a spirit of intolerance."[26]

An examination of the *Proceedings* of the National Conference of Catholic Charities between 1925 and 1930 reveals a considerable amount of space still being devoted to the role of the volunteer. Certain things, however, distinguish these discussions from previous ones. For one, there is recognition of a proper place for both the volunteer and the trained worker in Catholic social service. The volunteer is less frequently referred to as a "lunkhead," or a "stupid boor."[27] The necessity of training for the social worker, whether volunteer or professional, is almost universally admitted although questions might still be raised about the nature, amount, and source of this training. If the old problems were still present, they were at least being discussed in a more friendly atmosphere. Many who were volunteers originally had become professional social workers, particularly those whose natural ability in this line together with their experience made them especially valuable to their organizations.[28] The fact that the meetings of the National Conference of Catholic Charities provided a forum for the airing of conflicting views on these topics was in itself an important factor in lessening tensions.

Relations between volunteers and the diocesan bureaus, however, did not improve greatly in the years from 1925 to 1930. Unfortunately, there were many volunteers who still brought only good will to their tasks and were lacking in any understanding of the problems with which they had to deal. Others frequently stepped aside either through an inferiority complex or because they felt that their efforts went unappreciated. Some were not interested in cooperation with one another let alone with the various agencies. Monsignor John R. Mulroy, director of Catholic Charities in Denver, Colorado, thought that the answer to the problem was "to develop the sense of responsibility in the volunteer by training and more training."[29] It should not be forgotten, Monsignor Mulroy declared, that "the spirit of the Church is for volunteer social work and this spirit cannot be gainsaid, but the spirit of the Church likewise is for organization. In all her works she has found organization necessary."[30]

The opposition of the volunteer worker to the professional in earlier years had been characterized by an attack on the whole idea of social service as contrary to Christian tradition. Now that it was generally accepted that modern techniques and methods could be Christianized, a more subtle source of friction developed between the two groups. The insistence upon the training of the volunteer had frequently been advocated in such a way that it was not hard for the volunteer to develop a sense of inferiority. Dr. Charles P. Neill, speaking at the annual meeting of the National Conference of Catholic Charities in 1930, tried to bring out this point when he said,

> We, of the volunteer group, do not face as much difficulty in cultivating a sense of humility as you of the professional group do. You of the professional side, both by word and conduct, have so drilled into us the sense of our inferiority that many of the volunteers have dropped out of the work, and many of those who have remained in it have developed the inferiority complex, and humility thus comes to them easily. But, if you on the professional side are going to acquire humility it will in very many cases require a conscious effort, and the younger you are the more difficult it will be.[31]

Another aspect of the inferiority complex of the volunteer was involved in the growing realization that even the trained lay worker could not supply the type of service required in Catholic social work. An article in the *Catholic Charities Review* in 1926 reminded its readers that "Catholic organizations, it must be remembered, are religious organizations. Their basic work is religious work. . . . By reason of their close association with the work of the Church, Catholic social work organizations need the leadership of the priest."[32] While the point of the article was that the same principles of training in social work that applied to the layman should apply to the clergy engaged in social work, the implication for the volunteers was a reinforcement of his inferiority complex.

It is not surprising, therefore, that the supply of volunteers in 1930 was less than it was in 1900. The volunteer who had initiated the movement in social work in the Church that had produced the trained expert had largely disappeared. One possible explanation for this may have been that in the earlier days daughters of well-to-do parents did not seek employment as they were coming to do by the 1930's. Thus one important source of recruits was lost to the social service field. To a greater extent, however, the deficiency of numbers of volunteers was due to a situation which left the volunteer feeling that he was unappreciated, if not actually in the way.

For this reason many of the discussions of the role of the volunteer at the annual meetings of the National Conference of the years 1925 to 1930 tend to repeat the arguments of the previous five years. Much of the responsibility for overlapping and duplication of services was laid at the doorstep of the volunteer who failed to cooperate with the central bureau. However, Vincentians in particular were quick to point out the disadvantages of the young woman social worker in dealing with the male members of the family in certain types of cases. They felt that the "God-fearing and God-loving Vincentian, fellow-parishioner, and, perhaps, fellow-worker" was far more suited to the task.[33]

Occasionally, efforts were made to remind the delegates to the annual meetings of the National Conference that the "introduction of the trained worker has had a bad psychological effect on the volunteer workers, who have felt that the scientific treatment of poverty leaves no room for what they erroneously believe to be their own unscientific treatment."[34] Thomas F. Farrell reminded the delegates to the 1929 National Conference meeting that the real difference between the two was not the difference between scientific and unscientific workers but rather,

the two are related as the concave and convex sides of the same
reality which is the Charity of Christ. The trained worker is a check
on the possible excess of the emotions of the volunteer worker, and
the volunteer worker is a check on the possible defect of emotions
in the trained worker. . . . Exclude the trained worker and there is
danger of chicken-heartedness; exclude the volunteer worker and
there is danger of hard-heartedness.[35]

Some meeting of minds on this subject was developing by 1930
for at the annual meeting of that year, "at one of the very delightful
afternoon teas held during the sessions of the Conference the
volunteers and the professional workers decided formally to bury
the hatchet. They all agreed to work together in the future with
a spirit of mutual toleration for the attainment of their basic
objectives."[36]

The 1930's tended to focus even greater attention on the volunteer. There was, perhaps, a certain amount of justice in the turn
of events that now found "a very decided drift towards the use of
volunteers."[37] From the beginning of the National Conference the
emphasis had been on the need for the trained worker. The volunteer, in too many cases made to feel useless, had succumbed to
"centralization and the slow stifling of initiative" and had lost much
of his interest.[38] Now energies were being concentrated on the need
for volunteers and their potential not only in social work but also
in social reform.

Congested cities had proved more than the trained worker alone
could handle. There were now discussions on the limitations of
trained workers and suggestions as to how volunteers could help.
Mrs. Charles P. Neill, vice-president of the Christ Child Society
in Washington, D. C., called upon the professional social workers to
"act as commanding officers."[39] Dr. Neill pointed out that there
were many tasks the volunteer could handle thus relieving the
professional worker for tasks for which he was specially suited. To
those who claimed that the volunteer was too much trouble, Dr.
Neill observed that "there are volunteer workers who would try
the soul of anybody, and I know professional trained workers who
have tried my soul."[40] More and more the weaknesses of the trained

worker were discussed along with the weaknesses of the volunteer and the advantages of the volunteer received greater attention.

The personnel turnover in social service caused by the number of trained workers who would marry and leave the profession, and the difficulty the young woman social worker often experienced in dealing with the male side of family problems were considered to be at least as great a drawback as the uncertainty of volunteer service. The tendency to emphasize technique instead of attitude was likewise considered a trained worker's handicap. As Dr. Neill viewed it, if it were true "that in the general social movement or in the movement recognized in this National Conference of Catholic Charities, the professional has displaced the volunteer 100 per cent, it is a damning indictment of the movement. You cannot displace the volunteer and bring the movement to success."[41]

In 1933, Reverend Frederic Siedenburg, S.J., then executive dean of the University of Detroit, described the role of the volunteer in the new age as one of "personal and intimate service which the volunteer worker is particularly filled to give. The trained and paid worker is the symbol of society and of science; the volunteer worker is the symbol of charity and companionship."[42] Public service to the poor and the sick had expanded to a point where there was hardly any aspect of philanthropy that had not been invaded by the government. "The more personal and intimate elements of life are still untouched by public purse or service," Father Siedenburg observed, "and here the private agency and the charity volunteer have ample opportunity."[43]

The Diocese of Newark, New Jersey, in 1932 published statistics to prove the usefulness of the volunteer in their program.[44] Some twenty-six volunteer centers operating under the supervision of trained personnel distributed all relief and helped in the care of the diocese's twelve Catholic hospitals caring for 86,000 patients annually, 19 child-caring institutions for 3285 children, two correctional institutions, one Good Shepherd Home, and five homes for the aged. So successful was their program that the Reverend Ralph J. Glover, executive director of Associated Catholic Charities in Newark, reported that the "state, in administering its emergency relief program, has followed our lead and is extensively enlisting the aid of the volunteer."[45] Baltimore, Maryland, also reported successful incorporation of the volunteer into its diocesan program. Ninety-nine per cent of the relief work there was done by volunteers.[46]

Since volunteer work did not cost anything, the "depression-depleted coffers of private social agencies" after 1932, forced the agencies to "intensify their volunteer work because at the time their demands were greatest their finances were lowest."[47] It had long since been discovered that volunteers worked best when supervised by the agency staff, but the continuing tendency to single out the weak points of the volunteer while praising the strong points of the trained worker was condemned by the *Catholic Charities Review*. It was pointed out that the literature of volunteer social work was "either wholly critical or inspirational. It contains very few illustrations or descriptions of good volunteer work."[48] The *Review* recognized that it had "not done what it should to develop a real literature of volunteer work, a literature that is concrete, simple, and detailed," but that it would accept the challenge and try to remedy the situation.[49]

The economic depression of the 1930's accentuated all social problems and proved that to a great degree many of them were economic problems. Because these problems were now being met by governmental action in a number of fields with insistence on some integrated planning with the various agencies, the volunteer was placed under even greater responsibility than he had been. It was necessary that he "become to a greater extent a student of social phenomena and of professional techniques."[50]

The increasing demands for social legislation to combat the results of the depression suggested a new role for the volunteer. It was hoped that he could be instrumental in the creation of an informed public opinion on prospective social legislation. He had the advantage because of the interest in social work and he could meet the "taxpaying and contributing public on a far better footing than does the trained worker. . . . He has no ax to grind nor can the ill-founded accusation of gain be attributed to him."[51] The volunteer had the advantage of appreciation of the human equation in social work and would not "permit dependents to be sacrificed for the theories of intellectual bondogglers."[52]

It was apparent by 1938 that along with a growing recognition of the increasing importance of the volunteer, there was a lessening of tensions between the volunteer and the professional worker. Much of the difficulty had arisen from a failure of each to understand the other's function and potentialities. The social and economic problems developing from the depression of the 1930's had brought the "realization that the two are so closely related and so interdependent that only when complete harmony and cooperation exists between them can the work of each be effectively accomplished."[53]

The volunteer was finding new opportunities in the expanding public programs particularly in rural areas. Small communities had traditionally solved their problems by individual or volunteer service. It was the large urban area that had made organization on the professional level necessary. Since there had been a tendency to ignore the rural areas the volunteer, until recently, lacked encouragement to develop his potential for good in this field. He was now being brought out of the "attic of oblivion" where he had been consigned "like overstuffed furniture."[54] Here, too, the volunteer could not only take his place in organized welfare work, and an active interest in social problems, but also could protect Catholic interest and principles.

There still prevailed in some areas the notion that the volunteer was a sort of a chore boy to do the tasks that specialized personnel had neither the time nor the inclination to perform. For the most part, however, the volunteer was accorded a definite place of his own in the field of social welfare. The fact that it was the volunteer who had been the pioneer in raising standards was coming to be more generally appreciated, and it was recognized that it was an "amateur spirit, a fresh zeal that does not always survive in the professional" that was the volunteer's chief asset.[55] It was this heritage of personal service which the volunteer was being asked to share with the expanding social programs of both public and private agencies.

The National Conference of Catholic Charities sought to encourage the recruitment and training of volunteers in the 1940's by sponsoring institutes for volunteers on the diocesan level. The annual meeting of the Conference in those years placed considerable stress on the role of the volunteer. There was a feeling that much of the work done by the professional could and should be done by the volunteer, thus relieving the professional of some of the great load under which he was working. There was a financial advantage also in the use of the volunteer since funds were not always available to provide for professional help.

Chicago in 1940 demonstrated what could be done by organizing volunteer workers under the supervision of trained personnel. Some 4000 active volunteer Vincentians in 325 parishes were caring for 8000 families per week.[56] The Family Welfare Association of America praised the work in its report and recommended the plan of the Chicago Catholic Charities to other cities.[57] The plan was described as " 'the most serious attempt on the part of any social agency in the United States to organize volunteers on a large scale for service to families in need . . . the Church is the force which inspires the volunteer, placing before him a constantly broadening vision of service and compensation in spiritual benefits which accrue to devoted and untiring efforts.' "[58]

World War II gave the volunteer ample opportunity to demonstrate his capabilities, and he more than lived up to expectations. There were, however, individuals who attempted to "make most of the service of private social welfare agencies a direct function of the government."[59] These were people who saw in the "war crisis a new opportunity of enlarging governmental control and responsibility; they would even take over a large part of the work done by volunteers under private agencies; they would rally the volunteers around governmental agencies without any respect or consideration for the rights of agencies under which these volunteers now operate."[60] The potential effect of such a development on the future of Catholic social programs made it increasingly necessary to insure sound training for the volunteer in Catholic social philosophy. In this way the volunteer who might serve on boards, committees, and in other public capacities would be able to represent the Catholic social agency more adequately.

The record of service of the volunteer during the war showed the advantage of giving him adequate training. This training was "the most important and, at the same time, the most difficult responsibility of the Catholic Charities."[61] The suggestion made by Monsignor A. J. Fussenegger, diocesan director of Catholic Charities in Indianapolis, was for the diocesan director of Charities to conduct his own institutes and see that the volunteer had a "clear knowledge of the objectives, problems, needs, and resources of the program which he enters."[62]

For this training program to work effectively it would be necessary for the professional workers to encourage the volunteer to enter the field of service. This encouragement was thought to consist of the professional's recognition of the contribution the volunteer could make, of eagerly accepting his services, and of giving him all the assistance and help he needed. It was the professional who was to arrange for the recruiting, training, and placing of volunteers. In the placing of volunteers it was Monsignor Fussenegger's opinion that,

> a volunteer should never be placed in a position where he is doing a job, or giving a service for which money is available. If money can be obtained to pay for a service, the proper personnel should be employed. Only in an emergency, when it is impossible to get help or an appropriation of funds, should volunteers be used. A volunteer is not to supplant the paid worker; his function is to supplement him.[63]

The Secretary of the National Conference of Catholic Charities spent some time in the years immediately after World War II in a search "for new signs of life among volunteer groups, particularly Conferences of the Society of St. Vincent de Paul."[64] He found much real interest in a number of parish Conferences of the Society and came to the conclusion that "they were making a real contribution to the building up of family life, to the prevention and treatment of delinquency, to the administration of public benefits in

their respective neighborhoods."[65] Monsignor O'Grady looked upon
these activities as "evidence of a new interest on the part of the
Catholic laity" and predicted that this would be a "new source of
inspiration in Catholic social work."[66]

At the 1950 annual meeting of the National Conference of Catholic Charities there was a panel discussion on training programs for
Vincentians. This was in keeping with the renewed emphasis on
volunteer activity and the need for adequate volunteer training.
One panel member, James Fitzgerald, executive secretary of the
Particular Council of the Detroit Society of St. Vincent de Paul,
was considerably disturbed by the subject which he said gave him
"a faint beginning pain in the neck."[67] He was even more disturbed
when he read the fine print in the program which said,

> Local conferences are frequently called upon to give people informa-
> tion regarding various available community resources. There is now
> a question of formalizing these training programs. At this meeting
> representatives of the Society will discuss various methods used in
> keeping members informed in regard to community resources.[68]

It had at last dawned on Mr. Fitzgerald why he was put on this
panel, and he was not happy that this was the first and only comment he had heard on his proposal for just such a training program
back at the 1921 annual meeting in Milwaukee.

> That the sole comment on that speech — even though the com-
> mentator was so knowledgeable a one as Doctor O'Grady — came
> twenty-nine years later, is small incentive for me to propose another
> training program. I didn't mind so much waiting around for twenty-
> nine years for some comment on the first program, but I really can't
> be accused of pique or impatience if I decline to hang around another
> twenty-nine years before anyone pays any attention to a second pro-
> gram which I might propose today. I just don't think I'll be here
> anymore. Especially since I realize that my second program will be as
> much out of date then as my first one is now.[69]

It was Mr. Fitzgerald's hope that "any formalized training programs for conference members will not be so technical as to take
any of the simple joy out of being an ordinary conference member
nor any of the warmth and common kindness out of the visiting of
the poor in their own homes."[70] He much preferred the philosophy

expressed by Billy Ban "when he dug his mother-in-law's grave only three feet deep: 'why make a toil out of pleasure?' "[71] Mr. Fitzgerald warned that one must be careful "to keep membership in our conferences a pleasure and no toil and we must follow St. Paul's advice to do the works of mercy smilingly."[72] No statement could better convey the meaning of the personal service contribution of the volunteer. It was this spirit that Monsignor Fischer had in mind when in 1957 he paraphrased Pius XII's Christmas Message of 1952 and declared that "we must lead our fellow workers back home and our fellow Catholics everywhere to a revival of the spirit of personal charity."[73]

Experiments in the use of volunteers continued. The National Conference office undertook in 1957 a number of projects using volunteer services in children's institutions. There was still some reluctance on the part of the sisters of some institutions to use volunteers to their maximum capacity. It was the hope of the Conference that the projects would "serve as real demonstrations of the potentialities of volunteer services in children's institutions. . . . We have made only slight beginnings in utilizing the potentialities of our lay volunteers in the work of Catholic children's institutions."[74]

The first training program for group mothers in Catholic institutions for children was held at John Carroll University in Cleveland, Ohio, July 27 to August 7, 1958. Included in the program were sessions on training programs for college student volunteers. The results were what had been hoped for. The sisters "received a picture of volunteer services they had never thought was possible. . . . The only volunteer services they had considered at all successful were those given to fund-raising, and running errands, such as taking people to clinics. They never thought of volunteer services as playing an important role in the lives of children."[75]

Notes — Chapter V

1. *Catholic Charities Review*, Oct., 1936, Vol. 20, No. 8, p. 255.
2. Monsignor John O'Grady, "Lay Participation in Catholic Charities," *Catholic Charities Review*, Dec., 1925, Vol. 9, No. 10, p. 383.

3. Rose J. McHugh, "The Proper Relation between the Volunteer worker and the Courts," N.C.C.C. *Proceedings*, 1920, p. 277.
4. Robert Biggs, "Family or Children's Agencies, Which?" N.C.C.C. *Proceedings*, 1922, p. 167.
5. *Catholic Charities Review*, Oct., 1920, Vol. 4. No. 8, p. 239.
6. James Fitzgerald, "Recruiting and Training the Volunteer," N.C.C.C. *Proceedings*, 1921, p. 89.
7. *Ibid.*, pp. 89–90.
8. *Catholic Charities Review*, Dec., 1925, Vol. 9, No. 10. p. 383.
9. N.C.C.C. *Proceedings*, 1921, p. 98.
10. *Ibid.*, p. 96.
11. *Ibid.*
12. *Catholic Charities Review*, Dec., 1925, Vol. 9, No. 10, p. 383.
13. *Ibid.*, May, 1923, Vol. 7, No. 5, p. 162.
14. *Ibid.*
15. *Ibid.*
16. *Ibid.*, p. 161.
17. Monsignor William J. Kerby, "Trends in Social Work," N.C.C.C. *Proceedings*, 1926, p. 14.
18. Monsignor John O'Grady, "Lay Participation in Catholic Charity," N.C.C.C. *Proceedings*, 1925, p. 262.
19. *Catholic Charities Review*, Dec., 1925, Vol. 9. No. 10, p. 380.
20. *Ibid.*
21. Monsignor John O'Grady, "Lay Participation in Catholic Charity," N.C.C.C. *Proceedings*, 1925, p. 257.
22. *Ibid.*
23. *Catholic Charities Review*, Dec., 1925, Vol. 9, No. 10, p. 382.
24. Monsignor William J. Kerby, "Trends in Social Work," N.C.C.C. *Proceedings*, 1926, p. 16.
25. *Ibid.*
26. *Ibid.*
27. *Catholic Charities Review*, Sept., 1919, Vol. 3, No. 7, pp. 203–204.
28. N.C.C.C. *Proceedings*, 1928, p. 394.
29. *Ibid.*, p. 385.
30. *Ibid.*
31. Dr. Charles P. Neill, "The Volunteer in the New Age," N.C.C.C. *Proceedings*, 1930, p. 39.
32. *Catholic Charities Review*, Feb., 1926, Vol. 10, No. 2, p. 69.
33. Val. Blatz, Jr., "New Phases of Volunteer Work," N.C.C.C. *Proceedings*, 1929, p. 24.
34. *Ibid.*
35. *Ibid.*
36. Editorial, "The Return of the Volunteer," *Catholic Charities Review*, Oct., 1930, Vol. 14, No. 8, p. 206.
37. *Ibid.*
38. Mrs. Leon C. Finck, "What is Being Done in Social Welfare," N.C.C.C. *Proceedings*, 1931, p. 58.
39. Mrs. Charles P. Neill, "Methods of Securing and Holding the Volunteer," N.C.C.C. *Proceedings*, 1930, p. 71.
40. *Ibid.*, p. 35.
41. *Ibid.*

42. Reverend Frederic Siedenburg, "Catholic Lay Action," N.C.C.C. *Proceedings*, 1938, p. 382.
43. *Ibid.*
44. N.C.C.C. *Proceedings*, 1932, pp. 252–253.
45. *Ibid.*
46. *Ibid.*, p. 308.
47. N.C.C.C. *Proceedings*, 1938, p. 382.
48. *Catholic Charities Review*, Oct., 1937, Vol. 21, No. 8, p. 237.
49. *Ibid.*
50. N.C.C.C. *Proceedings*, 1938, p. 383.
51. *Catholic Charities Review*, Oct., 1936, Vol. 20, No. 8, p. 256.
52. *Ibid.*
53. *Ibid.*, Feb., 1938, Vol. 22, No. 2, p. 44.
54. *Ibid.*, Oct., 1937, Vol. 21, No. 8, p. 249.
55. William Lamers, "Relationship between Volunteer and Professional Leadership in Catholic Youth Organization," N.C.C.C. *Proceedings*, 1938, p. 148.
56. N.C.C.C. *Proceedings*, 1940, p. 19.
57. *Ibid.*, p. 20.
58. *Ibid.*
59. *Catholic Charities Review*, Sept., 1942, Vol. 26, No. 7, p. 181.
60. *Ibid.*
61. Monsignor A. J. Fussenegger, "Necessity for a Corps of Volunteers," N.C.C.C. *Proceedings*, 1946, p. 201.
62. *Ibid.*
63. *Ibid.*, p. 200.
64. Monsignor John O'Grady, "The Conference and Trends in Catholic Social Work at the Present Time — Challenges Ahead," N.C.C.C. *Proceedings*, 1948, p. 13.
65. *Ibid.*
66. *Ibid.*
67. N.C.C.C. *Proceedings*, 1950, p. 265.
68. *Ibid.*, p. 266.
69. *Ibid.*, pp. 266–267.
70. *Ibid.*, p. 268.
71. *Ibid.*, p. 269.
72. *Ibid.*
73. *Catholic Charities Review*, Oct., 1957, Vol. 41, No. 8, p. 9.
74. *Ibid.*, Jan., 1957, Vol. 41, No. 1, p. 1.
75. *Ibid.*, Oct., 1958, Vol. 42, No. 8, p. 5.

CHAPTER VI

Growth of Diocesan Charity Organization

FOR the National Conference of Catholic Charities to achieve its objectives it was necessary that the national office reach the ordinary Catholic on the parish level through some form of diocesan organization. The Council of Trent had reemphasized the traditional role of the bishop in overseeing all measures for relief of the poor, but it had not spelled out the manner in which this was to be accomplished. It would not be enough for the National Conference to advocate the raising of standards, warn against duplication and overlapping of functions, encourage preventive as well as relief work, and support good social legislation based on Catholic principles if there were no machinery to carry these things out on the local level.

Since most Catholic charitable institutions in the United States had grown to meet specific needs as they arose, there was a haphazard development of institutions and services rather than implementation of any well-thought-out plan. Each organization had become accustomed to having its own way without very much concern for the others. A National Conference of Catholic Charities might preach against this situation, but it would be powerless to act in a particular diocese without the active support of the bishop of that diocese.

This need on the local level for some type of central organization further strengthened the desire for development of the diocesan central bureau. The need was first felt in the child-care agencies, where between 1895 and 1912 central child-care institutions were established in six cities. Before long it became apparent that the work with children could not easily be separated from other forms of welfare work. The need for a centralized system under diocesan

Left to right: Monsignor Kerby, Bishop Shahan, and Monsignor O'Grady on the steps of McMahon Hall, Catholic University

This picture was taken at a meeting of the Continuing Committee of the Directors of Catholic Charities. (Name later changed to Standing Committee.) St. Louis, Missouri, April 21, 1936.

Seated, left to right: Rev. Robert P. Barry, Director of the Catholic Charitable Bureau, Boston, Mass., Rev. Edwin L. Leonard, Director, Catholic Charities, Baltimore, Md., Rev. John J. Butler, Director, Catholic Charities of St. Louis, Rt. Rev. Msgr. John O'Grady, Secretary, National Conference of Catholic Charities, Washington, D. C., and Very Rev. Msgr. John R. Mulroy, Director, Catholic Charities, Denver, Colorado.

Standing, left to right: Rev. Ralph J. Glover, Executive Director, Associated Catholic Charities of Newark, N. J., Rev. Bryan J. McEntegart, Director, Division of Child Care, Catholic Charities, Archdiocese of New York, Rev. William H. Meegan, Director, Catholic Charities, Buffalo, N. Y., and Rev. Francis Egan of St. Louis (not a member of the Committee).

auspices embracing not only child welfare but also recreation, health, and other related services was then recognized. In the dioceses of Boston and Hartford the religious care of children placed in foster homes by public agencies was a problem demanding special attention. In large cities like Philadelphia and New York the establishment of juvenile courts had resulted in the Catholic organizations in those cities employing full time workers to act as their representatives in the courts. The Strong Commission in New York, 1913 to 1914, whose "real purpose . . . appeared to be the secularization and paganization of all the charities of the great state of New York by showing incompetencies, abuses, and corruption in privately operated charities," was another convincing argument, according to Monsignor Mulroy, for coordination and centralization on the local level.[1] By 1928 some thirty cities in the United States and Canada had adopted some form of local central bureau of charities.

Up to 1910, therefore, the concern for the spiritual welfare of dependent children would appear to be the chief cause for a diocesan bureau. Between 1910 and the end of World War I the development of a number of departments of public welfare on the state and local level created the necessity of having some kind of central organization to deal with them. In this period occurred the most rapid increase of central bureaus.

There was a gradual realization during this period that Catholic institutions were not sufficient in themselves to exercise the broad influence that was expected, unless more attention were given to noninstitutional or extrainstitutional activities. "A far greater influence in human welfare is being exerted by such agencies nowadays," said Reverend M. J. Scanlon, Diocesan Director of Charities in Boston in 1918, "than by the time-honored charitable institutions and . . . the larger field where there is close and intimate touch with the multitudes of struggling people in and about their houses, is the urgent need of our time."[2] The great advantage of the diocesan bureau was that "under episcopal direction and with its encouragement [it] can reach out to every corner of the diocese where there is a charitable problem to be met and solved."[3] It was clear, too, that the rapid growth of public and other private agencies might preempt the field unless action were taken by the Catholics. There was no denying that social service as distinct from charitable institutions had been considerably in the hands of those outside the Church. "To offset the all too evident lack of Catholic agencies to handle Catholic cases, the diocesan charitable bureau comes in very providentially."[4]

Evidence that something was being done about the lack of co-ordination among Catholic agencies could be found in the growing number of appointments of diocesan directors and the establishment of diocesan bureaus of charity. Father Scanlon in 1918 looked upon this development as "historically just a revival of an ancient institution and the reassurance of diocesan responsibility for the success or failure of the good work within its confines."[5] Perhaps the most important development, however, came in 1916 when the diocesan directors came together as a group at the biennial meeting of the National Conference of Catholic Charities. Many of the pioneer lay leaders were not very happy with the creation of a committee of diocesan directors within the framework of the National Conference of Catholic Charities,[6] but there was fear that the Conference might fail because of the lack of the support of the clergy. The incorporation of the directors into the National Conference assured the support of the clergy and made them the link between the National Conference and the local level.[7]

The *Catholic Charities Review* in 1920 took notice that there was a great deal of talk about this failure of the clergy to support social service movements, and expressed doubt that there was any real foundation to the charges.[8]

> Priests are naturally unwilling to cooperate in a work in which they are not given an active voice. They cannot and should not be expected to surrender their leadership in charity as in other religious works to lay organizations. Wherever diocesan charities are well organized the priests are ever ready and willing to cooperate. They are anxious, and rightly so, to see the integrity of their parish maintained. They are anxious to see as much work as possible done by the parishes.[9]

Although there were not more than five priests who were connected with parishes at the first meeting of the National Conference in 1910, there were twenty-six at the 1920 meeting.

In the period between World War I and the beginning of the depression of 1929 the extension of the idea of a diocesan director and a central bureau of charities raised a number of questions as to the authority of such offices and their relation to existing charitable institutions. The directors of charity acted immediately under their respective bishops and had as their principal task the fostering and supervision of all charitable activities of the diocese and direction over related matter referred to them by priests or laity. Since most charitable institutions already were legally incorporated in their respective states, the relation of the diocesan director to them would have to be determined in each instance by the particular bishop. The extent of the director's authority or supervision would likewise have to be determined in each instance. Consequently, there was no uniform pattern applicable to all dioceses.

If the sound development of Catholic participation in social work required a central organization with a priest in charge devoting full time to a well-thought-out program, it was even more important that active episcopal support be given. In 1925, Monsignor O'Grady observed that "it is a well recognized fact of Catholic history that no work of any single individual or group can assume any degree of stability until it becomes an integral part of the official work of the Church."[10] Monsignor O'Grady, as executive secretary of the National Conference of Catholic Charities, had been making efforts to establish diocesan bureaus of charities and study the operation of those already in existence. It was his judgment that the "experience of the past few years has also taught us that the formal approval of the bishop is not sufficient for the success of a diocesan program of Catholic charities. The work must have his active support. It must be done in his name and under his leadership."[11]

As the head of the agency through which the bishop directed the charitable activities of his diocese, the diocesan director has as his objectives the coordination and correlation of the work of all Catholic agencies in the diocese; direction of work in casework,

group work, health, and social action; official representation of the
diocese in dealing with other agencies in the community; continuing
study of social conditions; responsibility of organizing all, professional and volunteer, who are engaged in social work.[12] One of the
chief tasks of the central bureau would be to induce the "normal
agencies of the Church to assume an increasing share of responsibility for the poor and the handicapped."[13] If effective casework was
encouraged, then good example would be given to the parish and
volunteer organizations and Catholic social work would be made an
integral part of the everyday activities of the Church. Another major
task was the cooperation with other agencies in analyzing and
removing the causes of social problems.

Not all of the diocesan bureaus in the period prior to 1925 began
with a definite policy as to exactly what work would be done.
Usually they undertook all kinds of tasks. The workers attached
to the bureau attended case conferences, juvenile court sessions,
engaged in child welfare work, organizational activities, and even
occasionally recreational work. For this reason one of the early
problems of the diocesan bureau was that it soon became overloaded with work. This condition was aggravated by the lack of
trained Catholic social workers. About the most that many of the
bureaus were able to do under these conditions was to make the
initial visit and take care of emergencies.

The transition from the child-care program, which was characteristic to most institutions, to a diocesan program concerned with
family welfare was not an easy one. Before 1925 some thirteen
dioceses had given recognition to the principle that social work for
the family was the basic form of social work.[14] Monsignor O'Grady
observed that in 1925 there was not as much respect as there should
have been for social work techniques and standards even among
those who presumably were committed to their use.[15] A tendency
to depend too exclusively on volunteers was symptomatic of this
condition. Thus even well-planned programs would fail to attain
their objectives.

A warning against other possible difficulties in the establishment of diocesan programs had been sounded by Rev. M. J. Scanlon, Diocesan Director of Charities in Boston, as early as 1920.

> It would be idle to assume that this new development augers well in every particular for Catholic Charities. Practically all our Catholic charitable works owe their beginnings to private initiative and not to official promptings. . . . Too much coordination and too much supervision and too much efficiency may very easily lessen the warmth of our Catholic people's devotion to good works leaving us with an elaborate form of administration, but with very meagre substance of actual charitable work. We say this not in discouragement of the present trend toward a more perfect organization of Catholic charities, . . . but rather as a warning against the possible and not altogether unlikely assumption that the cause of charity can be harnessed to the paraphernalia of the department store or of the steel industry.[16]

Nineteen years later the Most Reverend John J. Mitty, Archbishop of San Francisco, issued a similar warning against the dangers of excessive organization. "It is becoming true," he said, "that the rating of our agency depends principally upon the physical setup of our organization, the training which our social workers have, the professional organizations they belong to, the type of case histories we keep, the statistics we furnish, the case loads, the adjustments we make for our clients, and not so much upon the love we have shown to those who need our help."[17] This condition he attributed to the ease with which social work can slip into routine in its following of rules and regulations.

At the 1926 annual meeting of the National Conference of Catholic Charities a discussion of the pitfalls of organization brought out that seldom did the annual reports of Catholic agencies mention any of the spiritual good they were attempting to accomplish.[18] It was noticed that nonsectarian workers reported it because "for them it was like a whiff of sweet perfume, it is something exceptional."[19] While the chief complaint about the agency's annual report was the lack of scientific analysis of service and finances, it was suggested that it would be wise to "report the spiritual good done, for it will be a potent factor in gaining the good will of parish priests, who are now looking upon our work with doubt and misgivings."[20]

Of all of the problems attendant upon the development of the diocesan bureau of charities, perhaps the most significant in the 1920's was the overloading of the central office. The remedy for such work loads was not a larger and better trained staff but rather a recognition of the essential function of the central bureau as an educational one. Not enough effort had been spent in getting across to both priests and laity "that the central organization is not intended to relieve them of all their obligation in regard to individuals and families in need of assistance."[21] In many dioceses there was little contact between the central bureau and the various child-care institutions. Little effort was made to bring the religious together to discuss problems and no one from the central office assumed responsibility for keeping the sisters informed of advances or new developments in the field of social work. There was great need for the central bureau to arrange for a pooling of experience among those engaged in diocesan social work. The overloaded central bureau was thus diverted from its principal tasks.

What was happening was that various lay organizations and parish priests were passing on a greater share of their work to the central organization. According to Monsignor O'Grady the task was to get "our priests and laity to recognize that the central organization is not intended to relieve them of all their obligations in regard to individuals and families in need of assistance."[22] The line of reasoning which prompted the unloading of the problems of the parishes and volunteer organizations on the central bureau was, "since we are supporting these large large downtown organizations, and turning over large sums of money to them every year, why not make them work for what they are getting."[23] Monsignor O'Grady observed, too, that "the Sisters in the parochial schools in many places are beginning also to catch the contagion. They have at last found a means of relieving themselves of all responsibility for their truant, backward and unruly children."[24]

Inefficiency in the operation of the central office was a natural result of this overloading. Emergency cases frequently comprised over seventy-five per cent of the total number of cases.[25] Instead of each organization in the diocese gaining a new consciousness of its respective duties there was a general undermining of responsibility. "One of the great fundamental aims of every central organization should be to cause an increasing amount of social and charitable work to be done through the ordinary mechanism of the Church in its parish organization," declared Monsignor O'Grady.[26] But, because many of the central offices felt they had to make too many promises in the beginning of what they would do in order to justify their existence, the central office must bear its full share of responsibility for the resulting confusion and inefficiency.[27] The end result was that the central bureau was becoming one of many agencies and often competing with them. This was a serious departure from the original purpose of the central bureau and if long continued would result in another organization being created to do what the central bureau was supposed to do.

The diocesan organization of Catholic charities went through definite stages in its development. The early stage appeared to be one in which it was supposed to render certain services not being offered by any other agency. "It was supposed to eke out its existence in a twilight zone. It dare not trespass on the traditional reservations of the institutions or the volunteer agencies."[28] The second stage was a kind of rule-making stage in which the relationships of the agencies to each other and to the central bureau were outlined. The third stage was characterized by a general acceptance of certain principles governing the relationships of the various organizations such as, agreement that there was a need for social investigation, that the full-time worker did have a place in the volunteer agency, and that there should be greater concern for standards of service. By 1930 most diocesan organizations had reached this third stage.

There was growing recognition by diocesan agencies of the authority of the central bureau to start new charitable activities, if needed, and to discourage those that had outlived their usefulness. In this latter capacity the relationship of the central bureau to the institution run by a religious community needed clarification.

The central bureau could not function without the help of the institution, and the institution came to recognize that it could be helped tremendously by a properly run central bureau even if this meant a change in the type of work the institution might be asked to do. Interpreting the Catholic institution to the public came to be the responsibility of the central bureau, and to do this in an age that was critical of institutional care of children required insistence on high standards of work. By the beginning of World War II there was growing confidence in the work that was being accomplished in child-care institutions and it was felt that "The most prejudiced and critical person is disarmed by a visit [to the institutions in question]. . . . They must be seen to be known and appreciated. It is our problem to bring the world to the doors of our institutions. There is no problem after that."[29]

It was pretty well agreed by diocesan directors of Catholic charities in the 1930's that among the results to be achieved by a well-organized central bureau were the raising of standards, elimination of overlapping, fostering of preventive as well as remedial measures, improvement and extension of family welfare work with the emphasis on family rather than institutional care where it was advisable, and the promotion of social legislation based on Catholic principles. This last function became increasingly important after the depression of 1929 and the National Conference of Catholic Charities worked closely with the directors of Catholic charities to accomplish this end.

The Archdiocese of Cincinnati in 1926 demonstrated what could be accomplished through cooperation with the National Conference in setting up a diocesan program. Monsignor O'Grady had examined the local situation and presented a program in November, 1926, which was approved by the Archbishop and accepted as the official program of the archdiocese.[30] Great progress had been made by the archdiocese since the establishment of the Bureau of Catholic Charities and Social Service in 1915, but as one of the pioneer organizations in the field, the Bureau has experienced the difficulty of lack of any real authority except that which it won by patient and persevering work, in overcoming the handicap of insufficient funds.[31] As a result a number of children's institutions had refused to recognize the Bureau or be guided by its policies. All of this was now changed, and the reorganized Bureau was now backed by the authority of the Archbishop.

In 1937 there were sixty-eight diocesan bureaus organized in thirty-five states,[32] a growth which kept pace with a similar trend toward coordination and centralization in public welfare. Because of the expanding role of the government in public welfare, it was imperative that the Church have a central bureau of charities with authority to deal with public and other private agencies in matters affecting the lives of a large number of Catholics. There was, however, an understandable lag in organization in dioceses covering large areas where problems of transportation made it difficult to deal with scattered populations.[33]

Sister Victoria Francis of the Foreign Missionary Sisters of St. Dominic, Maryknoll, New York, remarked at the annual meeting of the National Conference of Catholic Charities in 1937 that there was a considerable change from the atmosphere of twenty years before where "organized charity" had been equated with a major heresy.[34] "Now, if every Catholic," she continued, "thoroughly understood that the Church itself stands for 'organization'; that it requires those who serve the Church to be properly 'trained'; that the Vatican itself 'keeps records' most efficiently; perhaps such terms as 'organized charities' and 'trained workers' and 'case records' would send fewer chills down the spines of those who in this respect tend to be more Catholic than the Pope."[35]

The central bureaus of charities during this period of the 1930's were soon faced with a new problem. The economic crisis had placed heavy burdens on the private agencies and the work of systematization and coordinating of agencies sponsored by the National Conference of Catholic Charities had not progressed to a point where there was complete understanding of the role of the central agency. The popular concept of measuring the worth of any organization in terms of money spent left the central bureau in a difficult position. There was little money to distribute, and governmental agencies were assuming a greater share of responsibility for relief. The private agencies, therefore, had begun to direct much of their attention to the study of social causes; as a result, they appeared to the average observer to be doing very little to help relieve economic distress.

Much misunderstanding of the role of the central bureau thus developed. That it was necessary to have a diocesan bureau as the official organ for studying social problems, and as the only proper agency for dealing with social problems, and as the only proper agency for dealing with state and municipal organizations was not always appreciated. Teamwork was difficult to achieve when the central bureau was not always recognized as the planning body with responsibility for a unified diocesan program. The affiliated agencies often neglected their role as the interpreter of the diocesan program even when they did understand and appreciate it.

The decade of the 1930's, however, was not without its advantages. With the governmental agencies carrying most of the burden of relief there was an opportunity for the Catholic agencies to turn to efforts to supplement the pastoral ministry of the Church. Educational programs acquainting Catholics with the benefits available under the new governmental programs gave the central agency the opportunity to do some of the things for which it was originally intended. There was also a greater concern for the problems of family relief. There was, likewise, a questioning of limiting the primary responsibility to children because the result of the failure to know the family problem was to limit work to relief and neglect prevention.[36] Then there was, also, a very noticeable increase in the participation of the younger clergy in social work and social movements. One of the important functions of the National Conference of Catholic Charities was to foster and promote developments such as this. The diocesan directors of charities had pledged themselves in 1935 to exert every effort toward having priests and religious released from diocesan work in order to prepare themselves for service in the field of social work.[37]

The relation of the layman or volunteer in social work to the diocesan bureau raised questions that did not always have easy answers. Since one of the great contributions of the Society of St.

Vincent de Paul had been the insistence on coordination and centralization of Catholic charitable activities, it was surprising that at least one person subscribed to the impression in 1920 that "the dawning era marks the day of increasing activity on the part of the laity in social work."[38] Fears on the part of some that a central organization would interfere with the operations of the Vincentians were not realized in most of those areas where the diocesan charities were properly organized. In fact, the Society seemed to be doing better work in those places than in the dioceses which were unorganized.[39] Much of the central bureau's relief work could be done through the Society and thus increase the Vincentians' opportunities for service.

Under the stress of daily activities, however, it was not unlikely that the central office would overlook its mission to the laity, and place less emphasis on the recruitment of the volunteer layman, particularly in an age when the trained worker appeared to be in conflict with the volunteer. Moreover, according to Monsignor O'Grady, it was no easy task to integrate diocesan organizations which "were exceedingly jealous of their own rights and prerogatives and were greatly afraid lest their identity be lost in the new program."[40] Since the viewpoint of the volunteer was fairly typical of the viewpoint of the average layman, the diocesan bureau failed to be understood by the rank and file. Mutual misunderstandings of viewpoint and objectives contributed to the view that the layman was being excluded from the field of social work. In 1930 this idea was expressed by a Community Chest worker when he said, "The St. Vincent de Paul members were very active before, but now you have a director of Catholic Charities serving on all committees. This is not giving the men a chance to be represented."[41]

Since coordination of the charities of a diocese was essential, it was necessary for the Society of St. Vincent de Paul to find its niche. It was difficult, however, for many of the members to discover just what this was. The Society, nevertheless, continued its loyal support of the National Conference of Catholic Charities, arguing that none "can fail to profit by attendance at the National Conference" and that as Vincentians they "should preach its value to others, who may know of the purpose of the Conference only in a very hazy way."[42] In 1933, the Reverend John C. Carr, director of Catholic Charities in Buffalo, declared that the future of the Society of St. Vincent de Paul lay in the spiritual perfection of its members, cooperation with other agencies, ability to use the newer techniques in social work, and the extension of the Society into every diocese and parish.[43]

While there was recognition that the role of the layman should be a significant one, there were not too many successful attempts to enlist his support. In 1925, Monsignor O'Grady made the suggestion that the first step toward securing the layman's assistance was the organization of an active board of directors in conjunction with the central bureau of charities.[44] It was Monsignor O'Grady's belief that, instead of having the boards of directors selected by the bishop, as they usually were, it would be wiser "to consider the possibility of having the board selected by the membership of the organization . . . the rank and file of the membership would [then] feel a keener interest in the organization if they had an active voice in selecting its officers."[45] Such a board should not be a mere figure-head but "pass on the budget of the organization and all its major policies, leaving the details of administration to the Director."[46]

Despite this and similar suggestions, it would seem that the interest of the laymen in diocesan social work declined rather than increased after the 1920's. Monsignor O'Grady, in 1925, warned against an approach to social work "in the name of standardization and coordination" that would "shut out all thinking on the part of our laity."[47] It was Monsignor O'Grady's idea that it was essential that the laity be given an "important part in the development of standards and policies."[48] He suggested the presentation of programs in "the form of counsels rather than of laws, hoping that in time, and as a result of a gradual educational process they will come to select the better and wiser course."[49] He advised patience in the "hope that our lay organizations, which do not seem to see the need of organized Catholic work, may change their viewpoint, rather than run the risk of alienating them forever!"[50] If the laity were to be allowed "to participate intelligently in our work," argued Monsignor O'Grady, "their services must not be confined to the raising of money. Intelligent men and women of today will not take a very deep interest in our charities if their opinions do not have some influence on programs and policies."[51]

The later years, however, did not see a great deal of change in the status of the layman or volunteer. At the Executive Committee meeting of the National Conference of Catholic Charities in 1943, Miss Marguerite Boylan contended that while the Conference had developed leadership among the priests and the sisters, it had failed to develop lay leadership throughout the country.[52] She thought that it was time that greater efforts be expended to develop "a devoted, intelligent, strong lay group."[53] Monsignor O'Grady, at this meeting, attributed the failure of the Conference to develop a strong lay leadership to "the tide of the times."[54] This tide, he thought, had now turned and lay leadership in the local community was developing and could be encouraged by the National Council.

Given the conditions that existed, the centralization of the 1920's and 1930's in the development of Catholic social service was probably a necessary one. The stress on standards also had to be emphasized. The price, however, was not only the failure to develop a strong lay leadership but the setting of a pattern that remained unchanged until after World War II. There were no replacements for the "old-timers" like Thomas Mulry, the New York contractor; Edmond Butler, Mr. Mulry's chief lieutenant; Robert Biggs, a Baltimore businessman, who was in a sense an originator of central offices for Catholic Charities, Timothy Hurley, editor of the Juvenile Court Record, among the Catholic laymen active in the first White House Conference on Children in 1909. At this White House Conference there were 43 Catholics among the 216 attending it, and 23 of them were Vincentians.[55] Dr. Thomas Dwight, a Harvard anatomy professor, has no successor today "who manifests consistent or pressing personal interest in the apostolate of Catholic social service."[56] Jack J. Spaulding, an Atlanta lawyer, and many others that might be mentioned were among those who gave the Society of St. Vincent de Paul a leadership in the years down to 1915 that it has since tried hard to regain.

During the early development of the diocesan organization of charities the layman was not the only one who appeared to be relegated to a secondary position. The pastor of many a parish was also convinced that he was being assigned a minor role in the scheme of things. While it was admitted that the parish had the primary responsibility for taking care of the needs of its own people, urban growth was producing a situation where frequently the parish with the greatest needs had the least resources. Some problems, moreover, tended to transcend parish boundaries. A central bureau could be a great help in dealing with such a situation but serious misunderstandings between the parish and the central bureau arose and made coordination difficult.

Few pastors in the 1920's tended to question the need of a city-wide organization to deal with juvenile delinquency or with investigation of applicants for admission to the various child-care institutions.[57] When, however, existing parish organizations needed additional finances to handle relief problems, the pastor frequently felt that he was already doing all that could be expected of him. One of them was quoted by Monsignor O'Grady as saying, "if I only had all that I contribute to the diocesan charities I could care adequately for my own poor and have a large surplus left over."[58]

As a result of his contact with the clergy in the parishes, Monsignor O'Grady was of the opinion that much of the blame for the misunderstanding could be placed at the doorstep of the diocesan organization. "When I find a large number of pastors," he said, "opposed to a central Catholic relief organization I have strong suspicion that the agency is not doing good work or is failing to present its results in a telling way."[59] He did not feel as some did that there was no hope of converting the older clergy. Although he did approve of introducing the concept of social work in the seminaries he felt that the best means of winning over the clergy was by "actual and tangible results."[60] His advice was that, "When we do a good piece of case work in a Parish we should call it to the attention of the Pastor. If we fail the first time let us not be discouraged. Good work will win him over in ninety-nine cases out of a hundred."[61] As Monsignor O'Grady saw it the priest in the parish did not think in terms of expansive programs but "his ordinary everyday experience predisposes him to think in terms of concrete realities."[62]

To a certain degree many of the difficulties in the relation between the parish and the central bureau could be traced to lack of communication between them. Many of the parish organizations were still under the impression that temporary relief was the limit of their obligations. The movement sponsored by the National Conference going beyond relief into the whole subject of family welfare was not well understood. The lines of communication between the National Conference and the parish level were by no means well established. The Vincentians were, of course, in contact with the newer developments but there was almost no contact between them and the various women's organizations engaged in parish relief.[63]

The National Conference of Catholic Charities needed interpretation on the parish level and this was not being done effectively. A caseworker representing the diocesan bureau was not likely to promote understanding of the work of the bureau when she urged a pastor to validate a marriage in which there were five children, when the pastor already knew that the man in question had a wife and three children in another country.[64] Despite some areas of understanding, the gulf between the parishes and the central bureau was still quite wide in the late 1920's. The parish often assumed that it was perfectly capable of dealing with its own problems, which it frequently conceived only in terms of relief. The assistance of an agency and full-time professional help was neither wanted nor considered necessary. There were also pastors who expected too much from the central bureau. When the expectations were not fulfilled the result was criticism of the bureau.

The National Conference meetings in the late 1920's devoted considerable time to a discussion of the problem of the relation of the parish to the diocesan bureau. In 1927 the Conference made an effort to have the parish considered as a social unit. A number of parish programs had shown some progress in this direction in the previous ten years and gave considerable promise for the future.[65]

Reverend Edward R. Kirk, director of Catholic Charities in Newark, New Jersey, in 1927 declared that it was necessary for the parish priest to realize that he needed the assistance of a diocesan organization to help him fulfill his responsibility. "It is no longer possible," he said, "for the priest to be Doctor, Lawyer and Social Worker. In these days of floating population, varied nationalities and general hurry and turmoil, no one person can expect or should expect to be able to deal with the thousand and one difficulties which arise in a parish, and it is here that the Bureau comes to his assistance and should extend courtesy, cooperation and consecration."[66]

There was no question but that the wholehearted cooperation of the clergy was essential if the National Conference of Catholic Charities was to have influence on the local level. The training of the clergy in social work and the force of episcopal authority might effect some kind of cooperation but as Father Carr, Diocesan Director of Charities in Buffalo, in 1928 said, this "does not appeal to the heart."[67] Part of the difficulty as he saw it was that "the status of a director of charity is not clearly defined. No mention of it is made in the new code or in any of the diocesan statutes that I have seen."[68] Father Carr's opinion was that success might be attained "in spite of the opposition of some of the clergy, but we cannot succeed in the face of opposition of the majority."[69]

Monsignor O'Grady's experience led him to believe that in general too much was being expected of the central office by the parish because of the misunderstandings of the role of each. He was of the opinion that much of the overloading of the central bureau was the result of the bureau's assumption of "a part of the pastoral responsibilities of the priest."[70] He felt that pastors had not been made aware that it was not the duty of the central bureau "to furnish funds to pay rent, provide food and fuel and clothing for the poor of the parish."[71] What the pastor should expect, according to Father Edward R. Kirk, was "the most exacting courtesy" and there should be "recognition on both sides that this great effort to solve social problems is too big for personalities."[72]

The 1930's, however, did not see any great improvement in the relationship of the parish and the central bureau. It is true that there were isolated developments like the study made of Catholic Charities in Chicago in 1933, where the effective coordination of the Central Charity Bureau and the Society of St. Vincent de Paul presented unusual opportunities for both.[73] This study made by the Family Welfare Association of America at the request of the Emergency Welfare Fund of Cook County, concluded that the "community at large should be better acquainted with the spectacle of 4,000 men visiting weekly approximately 8,000 families in which state and private funds are maintaining life."[74] Reverend William O'Connor, diocesan supervisor of Catholic Charities of Chicago, felt that the cooperation of the two organizations presented "an unusual opportunity for effective organization of the contributions of trained and volunteer workers, and if such trained workers were infused into the staff, the Central Charity Bureau has an opportunity to develop within a reasonable time an organization which may well become a pattern for the Catholic social machinery of the country at large."[75]

Yet, in 1940, the *Catholic Charities Review* could still ask the question, "Why are our priests and people not more interested in our program?"[76] The answer given was, "Their own problems have been taken away from them."[77] The Review concluded that the central bureau had assumed parish responsibilities. A partial explanation for this was found in that a Catholic social agency differed greatly from a public or other private social agency. The Catholic agency could not assume, as it had apparently done in imitation of the public agency, exclusive responsibility for its cases. The Catholic family seeking assistance was primarily the responsibility of its pastor. The parish priest was not a resource of the central agency. "We are one of their resources," declared the *Catholic Charities Review*, "to think otherwise or to act otherwise is to assume a responsibility which church law has placed on the pastor."[78] The *Review* warned that, "it will be a sad day when parish priests and their people cease to say 'our poor' and speak rather of 'your cases.' "[79]

One exception to the usual pattern of the development of diocesan organization of charities, however, can be found in the Archdiocese of St. Louis. The site of the first American foundation of the Society of St. Vincent de Paul became the place where the steady growth of the Society early demonstrated the necessity of a central bureau as a clearinghouse for the Society's work. This bureau, established in 1919, developed to meet the increasing demands placed upon the Society. A series of natural disasters further strengthened the need of central organization. The Ordinaries of the Archdiocese had always given strong support to the Vincentians and this was especially true after 1903 when the Most Reverend John J. Glennon became Archbishop of St. Louis. A sound relationship therefore developed between the Vincentians and the professional staff of the diocesan bureau of charities demonstrating the kind of cooperation to be hoped for in the organization of diocesan charities.

Perhaps the fact that the Catholic Church in the United States grew in such a way that isolated communities developed, prevented a spirit of cooperation from being easily achieved. This would be especially true where immigration tended to swell the ranks of Catholics. Catholic work of all kinds had been noticeably individualistic, and many diocesan charitable agencies tended to isolate themselves from each other. While the National Conference of Catholic Charities had tried to bring home the necessity of coordination, it still had a long way to go by 1940 to achieve its goal.

Notes — Chapter VI

1. Monsignor John R. Mulroy, "The Meaning of Coordination in Catholic Charities," N.C.C.C. Proceedings, 1936, p. 259.
2. Reverend M. J. Scanlon, "Diocesan Charities and their Organization," Catholic Charities Review, Dec., 1918, Vol. 2, No. 10, p. 300.
3. Ibid.
4. Ibid.
5. Ibid., p. 298.
6. Ibid., Mar., 1960, Vol. 44, No. 3, p. 4.
7. Ibid., Sept., 1920, Vol. 4, No. 7, p. 201.
8. Ibid.
9. Ibid., p. 202.
10. Monsignor John O'Grady, "Lay Participation in Catholic Charity," N.C.C.C. Proceedings, 1925, pp. 253–254.
11. Ibid., p. 254.
12. Marguerite T. Boylan, Social Welfare and the Catholic Church (New York, 1941), p. 3.

13. *Catholic Charities Review*, May, 1925, Vol. 9, No. 5, p. 189.
14. O'Grady, "Lay Participation," N.C.C.C. *Proceedings*, 1925, p. 255.
15. *Ibid*.
16. *Catholic Charities Review*, Oct., 1920, Vol. 4, No. 8, pp. 238–239.
17. O'Grady, "Lay Participation," N.C.C.C. *Proceedings*, 1925, p. 5.
18. Victoria Larmour, "What our Annual Reports do not Report," N.C.C.C. *Proceedings*, 1926, p. 100.
19. *Ibid.*, p. 103.
20. *Ibid.*, p. 104.
21. O'Grady, "Lay Participation," N.C.C.C. *Proceedings*, 1925, p. 259.
22. *Catholic Charities Review*, Dec., 1925, Vol. 9, No. 10, p. 381.
23. Monsignor John O'Grady, "The Evils of Centralized Responsibility," *Catholic Charities Review*, May, 1925, Vol 9, No. 5, p. 187.
24. *Ibid*.
25. *Ibid*.
26. *Ibid*.
27. *Ibid*.
28. *Ibid.*, Mar., 1928, Vol. 12, No. 3, p. 92.
29. Reverend William A. O'Connor, "Problems Facing Catholic Charities Today," *ibid.*, Mar., 1940, Vol. 24, No. 3, pp. 73–74.
30. *Ibid.*, Dec., 1926, Vol. 10, No. 10, p. 389.
31. *Ibid*.
32. Marguerite T. Boylan, "The Diocesan Bureau of Social Welfare," N.C.C.C. *Proceedings*, 1937, p. 129.
33. *Ibid.*, p. 130.
34. Sister Victoria Francis, "The Responsibility of Religious for Interpretation of Social Work to Members of the Community," N.C.C.C. *Proceedings*, 1937, p. 145.
35. *Ibid*.
36. Florence M. Mason, "The Future of Catholic Charities Bureau," *Catholic Charities Review*, Nov., 1947, Vol. 31, No. 9, p. 233.
37. *Catholic Charities Review*, Oct., 1935, Vol. 19, No. 8, p. 259.
38. *Ibid.*, Sept., 1920, Vol. 4, No. 7, p. 226.
39. *Ibid.*, p. 202.
40. Monsignor John O'Grady, "Lay Participation in Catholic Charity," *Catholic Charities Review*, Dec., 1925, Vol. 9, No. 10, p. 379.
41. Address of Monsignor O'Grady reprinted in *Catholic Charities Review*, Jan., 1930, Vol. 14, No. 1, p. 25.
42. *Catholic Charities Review*, Sept., 1920, Vol. 4, No. 7, p. 226.
43. Reverend John C. Carr, "The Society of St. Vincent de Paul, Its Future," N.C.C.C. *Proceedings*, 1933, p. 520.
44. *Catholic Charities Review*, Dec., 1925, Vol. 9, No. 10, p. 381.
45. *Ibid*.
46. O'Grady, "Lay Participation," N.C.C.C. *Proceedings*, 1925, p. 260.
47. O'Grady, "Lay Participation," *Catholic Charities Review*, Dec., 1925, Vol. 9, No. 10, p. 383.
48. *Ibid*.
49. *Ibid.*, pp. 383–384.
50. *Ibid.*, p. 384.
51. O'Grady, "Lay Participation," N.C.C.C. *Proceedings*, 1925, p. 259.
52. "Minutes of the Executive Committee," Nov. 12, 1943, p. 4.
53. *Ibid*.

54. *Ibid.*
55. *Catholic Charities Review*, Sept., 1957, Vol. 38, No. 7, p. 158.
56. *Ibid.*
57. *Ibid.*, Feb., 1923, Vol. 7, No. 2, p. 65.
58. O'Grady, "Lay Participation," N.C.C.C. *Proceedings*, 1925, p. 256.
59. *Catholic Charities Review*, Feb., 1923, Vol. 7, No. 2, p. 64.
60. *Ibid.*, p. 65.
61. *Ibid.*
62. *Ibid.*, p. 64.
63. O'Grady, "Lay Participation," N.C.C.C. *Proceedings*, 1925, p. 258.
64. N.C.C.C. *Proceedings*, 1928, p. 70.
65. *Catholic Charities Review*, June, 1927, Vol. 11, No. 6, p. 229; Mar., 1930, Vol. 14, No. 3, pp. 76–77.
66. Reverend Edward J. Kirk, "What Pastors May Expect From Diocesan Organizations of Catholic Charities," N.C.C.C. *Proceedings*, 1927, p. 313.
67. N.C.C.C. *Proceedings*, 1928, p. 68.
68. *Ibid.*
69. *Ibid.*
70. Monsignor Francis J. O'Hara, "What Pastors May Not Expect From Diocesan Organization of Catholic Charities," N.C.C.C. *Proceedings*, 1927, p. 317.
71. *Ibid.*
72. *Ibid.*, p. 313.
73. Reverend William A. O'Connor, "Problems Facing Catholic Charities Today," *Catholic Charities Review*, Mar., 1940, Vol. 24, No. 3, p. 73.
74. *Ibid.*
75. *Ibid.*
76. *Ibid.*, p. 71.
77. *Ibid.*
78. *Ibid.*, p. 70.
79. *Ibid.*

CHAPTER VII

The N.C.C.C. as an Information and Research Center

THE NATIONAL CONFERENCE OF CATHOLIC CHAR-
ITIES, according to Monsignor Mulroy, has from its origin been a
"providential coordination" of "scholars and teachers of Christian
social philosophy" and of "those intensely active exponents applying
that same philosophy to the problems of American life."[1] The work
of the executive secretary of the Conference, the Diocesan Directors Committee, and the Conference of Religious provides the
direct contacts on the local level; the annual meeting provides the
national forum for those who are in a position to contribute to
Catholic social thought and action. Monsignor Mulroy in 1940
referred to the National Conference as the "living voice for the
accurate statement of the Catholic philosophy of social work" operating through its annual meeting to become the "spokesman for
the Church, the advisory body for priests, religious orders of men
and women, and for the Catholic laity in all matters pertaining to
social work."[2]

The annual meeting quickly became one of the most important
instruments through which the National Conference exercised its
influence. From 1910 to 1920, the meeting was held every two
years. After that time the need for an annual pooling of experience
and information was recognized. This annual meeting has proved
to be a fairly reliable barometer of Catholic charities activities. "It
registers its strength and its weaknesses, its cross currents and its
drifts, its successes and its failures," commented the Editor of the
Catholic Charities Review in 1930.[3]

For the most part the programs of the early years were arranged around the so-called topic committees. There was a committee for each of the following subjects: families, sick and dependent children, social and civic activities, women's activities, and delinquency. At each meeting various papers were presented under each of these headings with a general session devoted to topics of common concern. The Diocesan Directors of Catholic Charities and the Conference on Religious each held its own separate sessions, as did the Society of St. Vincent de Paul.

In the late 1930's the National Conference undertook to schedule regional meetings designed for workers in Catholic charities who confined their discussions to actual practices in the field of social work. These were held at irregular intervals and led to the conviction by 1948 that perhaps state meetings would be extremely useful.[4] In 1948 also some twenty conferences were held between representatives of the National Conference and local Catholic Charities staffs.[5] Three institutes for the Sisters and lay workers of child-caring institutions were also sponsored by the National Conference in that year. There was willingness on the part of the National Conference to arrange for more of these meetings "if it were in a position to provide the necessary service," but Monsignor O'Grady felt that the Conference was already "holding as many meetings as it can possibly service."[6] The great advantage of the regional meeting was that it provided "ample opportunity for all the delegates to secure a complete airing of their problems."[7] At the Denver regional meeting in 1955 which represented ten dioceses and seven states, the consensus was that "we need more meetings like this. It makes the message of the Conference more real for us. It gives us a chance of discussing our problems with those whose problems are close to our own."[8]

The success of regional meetings reflected not only a natural development in the expansion of the influence of the National Conference but also some dissatisfaction with the program at the annual meetings. There had been complaints from time to time that the program topics had been too technical for the type of audience that attended the large section meetings.[9] It was thought that discussion groups would have been better able to handle some of these topics. In preparation for the Houston meeting in 1941 the Executive Committee of the National Conference thought that it would be proper to discuss the entire program with the Chairman of the Program Committee.[10] The then current problems of volunteer service, housing, health gave an excellent opportunity for making it a "non-technical Conference that would reach our priests and our lay people."[11] It was the hope of the local committee that the broad appeal of the topics would do a "missionary piece of work for the Southwest."[12] The Executive Committee hoped that a sufficiently varied program could be arranged to meet the needs of professional workers, volunteers, and the laity as a whole.

The success of the arrangements for the Houston meeting appeared somewhat doubtful since the Executive Committee found itself still discussing the nature of the program for the annual meeting in 1943. Moreover, the Committee now found itself debating whether they should hold the annual meeting at all in view of the wartime travel restrictions. While the Executive Committee agreed that the meeting should be held, if at all possible, the Society of St. Vincent de Paul was somewhat lukewarm on the whole idea of annual meetings of the National Conference.[13] Members of the Particular Councils had been questioned on the advisability of holding the 1943 meeting and had been pretty much divided in their opinion. That the Vincentians were becoming somewhat disenchanted with the National Conference can be seen in the statement in the minutes of the Executive Committee of the National Conference at the meeting in April, 1943, to the effect that, "there is a question of the value of an annual meeting for the Vincentians and also the value of a publication due to the fact that few members attend the meeting and there is a question as to how many read the publication."[14] The Vincentians, however, agreed to cooperate if the meeting was held.

At one of its meetings in 1943 the Executive Committee discussed the question raised by Monsignor O'Grady of the desirability of a more unified program. The six topic committees made such unity difficult with each accustomed to prepare its own program independently of the others. Monsignor O'Grady suggested that a subcommittee of the Executive Committee be appointed to plan the program in consultation with the chairmen of the various topics committees.[15] Monsignor O'Grady noted that the functions of the topic committees were not clearly defined in the constitution of the National Conference, but they should "become more active in dealing with Catholic practices as such."[16] The Executive Committee's discussion centered around the advisability of the topic committees assuming the role suggested by Monsignor O'Grady. It was agreed that unless these topic committees gathered material and formulated ideas from the Catholic point of view in their respective fields they were not fulfilling the needs of the National Conference. It was finally decided to retain the committees as functional committees and provide a coordinating program committee for the annual meeting.[17]

In 1944 concern was expressed by Monsignor O'Grady in the agenda of the Executive Committee in June that there was a real need for "description of Catholic practices as they are within the field rather than theoretical discussions and speeches."[18] Such a question was bound to raise the basic issue of just what group or groups the National Conference was trying to serve. The increasing attention paid to the recruitment of volunteers since 1935 called into question the advisability of gearing a program at the annual meeting too exclusively to the professional worker. If the volunteer group made up the largest element in the National Conference membership they were certainly entitled to at least a corresponding share in the program.[19]

As long as the topic committee arrangement persisted, however, it seemed unlikely that there would be any real solution to the problem of getting sufficient material of general interest on the program of the annual meeting. The agenda for the meeting of the Executive Committee in 1945 noted that, "there is a tendency to develop the programs of our annual meetings on the assumption that our Conference membership is basically a professional social work membership."[20] Actually only a small number of members of the Conference were professional workers.

At the meeting of the Executive Committee in 1946 it was recommended that the topic committees continue to work with the Executive Committee as they had in the past year.[21] The object was a more unified approach in formulating the program for the annual meeting. The tendency was to get away from the practice of previous years which developed many topics with little or no relationship to each other. In 1947 the "Minutes of the Executive Committee" show a greater role being taken by the Executive Committee in offering suggestions and plans for the program of the annual meeting. In 1948 more pointed observation was made by the Executive Committee to the effect that many of the section meetings had been failures "because of inadequate service. Speakers have not been selected with sufficient care. The national office has not been able to give them the direction they need in preparing their papers."[22] On this latter point it was noted that a special effort had been made in the current year to have the papers turned in ahead of time. However, the staff was not adequate to examine all the papers, some of which "were of a very inferior quality and really should never have been read at our Conference."[23]

A matter of major importance for the 1949 annual meeting was the desire of the Society of St. Vincent de Paul for more meetings of its own. The Vincentians were "not satisfied with the program as it has been operated in the past few years."[24] It would appear that the development of the section meetings since about 1941 to meet the needs of the professional workers had led to the contention of the Society of St. Vincent de Paul that the annual program had been prepared "without any recognition of the problems of the Society."[25]

The questions raised about the nature of the program of the annual meeting, the groups that the National Conference was intended to serve, and their relation to each other led to the appointment by the Executive Committee in 1947 of a Committee on Interpretation of the Constitution under the Chairmanship of G. Howland Shaw, then treasurer of the National Conference. This committee was instructed to "draw up a statement explaining the relationship of the Director of Catholic Charities and of the Conference of Religious to the National Conference of Catholic Charities, in order to clarify this relationship in the minds of Conference members."[26] It was also asked to "define the various types of Conference membership, setting forth the benefits which members receive from each type, so that the Conference members will have a better understanding of the type of membership they hold and what they might expect in return for this membership."[27]

In a progress report on the committee's deliberations Mr. Shaw in October, 1948, said, "that as the Committee progressed in its discussions it seemed clear that what was needed was not a definition of the relationship of the Conference to these groups but rather a provision which would assure their closer participation in program building. This, he said, focused the Committee's attention on Article IV of the By-Laws which relates to Topic Committees."[28] Mr. Shaw, however, felt that it would be beyond the Committee's authority to "go into the question of program building or to make recommendations for radical changes in the Constitution which this would necessitate."[29] Upon Mr. Shaw's recommendation the Committee on Interpretation of the Constitution was enlarged so that it represented adequately the Directors of Catholic charities, the Conference of Religious, the Society of St. Vincent de Paul and other groups in the Conference.[30]

Another report of the Committee on Interpretation was submitted to the Executive Committee in April, 1949. Article II on the objects of the National Conference was to be changed to read as follows:

> This Conference shall provide a forum for discussing the application of Catholic thought and action in the fields of health, welfare and recreation, and shall stimulate research and the publication of material on these subjects. It shall not vote on any question.[31]

There was discussion on the "health, welfare and recreation" clause on the ground that it was not inclusive enough and the term "social welfare" was thought to have other disadvantages although it was perhaps preferable. The question of the National Conference voting or not voting on issues caused some discussion but it was finally agreed to exclude the sentence, of Article II "It shall not vote on any question" from the revised Constitution.[32] It was recognized that its inclusion might offer protection against any misunderstanding in "an organization like the Conference where strong, independent groups such as the Directors of Catholic Charities and the Conference of Religious are so closely associated with it."[33] However, it was assumed that the groups which made up the Conference were so "closely associated in a partnership that they would reach agreement among themselves on important issues" while it would be necessary for the Conference to vote if it were to make recommendations to the Administrative Board of Bishops on legislative proposals on the national scene.[34]

One of the recommended changes in the constitution was the appointment of a "Program Committee to consist of nine members of the Conference, representative of the several groups and activities of the Conference."[35] Since this committee was to take the place of the topic committees, whose members were elected, the question was raised as to whether the new Program Committee members ought to be elected. The opinion was that an appointed committee would make for a "smoother, and more efficient change-over in program planning."[36] A second draft of the new constitution was submitted to the membership of the Conference through publication in the *Catholic Charities Review* in September, 1949, and also was sent to the members who did not receive the *Review*. Recommendations of the members were considered by the Committee and as a result certain changes were made. The proposed new Constitution and By-Laws, including these changes, was unanimously approved by the Executive Committee at a meeting on November 18, 1949.[37] It was approved by the membership of the Conference at the Annual Business Session on November 19, 1949.

Operating under the new constitution, the Program Committee began to eliminate what Monsignor O'Grady called the "oracle" approach in favor of panels and workshops. There was a growing distaste for speeches and prepared papers. The object was to get greater participation by using patterns which permitted the widest possible contact among those concerned in a particular field. The Conference of Religious had experimented with workshops and found them most useful. The multidiscipline approach, using the local court as a center of leadership in dealing with the problems of family life, had been tried at the annual meeting in Cleveland in 1952, and found quite useful. According to the *Catholic Charities Review*, this meeting "whetted the appetites of the participants for further discussions of this type."[38] By 1953 there was expressed a desire for program continuity at the various annual meetings and the feeling that "perhaps the workshops will eventually constitute the core of our meetings."[39]

In the years after 1954 the problem of making the annual meeting more effective appeared to be chiefly one of technique.[40] The problem of planning a meeting so that all levels of professional competence were adequately provided for was a difficult task at best, but it was becoming clear that the workshop was "the very meat of the Conference program."[41] One "obvious shortcoming" of the Pittsburgh meeting in 1954, for instance, "was the lack of adequate machinery for a grassroots evaluation or criticism."[42] This lack of opportunity for "free communication or exchange of ideas" was "probably the biggest obstacle" in conducting these conferences but it was hoped that the workshop would "lead to the development of the art of communication."[43]

Another lesson from the Pittsburgh meeting was that there was probably "too much complacency in Catholic Charities."[44] Too many gave the impression that everything was going well. There was, however, some evidence of self-examination of both the work and motives of Catholic charities that argued well for the future.

The annual meeting held at Grand Rapids in 1955 showed some hopeful signs. The theme of the Conference, "Christian Neighborhood Service"; the method of planning which solicited ideas from all members; the combination of workshops, sectional meetings, and general sessions — all of these features made this meeting a contribution to the community in which it was held as well as to the National Conference as a whole.[45] A great deal of the credit for this result could be attributed to the work of Monsignor Floyd F. Fischer, chairman of the Program Committee. Among recommendations of this committee was the suggestion that future committees be more representative of the various fields of social service. There was need of greater concern for group work, neighborhood organization, youth work, etc., in addition to casework and institutional programming.[46] A new feature introduced by this Program Committee was its use as an "evaluation committee." Five members agreed to circulate among the various scheduled sessions and pass judgment on the "facilities, audience participation and reaction, the skills of the speakers and participants, and program content."[47] Their conclusions would then be passed on to the National Conference Office and made available to the new program committee.

The Program Committee for the 1956 meeting added still further recommendations for improvement of the annual meeting. In March, 1956, *The Catholic Charities Review* carried notes on the minutes of the Program Committees meeting to the effect that,

> each member of the National Conference of Catholic Charities must recognize his responsibility to the whole Conference as being superior to his own preferences. For if each member of the Conference takes an active interest in its over-all program, the whole Conference as well as the individual activity will be enhanced. Conversely, a tendency to boycott the general program because of a specific dissatisfaction will serve to weaken the whole fabric of Catholic Charities and ultimately destroy the individual phase of the program.[48]

The Program Committee encouraged "positive criticism" as an "active crusade for improvement" of the entire Conference program.[49] All of this was by way of preparation for "integration" as a keynote of the 1956 annual meeting in Buffalo.

It was the plan of the Program Committee for the Buffalo meeting to devote the time formerly given to sectional meetings to two "integrated days." On these days it was hoped to achieve an integration "of all the components of the Conference in these important meetings — the laity, the Religious and the Priests."[50] The technique involved was to be the use of keynote speakers on selected topics before the general assembly with the group breaking up into small discussion groups, then reassembling in general session to hear the various reports. This "buzz session" technique was designed to give a greater interest of the individual in the Conference as a whole and "provide diversity as well as unity."[51]

The Board of Directors of the National Conference expressed

approval of the idea, Monsignor Fischer noting that the idea had been brought up at a previous meeting in 1953, at which time the "importance of respecting the sovereign rights of each group within the Conference" was emphasized by Edmond B. Butler of New York.[52] At that time Monsignor O'Grady noted that integration had long been one of the goals of the Conference and that a "difference of opinion on one point should not stand in the way of the goal of collaboration."[53]

At the 1956 meeting, integration raised the basic question of whether the whole field of social work could or should be professionalized.[54] The Society of St. Vincent de Paul had participated actively in the Conference sessions down to 1920 and then gradually became isolated over this issue of professionalism. Monsignor O'Grady concluded that "there are some basic concepts lurking behind the scenes in this whole question that will be reexamined whether we like it or not."[55]

Monsignor Raymond J. Gallagher, chairman of the 1956 Program Committee, felt that in their Buffalo meeting "the fondest hopes of the Program Committee were realized because there was a thorough mixing of the priests, religious and laity."[56] There was, moreover, "further integration of personnel from faiths and disciplines outside of our own group. Leaders from the various fields of social welfare, whether Catholic, Protestant or Jewish, performed a notable service to the Conference by active participation in the sectional meetings."[57] It was also gratifying to see so many Diocesan Directors of Charity and Vincentians participating in the "integrated days."

> It seemed to the members of the Program Committee that a formula had been reached which served the best interests of the Conference by providing the delegates ample opportunity to deal with their own specific problems, yet at the same time providing them sufficient opportunity to meet together about common social problems.[58]

The Catholic Charities Review praised the work of the Program Committee in preparing for the Buffalo meeting, declaring that, "for a number of years we have felt that our Conference, and welfare conferences as a whole, were in a rut. There were very few new ideas being projected. We were repeating the same old things we had been saying for 20 to 25 years."[59] A new atmosphere prevailed at this meeting and "our Program Committee has brought us a long way toward a new outlook in Catholic Charities."[60] At the meeting of the Board of Directors of National Conference in October, 1956, Monsignor Fischer, then president of the Conference, said that "he could not let the opportunity pass without telling Monsignor Gallagher that the kind of leadership he has given to the Program Committee and the contribution he has made to the National Conference will be the basic source of a new outlook in Catholic Charities, a new outlook in programming, and a new spirit in the Conference."[61]

The Program Committee in 1957, again under the chairmanship of Monsignor Gallagher, continued the idea of "integration" and came to the conclusion that one of the important discoveries of their recent experiment was the "desire for continuity between one Conference and another."[62] As a result, "this desire for continuity," said Monsignor Gallagher, "dictated much of our programming."[63] The ideas of community-wide planning and the awareness of the wider horizons of social welfare as areas in which Catholic social philosophy "should be spoken of loudly," carried through the 1956 and 1957 meetings were examples of what the Program Committee had in mind.[64] It was the resolve of the Program Committee "that it would continue to broaden the vista of charity that becomes our obligation as Catholics to behold, and secondly that they would ask for public review by our people as well as for purposes of enunciation for the nation that singular difference which prevails within our welfare service, and that is the high level of motivation of Christian personal service — dedication."[65]

In succeeding years the Program Committee continued its emphasis on integration, continuity, and the responsibility of the National Conference to provide for "participation on every level" as an end result of its activity.[66] Monsignor Gallagher cited the example of the Welfare Federation of Cleveland from which "there is a constant coming forth of outstanding Protestant laymen who consider it part of the fulfillment of their responsibility to the community to give six, eight, ten years of participation in various areas of welfare; whether it is committees for planning or whether it is the Community Chest for collection of funds, or whatever area of service it happens to be."[67] Monsignor Gallagher considered this a goal to be promoted among Catholics and felt it was the duty of the National Conference to "stimulate and promote it."[68]

Progress toward this goal was marked in subsequent annual meetings. In the 1958 meeting Monsignor Gallagher observed what he thought was evidence of "the wider vision of our people as to community problems," as well as the reaffirmation "of the conviction that neither competence nor compassion needs to be sacrificed in order to attain the other."[69]

Through its annual meeting and through the publication of its proceedings the National Conference of Catholic Charities exercised one of its major sources of influence. From the beginning of the Conference, however, other avenues of contact with those whom it sought to influence were envisioned. For this reason *The Catholic Charities Review* in 1916 became the official organ of the Conference, informing the membership through its articles, editorial comment, and news columns. A *Directory of Catholic Charities*, long delayed because of the great difficulty encountered in securing the necessary information, was finally published in 1922. It was the fond hope of Bishop Shahan that the Conference would "take an active and immediate part in genuine sociological research along the lines to which our conference is devoted . . . to increase the number of research papers and to stimulate the taste for research among our workers."[70] Monsignor Kerby, too, in all his writings had emphasized a weakness in what he called the literature of investigation, interpretation, and direction, warning that sound planning is impossible without factual data.

The early years of the Conference, particularly following World War I, saw a number of these factual surveys made, many of which were discussed at the annual meetings. In 1921 Monsignor Kerby's *Social Mission of Charity* appeared as an "important milestone in Catholic social work in the United States."[71] Monsignor O'Grady's *Catholic Charities in the United States* in 1931 is the first history

50th Anniversary Meeting of the National Conference of Catholic Charities, New York, N. Y.,
September 23 to 27, 1960.

Left to right: Cardinal Spellman, President Eisenhower, Rt. Rev. Msgr. John O'Grady, Secretary
of the Conference, and Rt. Rev. Msgr. George H. Guilfoyle, President of the Conference.

CHAIRMEN OF
THE CONFERENCE OF RELIGIOUS

Mother Miriam
Regina, S.C.,
1920–1935

Sister Katharine,
O.S.B., 1935–1940

Sister Agnita
Miriam, S.C.,
1940–1949

Sister Mary Charles,
R.S.M., 1950

Sister Mary
Theodore, O.S.F.,
1951

Mother Bernadette
de Lourdes, O.Carm.,
1952–1953

Sister Mary Albert,
S.S.J., 1954

Sister Victoria
Francis, O.P.,
1955

Sister M.
Immaculate, S.D.P.,
1956

Sister Jean André,
C.S.A., 1957

Sister Maria
Mercedes, S.S.N.D.,
1958

Sister Miriam
Cecilia, S.C.,
1959

Sister M. Anselm,
C.S.M., 1960

of Catholic Charities in the United States. Monsignor John M. Cooper's *Children's Institutions* was a study based on the experience of a hundred of the best institutions for dependent children in the United States. Reverend Edward R. Moore's *The Case Against Birth Control* was the result of a two-year study of the National Conference's Committee on Population Decline and Related Problems. In 1926 there was published a report of the Committee on Standards of Family Case Work in Diocesan Agencies under the title *A Program for Family Service in Diocesan Agencies.*

The depression of the 1930's, however, found the Conference so involved with problems of relief and social legislation that the practical necessity of the moment took precedence over research activity. There were surveys to gather statistics on family welfare and relief, but most of the publications of the National Conference centered around a series of memoranda sent to the Continuing Committee of Diocesan Directors of Charity (after 1939, the Standing Committee), keeping them informed on legislative and other developments on the national scene. The first of these bulletins was issued December 4, 1934. The bulletin was "prepared exclusively for the members of the Committee on Policies and Resolutions of the National Conference of Catholic Charities. It will be issued at regular intervals to present significant trends in present day planning for social and economic betterment."[72] These bulletins were found extremely helpful to the diocesan agencies, and late in 1943 the National Conference began a series of similar informational bulletins to child-care institutions. This latter move was in response to a charge that the National Conference was not doing as much as it should for these institutions.[73]

In 1942 a manual for volunteers, *A Call to Service*, was issued jointly by the National Catholic Welfare Conference and the National Conference of Catholic Charities. This manual was the outgrowth of a study of a subcommittee of the Executive Committee of the National Conference of Catholic Charities which had begun a study of Catholic volunteer women's organizations. The manual stressed "personal service" and was to be used in connection with institutes to promote volunteer programs.

Another example of the National Conference's cooperation with other Catholic organizations in an effort to serve as wide an area of activity as possible was the holding of an Institute for Catholic Prison Chaplains at Washington, D. C., in 1940. This institute was held under the joint auspices of the Federal Bureau of Prisons, Department of Justice, and the National Conference of Catholic Charities, in cooperation with the National Catholic Welfare Conference. Every aspect of the Chaplain's role as covered at this Institute and the Proceedings were immediately published by the National Conference in three parts: the reports of committees, principal addresses, and a summary of discussions on the committee reports. A similar Institute was held again in 1941 and its Proceedings were also published in the hope of providing a pool of experience for the chaplains.

Toward the end of World War II the National Conference was beginning to make studies of local communities. These area studies were to analyze the social and economic problems of Catholics and *The Catholic Charities Review* rather impatiently asked, "When will our people 'grow up' to make their own studies?"[74] Similar questions were being asked of the National Conference on the need for publication of more casework in the field of social work.[75]

After World War II the significance of the National Conference Office as an information center on Catholic charities in the United States was on the increase. A new type of Information Bulletin sent to all members who subscribed five dollars or more, began on January 24, 1947, covering such topics as child-welfare legislation, socialized medicine, international relief, immigration quota system, housing, and juvenile delinquency. Requests of all sorts began to pour into the Office of the Executive Secretary, including some from other countries in regard to Catholic social welfare in the United States.[76] One type of request, however, the National Office did not want: "We are not in a position to deal with personnel problems," said Monsignor O'Grady making it clear that the National Office was not an employment agency.[77]

In 1948 Monsignor O'Grady urged the Conference to "keep on exploring new avenues for research and publication," but it was not until the St. Louis, Missouri, Charities Office instituted a self-study in 1953 that he felt that there was real progress on "the way to a return to one of the original objectives of Catholic Charities."[78] This evaluation by the St. Louis agencies was made at the insistence of Joseph Cardinal Ritter, Archbishop of St. Louis. One of the most important results was that an understanding of the facts tended to remove much prejudice and bias.[79] "Most of all, the enthusiastic co-operation of everyone concerned," said the Cardinal, "has justified our experience. I give this as an example of what our people, motivated by a spirit of love and sacrifice can do. I hope that the interest and enthusiasm generated by this survey will continue to keep our Catholic Charities a leader in the field."[80]

The need for new studies in the 1950's was coming to be more widely recognized. The surveys of the 1920's were out of date and did not represent the type of research that was currently needed. Certainly one of the most significant of the new research projects in the 1950's was Beatrice M. Faivre's work on Gannondale, a small group-care institution conducted by the Sisters of Our Lady of Charity of Refuge in Erie, Pennsylvania. This study was begun by the superior of the institution, Mother Mary Agnes, early in 1955 when she gave approval to the Conference of Religious to conduct the study. The study on Gannondale was a worthy successor to *The Housemother* written by Sister M. Charles, R.S.M., sponsored by the Conference of Religious and published by the National Conference in 1954. This book had proved so valuable that it was translated into Italian and Spanish. The religious of Gannondale worked closely with the National Conference to tell the "story of their everyday work with adolescents, the difficulties they face, what they have achieved to date and the goals toward which they are striving in the future."[81] The institution showed great concern for counseling and the preparation of the girls for society when they returned to it. As Miss Faivre states, "this self-study . . . demonstrated its effectiveness because, as it progressed, some changes were immediately initiated whereas others were postponed until the climate for action was more favorable."[82]

Another institution that underwent an evaluation study, although not under National Conference auspices, was St. Michael's Home in La Crosse, Wisconsin, in 1957. This institution had been caring for neglected and dependent children in its present location for the previous forty years although the program had been operating in another location since 1872. A complete change of staff of the institution and of the Welfare Bureau of the Diocese in 1952, and the physical needs of St. Michael's led to an evaluation of the whole institution. The principal question raised was whether or not the institution should specialize in the "disturbed child." Out of the investigation came the answer that "shaping a program to the needs of the delinquent, the disturbed, and the adolescent in conflict was entirely warranted."[83] There were some lessons gained from the study and they pointed to the fact that

> An institution cannot be all things to all men, but its program must be flexible enough to be of real community service. No child care institution serving a particular area, can specialize to an extreme degree and still be a helpful resource. . . . It must make a real effort to serve those children for whom there is no other resource.[84]

These studies were among the signs of a new leadership being supplied by the religious communities. The Conference of Religious, one of the component elements of the National Conference of Catholic Charities and identified with it since 1920, had in the late 1940's assumed a new role with the creation of the Standing Committee for Religious in 1947. Although the primary reason for the committee's creation was to enable the religious to participate more actively in program planning for the National Conference annual meeting, it soon became apparent that one of the tasks of the committee would be the "assembling of first-hand material on actual practices in the field of Catholic institutional care."[85] The new leadership developed among the religious communities tended to regard the institutions they served "as community institutions caring for the child as part of the family of the community."[86] Since one of the tasks of the Standing Committee was educational, the emphasis on study and research into actual conditions was natural.

Like other groups in the National Conference of Catholic Charities the religious had found it necessary to meet the changed conditions of a new age. That they should form a separate unit in 1920 is understandable. As Sister Victoria Francis, O.P., chairman of the Standing Committee for Religious in 1955, stated it, "we can talk with each other more easily and more readily than we can with a mixed group."[87] The religious first had to get together and learn to communicate with each other. The modern age, however, "requires a much more public performance than in years gone by. It therefore necessitates," declared Monsignor Raymond J. Gallagher, "our reviewing attitudes and outlooks as they are related to the public life demanded of our Sisters."[88]

A factor creating a new problem faced by many of the child-care institutions staffed by the sisters in the 1950's was a decline in population in the institutions. This necessitated a reexamination of the programs of these homes. Some of the suggested courses of action were retraining those mentally defective children who were capable of retraining, specialized programs for retarded children, and institutional care for the emotionally disturbed child.[89] Monsignor Gallagher felt that a by-product of this approach would be an attraction to the convent of many who would see a life of opportunity in helping others. Study and research are necessary to determine the best program in each particular case.

Despite the opportunities for research and despite what had been accomplished, it was the contention of Monsignor Fischer in 1957 that "Catholic Charities is not measuring up to its responsibility in the production of scientific research that should accompany such a vast program of social services."[90] The studies of the aging — *Older People in the Family, the Parish and the Neighborhood* (St. Louis, 1955); Sister Mary Therese, O.P., *A Study of the Aging in a Cleveland Parish* (Washington, 1954); and Janet Bower, Ph.D., *Older People of St. Boniface Parish* (Buffalo, 1957) — excellent though they were, had just begun to scratch the surface.

"Many believe that we must have more research but are reluctant to recognize that research is something that they themselves can and should do," declared Monsignor Fischer.[91] He felt that there were too many assumptions underlying current Catholic social work.

It was the duty of the National Conference to carry out the object of Article II of the Conference's constitution to not only "provide a forum for discussing the application of Catholic thought in the general field of social welfare" but also to "stimulate action, research and the publication of material in this field."[92]

Monsignor Kerby in 1924 had made similar remarks about the necessity of research when he advocated "a thorough, scholarly study of every institution and agency, a review of its methods and results, an account of overlapping, unnecessary plants, neglected fields; a study of lines of development in given circumstances."[93] The National Conference would then be encouraging a real contribution to the elimination of the causes of poverty and distress by providing a solid factual basis upon which to make decisions. It would be doing this, as Monsignor Kerby put it, as "a broad civic and social duty."[94]

Notes — Chapter VII

1. N.C.C.C. *Proceedings*, 1940, p. 16.
2. *Ibid.*, pp. 16–17.
3. *Catholic Charities Review*, Oct., 1930, Vol. 14, No. 8, p. 206.
4. Monsignor John O'Grady, "The Conference and Trends in Catholic Social Work at the Present Time," N.C.C.C. *Proceedings.* 1948, p. 10.
5. *Ibid.*
6. *Ibid.*
7. *Catholic Charities Review*, Nov., 1955, Vol. 39, No. 9, p. 18.
8. *Ibid.*, pp. 18–19.
9. "Agenda, Executive Committee of N.C.C.C." for meeting, Apr. 28–29, 1941, p. 2.
10. *Ibid.*
11. *Ibid.*, p. 3.
12. *Ibid.*, p. 2.
13. "Minutes of the Executive Committee of the N.C.C.C.," Apr. 28, 1943, p. 10.
14. *Ibid.*
15. "Minutes of the Executive Committee of the N.C.C.C.," Nov. 12, 1943, p. 1.
16. *Ibid.*, p. 2.
17. *Ibid.*, p. 3.
18. "Agenda of the Executive Committee of the N.C.C.C.," June 12, 1944, p. 2.
19. *Ibid.*
20. "Agenda of the Executive Committee of the N.C.C.C.," Sept. 28, 1945, p. 3.
21. "Minutes of the Executive Committee of the N.C.C.C.," Aug. 24, 1946, p. 7.

22. "Agenda of the Executive Committee of the N.C.C.C.," Oct. 9, 1948, p. 2.
23. *Ibid.*
24. *Ibid.,* p. 1.
25. *Ibid.*
26. "Minutes of the Executive Committee of the N.C.C.C.," Apr. 29, 1948.
27. *Ibid.,* p. 2.
28. "Minutes of the Executive Committee of the N.C.C.C.," Oct. 9, 1948, p. 1.
29. *Ibid.,* p. 2.
30. *Ibid.*
31. "Minutes of the Executive Committee of the N.C.C.C.," Apr. 19, 1949, p. 2.
32. *Ibid.*
33. *Ibid.*
34. *Ibid.,* p. 3.
35. *Ibid.,* p. 4.
36. *Ibid.*
37. "Minutes of the Executive Committee of the N.C.C.C.," Nov. 18, 1949.
38. *Catholic Charities Review,* Nov., 1952, Vol. 36, No. 9, p. 205.
39. Thomas J. O'Donnell, "Reflections of a Program Committee Chairman," *Catholic Charities Review,* Oct., 1953, Vol. 37, No. 8, pp. 206–207.
40. Thomas J. O'Donnell, "The Pittsburgh Program — Some Reflections," *Catholic Charities Review,* Dec., 1954, Vol. 38, No. 10, p. 221.
41. *Ibid.,* p. 221.
42. *Ibid.,* p. 221.
43. *Catholic Charities Review,* p. 213.
44. *Ibid.*
45. Monsignor Floyd F. Fischer, "A Unique Conference," *Catholic Charities Review,* Dec., 1955, Vol. 39, No. 10, p. 17.
46. "Minutes of the Board of Directors of the N.C.C.C.," Nov. 7, 1955, p. 2.
47. *Ibid.*
48. *Catholic Charities Review,* Mar., 1956, Vol. 40, No. 3, pp. 19–20.
49. *Ibid.,* p. 20.
50. "Minutes of the Board of Directors of the N.C.C.C.," Apr. 24, 1956, p. 9.
51. *Ibid.,* p. 8.
52. "Minutes of the Board of Directors of the N.C.C.C.," Apr. 24, 1956, p. 5.
53. *Ibid.*
54. "Minutes of the Board of Directors of the N.C.C.C.," Apr. 24, 1956, p. 9.
55. *Ibid.*
56. Monsignor Raymond J. Gallagher. "The 1956 Conference," *Catholic Charities Review,* 1956, Vol. 40, No. 9, p. 7.
57. *Ibid.*
58. *Ibid.*
59. *Catholic Charities Review,* Dec., 1956, Vol. 40, No. 10, p. 2.
60. *Ibid.*
61. "Minutes of the Board of Directors of the N.C.C.C.," Oct. 27, 1956, p. 7.

62. "Minutes of the Board of Directors of the N.C.C.C.," May 9, 1957, p. 7.
63. Ibid.
64. Ibid.
65. Ibid., p. 8.
66. Ibid.
67. Ibid.
68. Ibid.
69. Monsignor Raymond J. Gallagher, "A Report of the 1958 Annual Meeting," Catholic Charities Review, Nov., 1958, Vol. 42, No. 9, p. 11.
70. N.C.C.C. Proceedings, 1916, p. 61.
71. "Why the National Conference of Catholic Charities," N.C.C.C. Secretary, Washington, D. C., p. 5.
72. "Confidential Memorandum to the Continuing Committee Directors of Catholic Charities," Dec. 4, 1934, Vol. 1, No. 1.
73. "Agenda of the Executive Committee of the N.C.C.C.," Nov. 12, 1943, p. 1.
74. Catholic Charities Review, Feb., 1944, Vol. 28, No. 2, p. 30.
75. "Minutes of the Topic Committees." Dec. 4, 1946, p. 7.
76. O'Grady, "The Conference and Trends in Catholic Social Work," N.C.C.C. Proceedings, 1948, p. 9.
77. Ibid.
78. Catholic Charities Review, Sept., 1953, Vol. 37, No. 7, p. 167.
79. Most Reverend Joseph E. Ritter, "Our Programs of Catholic Charities," N.C.C.C. Proceedings, 1953, p. 57.
80. Ibid.
81. Catholic Charities Review, May, 1955, Vol. 39, No. 5, p. 18.
82. Beatrice M. Faivre, Gannondale (Washington, 1959), p. 163.
83. Catholic Charities Review, May, 1957, Vol. 41, No. 5, p. 8.
84. Ibid., p. 9.
85. "The Conference of Religious 1920–1957" (Washington, 1957), p. 7.
86. O'Grady, "The Conference and Trends in Catholic Social Work," N.C.C.C. Proceedings, 1948, p. 13.
87. N.C.C.C. Proceedings, 1955, p. 150.
88. Monsignor Raymond J. Gallagher. "Challenges Facing our Religious," Catholic Charities Review, Feb., 1958, Vol. 42, No. 2, p. 16.
89. Ibid., p. 18.
90. Monsignor Floyd F. Fischer, "Catholic Social Work — Its Present and Future Role," Catholic Charities Review, Oct., 1957, Vol. 41, No. 8, p. 9.
91. Ibid.
92. Ibid.
93. Monsignor William J. Kerby. "Popularizing Social Work Among Catholics," N.C.C.C. Proceedings, 1924, p. 59.
94. Ibid.

CHAPTER VIII

The N.C.C.C. and Social Reform

"THE NATIONAL CONFERENCE OF CATHOLIC CHARI-TIES is a movement rather than an agency."[1] This statement appearing in a pamphlet designed to give a brief introduction to the National Conference points out rather clearly one of the basic objectives of the founders of the Conference in 1910. During the Conference's early history this objective appears at times to have been ignored or forgotten. The immediate need in 1910 was co-ordination and organization. After that, the necessity of promoting high standards of social work seemed to be the most important. Internal problems caused by the expansion of diocesan organizations of charities and the decreasing emphasis on volunteers for a time provided problems that focused the attention of the Catholic social worker on relief and the agencies and institutions concerned with it. A search for a cure for some of the modern social ills or at least a means of alleviating them was admitted to be a proper objective, but the time and energy of the Catholic worker was consumed in taking care of the immediate problem at hand, the dispensing of relief.

The founders of the National Conference, however, from the very beginning stressed the wider implications of the movement they had started. They never lost sight of the close relationship between charity and social justice. Mere relief of suffering was not their exclusive goal, nor was the Conference to be only an assembly of experts in the field of relief. The educational mission of the Con-ference was paramount in their minds and their hope was that it would be through the instrumentality of the National Conference that the laity could be reached and made active participants in the social movement. "They assumed," as Monsignor O'Grady said, "that Catholic Charities were the concern of all the people and not simply the preserve of a few."[2]

That, somehow, this idea had not developed and matured as well as had been expected can be seen in a comment in the September, 1950, issue of *The Catholic Charities Review* to the effect that "in this fortieth year we are getting a new perspective."[3] This new perspective was giving "technical processes their proper place in the program," and looking upon "Catholic Charities more and more as a movement in which all people must share."[4] The causes for this "new perspective" coming so late are not easy to assign. One of them, concerned with relief, has already been mentioned.

There was in addition, however, a strong conservative bent among many of the Catholic laity that was against the social service aspect of the movement. Monsignor White, one of the pioneers of the National Conference, spoke out in 1910 against those who said the Church ought not to concern herself with social questions because she has no program.[5] These people, Monsignor White said, denied the history of the Church. He also condemned those who at the other extreme would make of the Church a social reform club. Throughout the 1920's the Catholics as a whole were not taking any initiative in the matters of social legislation. They frequently rallied to support Church leaders when legislation opposed to Catholic interests was proposed, but "their work as a group has been," as *The Catholic Charities Review* observed, "very largely of the obstructionist character."[6]

In a letter to Monsignor Kerby in 1910, Dr. Charles Neill, then U. S. Commissioner of Labor, hoped that, "if this National Conference of Charities will from its beginning interest itself in the social and industrial causes of poverty and will prepare its members to take the attitude which Christianity and social sympathy and common sense suggest, the Conference will honor the Church and give noble service to the cause of humanity."[7] Monsignor William J. White was equally convinced that the Conference should "mark the beginning of a Catholic Social Reform Movement on national lines."[8]

Perhaps the early failure to convince sufficient numbers of those interested in charitable activities of study and research as the "first great need," deprived too many of the knowledge necessary for action in any program of legislative reform.[9] As Reverend M. F. McEvoy, diocesan director of Charities in Milwaukee in 1920, said, the result was that "though we have made great steps forward we still have not learned to put sufficient emphasis on prevention. . . . We should not permit conditions to exist that would make it necessary to bring that man or woman, boy or girl, to the door of the institution."[10]

In 1919, Monsignor Kerby pointed out that while "the prestige of the Church in respect of charity is very great. . . . An inheritance honors the ancestor rather than the descendant. It presents achievement in the former and good luck in the latter."[11] Accordingly, "the future asks of us with insistence to make our own distinctive contribution to the inheritance we shall pass on," and the monsignor added, "if we add nothing to it or if we make a serious mistake in what we attempt to add, the next generation will pay the penalty."[12] The contribution, as Monsignor Kerby saw it, was the "bringing about a timely adjustment of the new and the old," a clearer understanding of "complicated human rights," and a new view of "the function of the State, and of the possibility of large preventive measures in dealing with poverty."[13] It did not seem to the Monsignor that Catholic Charities could "remain remote from those processes nor indifferent to them."[14] Therefore, he hoped that the contribution of the generation for which he spoke would consist of "action upon the course of legislation and public administration in relief work, farsighted interpretation of social processes, higher standards of social justice and the arousing and sustaining of the modern conscience to the point of demanding effective reforms."[15]

In the 1920's, however, when most Americans had steady employment and rising wages, optimism and hope were too prevalent to cause many to worry about the next generation's heritage. This was true of Catholics as well as others. In an age when employee stockholding was encouraged, the psychological effects of wage earners' participation in large companies were very great.

Few people, as a result, concerned themselves greatly with social problems, and indicative of this lack of concern was the complaint in 1918 that the National Conference of Catholic Charities had found little time to discuss such things as the Settlement House problems. It was noted that there was no place for their discussion at the 1916 meeting either, and that a special meeting called for the purpose had attracted little attention.[16] Miss Margaret Tucker, a member of the Committee on Sick and Defective of the National Conference, observed that "this work is certainly not occupying the important place in the field of Catholic Charities that it should be, and that its future is anything but promising."[17] The Catholic settlement program, religious as well as social, "was looked upon as the work of the Catholic laity" and had depended, perhaps, too much on the volunteer who at the time was going into eclipse. There were those who questioned the value of the program[18] but it was equally true that general concern for such social problems was slight at the time. In the Archdiocese of New York in 1928, of the 3403 families totaling 15,313 individuals dealt with by Catholic Charities, "only thirty per cent were found to need cash relief while the balance were able to care for themselves after receiving service from Catholic Charities workers"; consequently it is not surprising that the Catholic layman could feel that relief was a sufficient manifestation of charity."[19]

While the individual Catholic limited his concept of charity to relief, the National Conference tended to limit its activities largely to the urban areas. The first concern of Catholic agencies had been to render effective service to immigrants in cities. Only slowly did agencies develop programs to include rural areas.[20] In 1929 not more than four dioceses had done much in the way of developing rural programs.[21] By 1938 only sixteen diocesan agencies appeared to have "fairly complete or partial coverage of rural areas."[22] Among the many reasons for this situation was the general complacency that was prevalent.

When a program for the diocese of Des Moines was proposed in 1924 the objections raised would indicate little knowledge of either rural or urban conditions. Some said, "there is no great need of a system of Catholic charity, Catholics are few, and as a rule responsible, self-respecting, proud and fairly prosperous."[23] Others replied that "Iowa is rich, and like the man in the Bible, 'hath need of nothing,' its fields are full of fat; it has no poverty and no problems."[24] There was little recognition of the view that held that "the social problems of the city are generally born in the country where the breakdown first occurs, and solution is sought in the city."[25] Nor was there any recognition that "there are rural problems in every country, in every district."[26]

The depression of the 1930's brought a rude awakening to those who had argued that there were no problems, whether rural or urban. It also gave an opportunity to the leadership in the National Conference to come out strongly on behalf of the social reform it had long considered necessary. Monsignor Robert F. Keegan, executive director of Catholic Charities of the Archdiocese of New York, in 1936 warned that "either we come to grips with the issues of the day as a professional body, or we vacate the leadership which is rightly ours."[27] He argued that, "social work, as a factor in American life and thinking, will not be worth its salt if it cannot transmute the realities of this depression into a new and constructive course of action."[28] Monsignor Keegan could see no alternative except some measure of social reconstruction and placed responsibility for such action squarely with the social workers. "In the past," he said, "we witnessed in social work the development of a philosophy of humanitarianism. This was succeeded by an era which placed emphasis on techniques. Today we behold social work concerned with the development of a philosophy of social and economic justice."[29]

Monsignor Keegan was convinced that "our social processes and our economic development no longer travel along parallel and equally mutual lines. They have clashed. Unless this conflict is resolved, our political order, under which they both have advanced, can no longer stand the strain."[30] Like Monsignor Kerby, Monsignor Keegan did not accept the nineteenth century view that "poverty and distress were due almost entirely to individual defects or individual misfortune."[31] Both believed that a much greater number of these cases could be shown to arise from the surrounding social and economic conditions.

Monsignor O'Grady, too, was concerned lest the conditions in the 1930's be looked upon as a temporary aberration of an otherwise sound society. "Are we at the mercy of economic laws," he asked in 1932, "or can we chart the course of our economic life? Many times, it would appear as if our national thinking were still dominated by the dismal eighteenth century concept of natural law."[32] Monsignor O'Grady argued that what was needed was a "drastic overhauling of the present economic structure," in accordance with *Quadragesimo Anno*.[33]

The Diocesan Directors of Charity meeting with the National Conference of Catholic Charities issued a statement which voiced the sentiments of the Conference leadership. They approved the trend away from the policies of nineteenth-century individualism as in keeping with rules of justice and Christian teaching. The directors believed that,

> The great depression revealed a great many defects in our economic system for which a permanent program is needed. It showed that our industrial structure had outgrown our legal and governmental machinery. . . . As prosperity returns we will have an insistent demand for a return to the social-economic thought of 50 years ago, loosely characterized as "rugged individualism." . . . We will have an increasingly vocal demand for the elimination of many forms of assistance for the workers and middle class. There will be the constant cry to Government from business. "Let us alone." . . . If Government does not establish some degree of restraint over these industries then the whole nation will continue to be economically and socially unstabilized. . . . The whole tendency of our times is toward the adoption of definite rules of conduct in industry and business relationship.[34]

Although the directors saw the need of social reconstruction, and through the National Conference sought to bring about a greater consciousness of social welfare problems, they were also aware of the danger of government control becoming so great that individual initiative would be choked off. They were, aware, too, that the private social agency could be swallowed up in an expanding program of government service. Therefore, while admitting the need of government assistance under certain conditions, the diocesan directors, through the National Conference, fought strenuously after the 1930's on behalf of the private agency. The relief problem of the thirties was well beyond the abilities of the private agencies to cope with. Government funds were necessary to handle the relief problem but since the source of the funds usually plays an important role in dictating their use, the private agency was in danger. This defense of the private agency was among the especially important accomplishments of the National Conference of Catholic Charities.

As a basic policy in their defense of the private agency, the leadership of the National Conference since 1935 stressed "benefits based on rights as against the expansion of public assistance as part of our social security program."[35] It was the firm conviction of the diocesan directors of Charities that the "constant expansion of public assistance would soon bring the Federal Government into all areas of American life."[36] The increased government services since the 1930's have had a heavy impact upon Catholic charity agencies as well as all other private agencies. It was to the task of supporting sound social legislation and avoiding the overpowering influence of the Federal Government that the National Conference of Catholic Charities has devoted its principal efforts since the thirties.

When the Social Security Act was before Congress in 1935, the two problems that required the greatest attention were the unemployed and the aged. Two suggested solutions to these problems were in conflict with each other from the beginning of the discussions on social security. One approach considered the problem as one of dependency and would have given out benefits on the basis of proved need. The other approach, generally favored by National Conference leaders, regarded the problem as one to be handled through some system of insurance. The insurance approach appeared at the time to be the best long-range approach but the immediate problem of relief had to be handled by grants-in-aid to the States for those who obviously had not had time to accumulate the necessary credits toward the insurance plan. The Social Security Act of 1935, as expanded in 1939, became a permanent piece of legislation and involved the government's recognition of its duty to attempt to prevent acute distress and provide some measure of security for an individual's later years. There remained, however, considerable difference of opinion as to the merits of insurance features when future amendments were discussed.

There were no objections from the National Conference to expanded benefits under the Social Security program so long as these benefits were based on rights. From time to time, however, revisions of the original Social Security Act were proposed which would revert to the needs test for benefits. Many of these revisions were sponsored by the same people who had worked for a general relief program in the early thirties.

One of these proposed revisions was the Wagner-Murray-Dingell Bill of the mid-forties. Monsignor O'Grady declared that support of Social Security "requires rather than prevents critical examination of methods proposed to achieve it."[37] This bill, he felt, "proposes methods, some good meriting support, others very bad, to be rigorously opposed. . . . Social Security should be able to be obtained without inordinate subjection of free men and free institutions to the State."[38] It was Title IV of the Bill to which particular exception was taken. This part of the bill would have turned over to the Federal Government major responsibility and control of general relief and eliminated established division of responsibility between federal and state governments. If passed in the form proposed, "it would sound the death knell for Catholic charity."[39] The proposal was considered by the National Conference to be particularly dangerous since it was made at a time when there was no serious public relief problem and when there was "absolutely no demand from the country for the entrance of the Federal Government into the field of public relief."[40]

Title XII of the same bill went even further. It would have eliminated established categories of Old Age Assistance, Aid to Dependent Children, and Aid to the Blind. Monsignor O'Grady pointed out the seriousness of this proposal, noting that "such extreme forcing of federal funds into the field of public relief, where they are not needed, and the inevitable federal control which is intended to follow, is the dream of the proponents of public welfare."[41] The great danger was that, "no State has moral fibre enough to refuse a grant of federal money," and to get this money "local control would be yielded."[42] Perhaps worst of all was the disposition, even of Catholics "to answer, 'let the State take care of them,' when reminded of their duty and the duty of the Church to serve the poor."[43]

Reverend William A. O'Connor, president of the National Conference of Catholic Charities and Archdiocesan Supervisor of Charities in Chicago, in an address June 8, 1944, on "Catholic Charities and Benefits Based on Rights" given at a Regional Meeting of the Conference in St. Louis, stressed the point that "economic security must not be bought at too great a price."[44] He referred to the Social Security Act as "a curious composite of benefits based on rights and of benefits based on needs," and the attempts to extend the benefits based on needs causes the controversy.[45] Quoting Franklin D. Roosevelt, who, in his January 5, 1935, message to Congress had urged that the Federal Government quit the business of relief, Father O'Connor took the stand that public and private agencies must maintain the established functional division of responsibility between them in the field of relief.[46]

Father O'Connor, moreover, made a plea to the Society of St. Vincent de Paul to play a special role in this question of public relief. "It is sad and disheartening," he said, "to hear Vincentians say that there is no work for their Conference to do today. . . . There was never more need for their spiritual activities. . . . But even in the field of material needs there is a great work for our Vincentians to do."[47] Because the Vincentians were closer to the poor in the parishes they were in a more advantageous position to do a better job than any central office. "A parish Conference of the Society of St. Vincent de Paul would find more work than it could handle if it undertook to visit regularly and faithfully only those poor who are receiving public benefits. . . . It is my considered conviction," continued Father O'Connor, "that the Church stands in greater need today of the help of her Vincentians than ever before in the history of our country."[48]

The National Conference of Catholic Charities held to the position that the Federal Government's interest in welfare programs should foster and develop the voluntary or private agencies services. This stimulation should include the encouragement to create private agencies where none existed.[49] The government "should supplement our efforts, not supplant them" stated Reverend John J. Lennon, director of the Department of Child Care, Catholic Charities of Archdiocese of New York.[50] "Only when all private efforts fail should the state make their responsibility its own," was the principle that Father Lennon advocated.[51]

On the matter of Social Security as well as other similar matters there were indications from the membership of the National Conference of Catholic Charities, according to Monsignor O'Grady, "they did not have sufficient opportunity to participate in matters of policy on a national level."[52] In 1946, at the annual Conference meeting, Monsignor O'Grady reminded the membership that the Conference was "to a large degree a forum for the expression and exchange of opinions," but that the "Directors of Catholic Charities, however, come together as the representatives of their Bishops to discuss common national problems."[53] Since the Director is "in a position to advise his Bishop locally about questions of diocesan policy, similarly the Directors nationally are in a position to advise the Bishops as a whole in regard to national policies."[54]

Monsignor O'Grady then announced that the directors of Diocesan Charities had developed a point of view on Social Security and their first task was to explain it to the Catholic social worker. He then stated that on full employment the directors were agreed that a program of public work should be provided by the Government "only when private enterprise with Government assistance and stimulation fails to provide continuous employment"; that the system of unemployment compensation was a "decided step in advance," but not all that it should be; that a federal work program was to be preferred to a grant-in-aid to the states for general relief;

that, since work programs and relief programs represent incompatible philosophies, both should not exist side by side; that Old Age and Survivors insurance should be extended.[55]

Between 1946 and 1948 there was a serious threat to the system of social insurance then in effect. Speaking at the National Conference annual meeting in 1948, Nelson H. Cruikshank, director of Social Insurance Activities of the American Federation of Labor, warned that there was a "steady drift in the direction of governmental charity."[56] He based his observations on activities in the 80th Congress, reports of the Hoover Commission, and the policies of Senator Robert A. Taft. On the contrary, Mr. Cruikshank contended that "the purpose of all aid, public or private, should be first to restore the individual's self-reliance."[57] He was "firmly convinced that the field of charity should be left to our humanitarian and religious institutions, while it is entirely appropriate for the government to help people help themselves through the instrument of social insurance."[58]

This 1948 meeting of the Conference in Boston gave hope that Catholic charities was beginning to fulfill its responsibility for participation and leadership in social movements, and for interesting the laity in this type of activity.[59] The commitment of the National Conference to a program of social insurance brought it into "the closest harmony with American labor," and Monsignor O'Grady observed that "this was part of the basic philosophy of the founders of the National Conference of Catholic Charities."[60] It was the hope of the leadership of the National Conference that the "transition from the old to the new in Catholic social work" would be carried out "at this stage better than we did in the 20's."[61] The test would be whether the transition could be worked out on the "basis of mutual respect of different groups," which Catholic social work of necessity must represent.[62] The hope "for the creation of a real movement," observed the *Catholic Charities Review* in 1950, "rests in an ability to develop through cooperative relationships."[63]

The efforts of those who sought to write into the proposed changes in the Social Security Act in 1949 the idea of a "needs test" for benefits and to place all forms of relief in the hands of the Government again met with opposition from the National Conference of Catholic Charities. Bishop Bartholomew J. Eustace of Camden, New Jersey, in 1949, argued for an expansion of benefits under Social Security but felt that "it must be admitted that anything, save Heaven and the Lakes of Killarney, can be purchased at too high a price."[64] Monsignor O'Grady in speaking of the proposed changes in the Act, when writing to Dean C. Acheson, then Vice-Chairman of the Commission on the Organization of the Executive Branch of the Government, declared that he could not conceive "of any more backward step in our national life than the substitution of a public assistance program for social insurance. To my knowledge," he continued, "no such backward step has been taken by any other country in the world. The whole drift in every country is to substitute benefits based on rights to protect the workers against the hazards of life, for a system of relief based on the needs test."[65]

In a bulletin to the directors of Diocesan Charities on March 28, 1949, there was included a copy of an address given by Monsignor O'Grady at the New England Regional Conference of Catholic Charities. The address, entitled "Implications of the Proposed Public Assistance Program," noted some changes in the general pattern of social welfare since 1910. Earlier the religious motives were still quite strong and local groups did a great deal of their own thinking. Secularization has, however, sapped much of the vitality from this field. There was a growing dependence on government bureaucracy noticeable, he said, even at the meetings of the National Conference. "One cannot fail to note what happens when Government experts appear at our meetings. They are regarded as great oracles. Everybody gathers around them. Everybody wants to stand in with them because some day they may need a job which the experts control."[66]

In order to ensure a hearing for the views of the National Conference a meeting between the Standing Committee of the Directors of Diocesan Charities was arranged with Oscar Ewing, Administrator of the Federal Security Agency for Thursday, May 5, 1949. The Standing Committee reiterated the views that had long been expressed by the National Conference; namely, (1) "voluntary organizations have a right to exist and expand as the need arises, (2) this right is a prior right with the government entering the field only if the need cannot be met by the voluntary agency, (3) the government has a responsibility to encourage the voluntary agencies."[67] Mr. Ewing appeared sympathetic toward the points of view expressed promising that nothing would be done to injure the programs of the National Conference. There was a feeling among the directors that much remained to be done in "interpreting our point of view to the leaders throughout the country on the national, state and local level."[68]

Necessarily bound up with the discussions on Social Security was the concern of the National Conference for the various proposals for care of the aged. Involved in the passage of the Social Security Act of 1935 was the question of whether assistance to the aged would be made available to private institutions providing care for the aged. Since some states had laws prohibiting assistance to private institutions the question of the relation of these laws to the Social Security Act was involved. There was also concern in the earlier days about including the workers of Catholic Institutions under Old Age Insurance provisions of the Social Security Act. The diocesan directors in the mid-thirties had three points of view on this question.[69] Some of them strongly favored inclusion of these workers, others wished to set up their own system, and another group preferred to await the results of the local Community Chests' study of the problem. In any case, it was agreed to promote statewide meetings on the subject.

Not until the mid-1940's, however, did concern for the aged take on the proportions of a major issue. In the early stages of discussion it appeared that there was some sentiment for an institutional program similar to that which Catholic charities had developed for dependent children in previous years.[70] It became clearer, however, as studies of the problem progressed, that the tendency of social work literature to look upon the problems of the aging as primarily pathological was a move in the wrong direction.

The Conference program for the care of the aged was in a sense a logical development of its previous interests. Child-care had long

occupied the center of interest in Catholic charities. Family counseling had come next, and it seemed to follow naturally that care
of the aged should now be of great concern. It was the opinion of
the Conference leadership that there was a "distinct danger that
we may look on large institutions as a panacea" in solving the problem.[71] Meanwhile, the National Conference kept close watch on
government proposals affecting the aged.

Another significant area of social legislation in which the National Conference took a decided interest was the field of public
housing. This interest had been shared with those engaged in professional social work even before the turn of the century. Housing
reform was, in a sense, merely one phase of professional social work.
It was the housing conditions in tenement and slum areas that produced the people who made charity organization societies necessary,
declared the social worker. Housing reform was therefore the key
to the rehabilitation of the urban community. Some of the early
reformers, like Lawrence Veiller, who wrote the first New York
State Tenement Law in 1901, were convinced that the reformers
must be organized because the exploiters were organized. Most of
them, however, were opposed to government subsidies. Leadership
in the National Conference agreed that better housing made better
family life and that this was certainly one of the important keys to
social reform. By 1930, this leadership believed that the formula
for success in better housing was to develop local authority under
state law as the administrative unit for a housing program. It was
further believed that federal funds would be necessary to make up
the difference between what the family could pay and the cost of
operating the project.

Monsignor O'Grady has had the undisputed leadership not only
of the Conference but also of the Catholic Church in the United
States in the fight for housing for low-income families. Together
with Mrs. Mary K. Simkhovitch, founder of Greenwich House in
New York, in the early 1930's he enlisted the help of others in-
cluding Gerard Swope, Harry Laidler of the League for Industrial
Democracy, Alfred E. Smith, Franklin D. Roosevelt and Mrs.
Roosevelt, and Herbert Lehman. Later Hugh Johnson, Fiorello La

Guardia, Senator Robert F. Wagner, and Harold Ickes were also converted to the ideas of the original group which "with no budget, but deep dedication to do something about housing needs, had a plan at the very beginning of the New Deal."[72]

From 1931 to 1937 it was the conviction of Monsignor O'Grady that the task of the National Conference was the pioneer one of interesting local groups in the housing problems. It was his hope that mass interest in the housing movement could be developed.[73] Some of the best Catholic leaders in the housing movement were produced in this early period, and it was their desire to keep it a volunteer movement, because they feared that in the long run a professional housing movement would weaken its chances of success. Among these Catholic leaders were Monsignor Edward R. Moore, an original member of the Housing Authority of the city of New York; Monsignor John R. Mulroy, who helped create the Housing Authority of the city of Denver; Monsignor Thomas O'Dwyer of Los Angeles, who helped lead the fight for adequate shelter there; Monsignor Thomas R. Reynolds of the Boston Housing Authority, who was a driving force in the movement in Boston; and Monsignor Leo A. Geary, who was an articulate member of the Buffalo Housing Authority.

In promoting a low-cost housing program Monsignor O'Grady argued that since the National Conference was heir to a tradition of interest "in wage legislation, trade unionism, workmen's compensation, child labor legislation," among other social movements, it was bound to follow in the footsteps of the pioneer leaders of the Conference.[74] The Conference had "contributed materially to the movement for old age security," and it was hoped that it would be able to do as much for the housing problem.[75]

The years 1939–1949 saw the professional housing movement growing and inclined to disregard the strength of the volunteer groups.[76] The "professional housers," according to Monsignor O'Grady, had difficulty in resisting the attacks of the real estate and home building groups with the same success as the volunteers. The enlistment of the forces of organized labor as well as various educational and religious groups and the support of Senator Robert

A. Taft effected the passage of the Housing Act of 1949 despite the many obstacles encountered.

Senator Taft's support was most important. The senator was convinced that a public housing program was the government's responsibility but he sought a substitute for the 1937 program. He had looked at the theory that if enough high-priced housing was built throughout the nation, the used-house market would be open to low-income families, and he also took a look at the proposal to issue rent certificates on the basis of a needs test to low-income families. These were the alternatives suggested by the critics of a low-rent public housing, which they denounced as "creeping socialism." On February 6, 1945, Monsignor O'Grady testified before the Taft Subcommittee on Housing and Urban Redevelopment. Personal Conferences between the two followed; and on April 11, 1946, when the Wagner-Ellender-Taft Bill was being debated in the Senate, Senator Taft rejected the alternatives to subsidized low-rent public housing and said he had found no method superior to that proposed in the bill before the Senate. Senator Taft, according to Lee Johnson, Executive Vice-President of the National Housing Conference in 1953, admitted the influence of Monsignor O'Grady on his thinking on public housing, saying that he had been convinced that rent certificates were not the answer and that a needs test "for elegibility for tenancy in low-rent public housing was unfair and degrading."[77]

The housing problem was closely related from the very beginning to slum clearance and slum analysis. Improvement in housing presupposed a solution to the slum problem. The slum problem in turn raised the whole question of the improvement of the city. It was in this manner that the movement for low-cost housing became tied up with urban renewal. Provisions for the redevelopment of cities were made in the Housing Act of 1949 and in the 1954 amendments to the Act the term "urban renewal" was substituted for "urban redevelopment" suggesting a more positive approach to the maintenance of good housing and health standards. The many problems, particularly relocation, that are connected with urban renewal were entering more and more into the discussions of the National Conference of Catholic Charities in the 1950's.

Two other areas of interest to the National Conference which were in a real sense related to the housing program were those of health services and race relations. The efforts that had been made from time to time since the 1930's to enact some form of health legislation had been of great concern to the leadership of the Conference. The diocesan directors were in substantial agreement with the statements of Reverend Alphonse M. Schwitalla, S.J., president of the Catholic Hospital Association in 1939, to the effect that any legislation should not affect the good relationship between public and private agencies, that there was need of some extension of the public health program, that caution be exercised by having administrative procedures follow the best available scientific procedures and not run ahead of them, that grants under Social Security be increased, that the number of hospitals be increased to provide a prudent reserve as well as effective capacity, that there be developed cooperative plans by public and private agencies on the care of the indigent, and finally that the individual be allowed a choice in his selection of plans of health insurance.[78]

Although nothing came of the legislative proposals in 1939, the discussion on a public health program continued, and in 1946 a National Health Bill (S. 1606) was proposed as a solution. Monsignor O'Grady testified before the Senate Committee on Education and Labor, which was holding hearings on the Bill in May, 1946. In his testimony he stressed what he considered some fundamental principles of social philosophy. The first objective, he said, was to encourage the individual to provide for his own health and then let government implement this voluntary effort without trying to supplant it.[79] He was opposed to extending the rural programs to the entire United States, feeling that the funds and services would be too thinly spread thus causing the rural areas to suffer. He was for universal coverage which would "be compulsory in fact, but voluntary in form."[80] This would mean, he said, "that all those who are now covered by voluntary programs can continue in their present status. It means an opportunity and an incentive to provide new voluntary programs."[81]

In general, the National Conference through its spokesman, Monsignor O'Grady, would sponsor a health program in which care would be "provided for the ordinary wage-earner without his having to sink to the level of a public assistance program."[82] Any such program should recognize the advances made by private endeavor in the field of health insurance and should provide the worker "with both medical and hospital care without a needs test."[83]

Two areas, labor and race relations, closely related to the social movements in which the National Conference played a major role, seem not to have received as much emphasis as one might perhaps expect. The interests of labor coincided with many of the objectives of the National Conference; but for the most part Labor and the National Conference seemed to proceed along parallel lines until the late 1940's. In the *Proceedings* of the annual meeting in 1947 the Conference devoted more space to the problems of labor than that of any previous year. Some thirty pages were devoted to such topics as the "Right of the Church to Speak on Social, Economic and Labor Problems," "The Church and Community Organization in the Labor Scene," "The Union and the Community," and "The Voice of Management in Labor." By 1951 the *Catholic Charities Review* remarked that the progress of participation of Labor in Catholic Charities was such that "the participation of Labor in the Conference is now not merely a token representation."[84] By then the *Review* could say that, "representatives of labor participate in all our meetings, including the meetings of the Board of Directors and the Directors of Catholic Charities."[85] The *Review* concluded that, "this means we are meeting with labor face-to-face in all problems and policies of Catholic social work."[86]

The important question as to the relation of the social programs being promoted by organized labor to the philosophy of Catholic charities had perhaps been responsible for the greater attention to labor in the recent years. The leadership of the Conference raised the question as to how well the Conference had presented its philosophy to Labor. At any event, "it was clear from the Washington meetings that labor participation in Catholic Charities has become a permanent fixture."[87]

In 1934, the efforts of the secretary of the National Conference to fulfill a pastor's request for material on race relations brought home to the Conference that little direct attention had been paid to the subject up to that time.[88] Almost nothing could be found in the *Proceedings* in the previous ten years, and there were only three articles in *The Catholic Charities Review*. The desirability of devoting greater attention to this problem was discussed at the meeting of the Executive Committee of the National Conference in January, 1935, and the immediate conclusion was to include some discussion of the race question in the annual meeting in 1935 at Peoria.[89] At that meeting the Conference of Religious held a session on child-care among Negroes and Mexicans. In general, in succeeding years more attention was devoted to Mexicans than to Negroes in the programs of the annual meetings. This was probably because of the urgency of the problems of Mexican labor in the dioceses of the Southwest. The annual meeting at Houston in 1941 devoted a part of the program to the treatment of minority groups particularly Negroes and Mexicans. In 1950, the annual meeting was planned for Miami, Florida, but was moved to Washington, D. C., when it was discovered that Negroes could not share the same housing facilities as the rest of the membership and probably would not be allowed to attend the luncheons.[90]

The Negro question was discussed at some length at the Peoria meeting in 1935. Reverend Francis J. Gilligan of St. Paul's Seminary, St. Paul, Minnesota, contended that "enough earnest words have been spoken about the ruthless violation of natural rights of individuals here and in other countries" and it was now time to speak on behalf of the Negro.[91] "And in order that our protest may not be merely verbal," continued Father Gilligan, "we should cooperate positively with agencies which are working constructively for the protection of those elementary rights."[92]

The "gist" of the problem as Father Gilligan saw it was the "terrifying specter of possible intermarriage," which he felt was in reality a specter that "lacks substance and form."[93] The basis of much of the prejudice blocking the Negro's progress, he thought, was the oft "repeated assertions that all Negroes are lazy, or ignorant, or immoral."[94] Father Gilligan went on to declare that "the practice indulged in by white individuals of repeating carelessly those statements is morally wrong."[95]

At the 1943 anuual meeting, the Honorable G. Howland Shaw, then president of the National Conference of Catholic Charities cautioned that "there are problems of the postwar period on which any compromise would be for us disastrous. One of these," he said, " — and it is an acid test — is the treatment of certain minorities in our American democracy: the treatment to be accorded to Negroes, Mexicans, Puerto-Ricans, Chinese and other 'Brothers under the Skin.' "[96] At that meeting Reverend John La Farge, S.J., then Associate Editor of America, recommended the setting up of a Catholic interracial council and a study group to get work under way immediately on this important issue.[97]

The interest of the National Conference of Catholic Charities in the movement for social reform was basic to its original objectives and it ultimately sought to relate the results of this reform to the parish and the pastoral ministry. Once the earlier emphasis of the National Conference on the conditions under which people lived was recaptured in the 1930's and expanded thereafter, it was clear that there were "certain types of problems . . . not being reached by the pastoral ministry."[98] Since it was the responsibility of the social worker and the pastor for "stimulating the type of parish organization that will be able to cope with the problems of the families" in a given area, it becomes necessary for both to understand the neighborhood of the parish.[99]

A renewal of the recognition of the significance of the neighborhood organization came with the realization of the necessity of providing closer contacts with the people than could be developed through a central bureau. A significant development along this line took place at the annual meeting in Buffalo in 1943. During that meeting the Executive Committee of the National Conference, on November 15, 1943, created a Committee on Neighborhood Organization.[100] Its purpose was to get the ideas of pastors on the local and neighborhood problems. Projects of all kinds as solutions to these problems were explored during the following six months, but there was some difference of opinion among pastors as to the extent of their obligation to participate in such projects.[101]

The expansion of blighted areas in the cities continued and threatened the Church's investment as well as the city's stake. By 1953 some progress had been made in analyzing the problems connected with blighted areas. Special meetings of pastors had been held at the annual meetings of the Conference in both 1951 and 1952. There was general agreement that discussion groups on the local level would give the pastors a better understanding of the possibilities in particular cases.[102]

The National Conference of Catholic Charities had been from its foundation concerned about certain problems not being reached by the parish, such as specialized services, adoptions, and the like. The enrichment of parish life was another of its objectives, and the challenge that it was not contributing as much as had been expected was met by this effort at establishing closer contact between the parish and the general social movement. The *Catholic Charities Review* declared that "at least part of the energy of Catholic Charities must be directed toward helping our parishes to meet their broader problems."[103] The reference was to housing, blighted neighborhoods and their related problems. The specialized services of the central bureau were not to be minimized, but the feeling was that the bureau could not "overlook the larger problems that are confronting us in the new day."[104]

One of the ways in which the religious communities could fit into this emphasis on neighborhood organization was to provide the health and social services for which many of them had been originally founded. A number of European communities had offshoots or foundations in the United States working on a neighborhood or parish basis. Many American communities had sprung up to fill the same need, such as the Dominican Sisters of the Sick Poor, the Missionary Sisters of the Most Blessed Trinity, and the Parish Visitors of Mary Immaculate. This last community had laid a foundation for new interest in parish work since its establishment in New York in 1920 by Mother Mary Theresa Tallon. These efforts could lay the foundation for a more systematic and analytical study of parish problems.

By 1956 the discussions of the pastors had resulted in certain conclusions. For one thing it appeared that the Catholic charities bureaus in many places had lost contact with the parishes. The rather close tie-up of the earlier days had disappeared. The discussions themselves were producing an amount of material that could be circulated among pastors and bring a better realization of what was being attempted. What appeared to be the greatest need was "more opportunities for communication between lay people and the priests in our parishes and the workers and priests in our diocesan agencies of Catholic Charities."[105] There was a danger that if the Catholic charities agencies were not sensitive to these broader social problems, the pastors might work for some organization which would thus isolate the central bureau in a limited field of activity and so destroy its traditional role of dealing with the social problems of the community.[106]

As an example of what leadership can contribute to a better relationship between the parish, the neighborhood, and the diocesan bureau, the *Catholic Charities Review* singled out The Work Conference on the problems of youth organized by Monsignor Raymond J. Gallagher in Cleveland in 1955.[107] Representatives of all agencies of the city and neighborhood leaders from all groups joined in the Conference with marked success.

If isolationism characterized Catholic charities in the United States in 1910, and the National Conference of Catholic Charities had as a primary objective the overcoming of this isolationism, then the Conference had accomplished only part of its task by its successes in the United States in the first forty years of its existence. A still greater task awaited it, for the isolation characteristic of 1910 still existed on the international level in 1950. It would have been impossible for Catholic charities to remain true to its mission while ignoring the wider field. Just as it had moved from relief to prevention to social reform nationally so now it turned its attention to similar problems on the international scene.

One of the earliest references to the international scene was in 1932 when the executive committee suggested that a European might be asked to be on the program of the annual meeting.[108] This limited approach to the problems of international charity was not substantially altered until World War II forced a recognition of the wider horizons. Dr. Parker T. Moon, professor of International Relations at Columbia University, had spoken at the 1933 annual meeting of the Conference about what a body of social workers could do to improve international relations.[109] This, however, was about the extent of the interest down to 1940.

Monsignor O'Grady, meanwhile, had made a trip to South American countries in the belief that the National Conference of Catholic Charities should establish closer ties with those countries. At the annual meeting at Houston in 1941 he suggested that representatives from South American countries be invited to participate. He was convinced that the Conference's outlook should be broadened.

The outbreak of World War II, however, had centered the focus elsewhere than Latin America. The real problems arose after peace had been declared and the displaced person along with the reconstruction of the war torn areas were items demanding immediate attention. Bishop Bryan J. McEntegart, Bishop of Ogdensburg, New York, in 1947, remarked after a visit overseas that, "to any fair-minded visitor in Europe today, one thing is plain. The relief and reconstruction of Western Europe is a task in which Americans must cooperate wholeheartedly unless they wish to desert every principle that is sacred to them."[110]

The displaced person became "a symbol of interest of Catholic Charities in a great international Catholic welfare problem," declared Monsignor O'Grady in 1948 at the annual meeting of the Conference in Boston.[111] The great task was to educate American public opinion toward the displaced person who for the most part comprised Jews, Poles, Ukrainians, Balts, and others from Eastern Europe. The education program of the National Conference stressed the right of asylum of people who were guilty of no crime, and their right of free choice as to their future place of resettlement. Monsignor O'Grady hoped that the National Conference Office would have "the resources and the courage to provide the leadership needed in this field."[112]

The difficulty of the educational task was highlighted as Monsignor O'Grady declared in 1947, by "certain prejudices that have modified our traditional policy" in providing asylum to persecuted people.[113] "Let us, as Catholics," he urged, "not be too quick to blame others for these prejudices. . . . Let us not take the easy way out by blaming others for the failure of Congress to take action"[114]

The Boston meeting devoted a great deal of its time to the international aspects of charity, and it was the opinion of Monsignor O'Grady that, "the Conference as the clearing house for Catholic Charities must always emphasize the international aspects of Catholic Charities."[115] It was clear, he thought, that "Catholic Charities can no longer isolate itself and remain true to its basic guiding principles. It must be interested in human needs independent of nationality, race or color."[116]

This concern for the broader aspects of charity manifested itself in an effort by the National Conference to bring about changes in the philosophy expressed in the McCarran-Walter Immigration Act which was passed by Congress over a presidential veto in 1952. It was the contention of the leadership of the National Conference of Catholic Charities that this act embodied the prejudices and discriminatory thinking of the immigration legislation of the 1920's. It was further contended that since little real analysis was made of the problem before the 1924 Act there was even greater need for a complete study of the issues. The Immigration Committee of the Diocesan Directors of Catholic Charities felt that some steps might be taken in this direction by the scheduling of conferences on a local basis. Such conferences on immigration policy were held at Lexington, Kentucky, November 9, 1957, Fargo, North Dakota, May 3, 1958, and Denver, Colorado, December 6, 1958. These were well attended by local civic and religious groups and took a firm stand in favor of nondiscriminatory policies on immigration. It was the hope of the sponsors of the conferences that a more wholesome attitude toward immigration in all parts of the United States could be developed. This concern for international charity was not limited to a mere sharing of goods with other nations. This would have been comparable to the old concept of equating relief with charity. Monsignor O'Grady insisted that Catholic charities "must also develop contacts with them; it must find ways and means of sharing experience with them. . . . We must look to the day when there will be a central organization of Catholic Charities for the entire world. We look to the day in which such a central organization will be operated directly under the Holy See itself."[117]

Whether because of foreknowledge or influence, Monsignor O'Grady turned out to be a good prophet. He visited Rome in 1950 as a member of a subcommittee appointed to draw up a constitution for a proposed International Conference of Catholic Charities. The first meeting of the International Conference was held in Rome in December, 1951. Its purposes were outlined to be, "promotion of coordination" of all Catholic charities, "exchange of information and documentation in the social field," and "representation of Catholic organizations and interests on the international level."[118] The central office was to be in Rome.

Within a short time after its establishment the International Conference acquired consultative status in the United Nations Economic and Social Council. At its 1957 annual meeting the National Conference of Catholic Charities voted to establish a "small international social welfare committee that will serve as a rallying center for United States thinking on all phases of this great subject of world Catholic Charities."[119] This committee was also to serve as an information center for National Conference members of matters concerning the International Conference.

In a very real sense the National Conference of Catholic Charities has done much in its relatively short life to develop the idea of charity in its broadest sense. It had accepted the challenge of the 1930's and taken an active part in the formation of social legislation. There was a danger, however, as Monsignor O'Grady said he had been told in the first years of the Conference's history, that Catholic Charities seemed "concerned largely with making itself into a defensive force."[120] The critic continued, according to Monsignor O'Grady, by pointing out that,

> Your people give the impression that they are always on the defensive. They seem to feel that they are constantly threatened in their defense, they are always looking for political weapons. I have never thought for one moment that this was your best asset. You have a great storehouse of tradition and achievement. You also have a basically sound philosophy of life. Your challenge is to make these fine qualities into a working program.[121]

There was considerable evidence in the record of the National Conference of Catholic Charities that as it approached its Golden Jubilee in 1960 it had accepted this challenge and was becoming a positive social force.

Notes — Chapter VIII

1. "National Conference of Catholic Charities" (Washington, 1952), p. 5.
2. O'Grady, *Catholic Charities* in the U. S., p. 433.
3. *Catholic Charities Review*, Sept., 1950, Vol. 34, No. 7, p. 168.
4. *Ibid.*
5. St. Vincent de Paul *Quarterly*, May, 1910, Vol. 15, No. 2, p. 207.
6. Monsignor John O'Grady, "The Future of Catholic Case Work," *Catholic Charities Review*, Mar., 1922, Vol. 6, No. 3, p. 95.
7. Dr. Charles P. Neill to Dr. Kerby, Aug. 8, 1910, in N.C.C.C. *Proceedings*, 1910, p. 178.
8. Monsignor William J. White, "The Reform Problems which the Church Should Meet," N.C.C.C. *Proceedings*, 1910, p. 174.
9. *Ibid.*
10. N.C.C.C. *Proceedings*, 1920, p. 80.
11. William J. Kerby, "New and Old in Catholic Charity," *Catholic Charities Review*, Jan., 1919, Vol. 3, No. 1, p. 8.
12. *Ibid.*
13. *Ibid.*
14. *Ibid.*
15. *Ibid.*, p. 11.
16. Margaret Tucker, "Catholic Settlement Work — An Analysis," *Catholic Charities Review*, Dec., 1918, Vol. 2, No. 10, p. 304.
17. *Ibid.*
18. N.C.C.C. *Proceedings*, 1914, pp. 224–225.
19. *Catholic Charities Review*, May, 1929, Vol. 13, No. 5, p. 163.
20. *Ibid.*, Jan., 1938, Vol. 22, No. 1, p. 13.
21. *Ibid.*, Sept., 1929, Vol. 13, No. 7, p. 230.
22. *Ibid.*, Jan., 1938, Vol. 22, No. 1, p. 13.

23. N.C.C.C. *Proceedings*, 1924, p. 21.
24. *Ibid.*, p. 22.
25. *Ibid.*, p. 23.
26. *Ibid.*
27. Monsignor Robert F. Keegan, "Facing Present Realities," *Catholic Charities Review*, Jan., 1936, Vol. 20, No. 1, p. 10.
28. *Ibid.*
29. *Ibid.*
30. Monsignor Robert F. Keegan, "Lay Participation in the National Conference," *Catholic Charities Review*, Oct., 1936, Vol. 20, No. 8, p. 256.
31. *Catholic Charities Review*, Sept., 1936, Vol. 20, No. 7, p. 230.
32. N.C.C.C. *Proceedings*, 1935, p. 298.
33. *Ibid.*, p. 71.
34. N.C.C.C. *Proceedings*, 1935, p. 298.
35. *Catholic Charities Review*, Dec., 1952, Vol. 36, No. 10, p. 225.
36. *Ibid.*
37. "Information Bulletin of the N.C.C.C. for Catholic Institutions," Feb. 6, 1944, Vol. 1, No. 2, p. 2.
38. *Ibid.*
39. *Ibid.*, p. 3.
40. *Ibid.*
41. *Ibid.*, p. 4.
42. *Ibid.*
43. *Ibid.*
44. *Ibid.*, June 8, 1944.
45. *Ibid.*, p. 4.
46. *Ibid.*, p. 5.
47. *Ibid.*, p. 8.
48. *Ibid.*, p. 9.
49. Reverend Bernard M. Brogan, "Catholic Philosophy of Child Care," N.C.C.C. *Proceedings*, 1946, pp. 84–85.
50. Reverend John J. Lennon, "Catholic Philosophy of Child Care," N.C.C.C. *Proceedings*, 1946.
51. *Ibid.*
52. Monsignor John O'Grady, "Catholic Agencies and Social Security," N.C.C.C. *Proceedings*, 1946.
53. *Ibid.*
54. *Ibid.*
55. *Ibid.*, pp. 61–63.
56. Nelson, Cruikshank, "Threats to Social Insurance," N.C.C.C. *Proceedings*, 1948, p. 97.
57. *Ibid.*
58. *Ibid.*
59. *Catholic Charities Review*, Nov., 1948, Vol. 32, No. 9, p. 234.
60. Monsignor John O'Grady, "The Conference and Trends in Catholic Social Work," N.C.C.C. *Proceedings*, 1948, pp. 15–16.
61. *Catholic Charities Review*, Dec., 1950, Vol. 34, No. 10, p. 249.
62. *Ibid.*
63. *Ibid.*
64. Most Reverend Bartholomew J. Eustace, "Charity, Industry and the Welfare State," N.C.C.C. *Proceedings*, 1949, p. 25.
65. Monsignor O'Grady to Dean Acheson, Nov. 22, 1948.

66. "Confidential Bulletin for Directors of Catholic Charities," Mar. 28, 1949.
67. Ibid., May 14, 1949.
68. Ibid.
69. Ibid., Nov. 17, 1937.
70. N.C.C.C. Proceedings, 1939, p. 14.
71. "Confidential Bulletin for Directors of Charities," Sept. 23, 1946.
72. Catholic Charities Review, May, 1956, Vol. 40, No. 5, pp. 10–11.
73. MS. Monsignor O'Grady, "Catholic Charities and Housing," p. 1.
74. Monsignor O'Grady, "The Conference and Trends in Catholic Social Work," N.C.C.C. Proceedings, 1948, p. 14.
75. Ibid.
76. O'Grady, "Catholic Charities and Housing," p. 1.
77. Lee Johnson, "Bob Taft — Champion of Low Rent Housing," Catholic Charities Review, Sept., 1953, Vol. 37, No. 7, p. 172.
78. "Confidential Bulletin for Diocesan Directors of Catholic Charities," Jan. 28, 1939.
79. Ibid., May 7, 1916.
80. Ibid.
81. Ibid.
82. Monsignor John O'Grady, "Catholic Agencies and Social Security," N.C.C.C. Proceedings, 1946, p. 65.
83. Ibid.
84. Catholic Charities Review, Jan., 1951, Vol. 35, No. 1, p. 9.
85. Ibid.
86. Ibid.
87. Ibid.
88. "Minutes of the Executive Committee of the N.C.C.C.," Jan. 30, 1935.
89. Ibid.
90. "Minutes of the Board of Directors of N.C.C.C.," Apr. 17, 1950, p. 2.
91. Reverend Francis J. Gilligan, "The Catholic Social Worker and the American Race Problem," N.C.C.C. Proceedings, 1935, p. 304.
92. Ibid., p. 305.
93. Ibid., p. 308.
94. Ibid., p. 309.
95. Ibid.. p. 310.
96. N.C.C.C. Proceedings, 1943, p. 15.
97. Ibid., pp. 114–115.
98. Catholic Charities Review, Mar., 1951, Vol. 35, No. 3, p. 55.
99. Ibid.
100. "Minutes of the Executive Committee of the N.C.C.C.," Nov. 15, 1943, p. 10.
101. Ibid.
102. Catholic Charities Review, Jan., 1953, Vol. 37, No. 1, pp. 3–4, N.C.C.C. Proceedings, 1953, p. 36.
103. Catholic Charities Review, Oct., 1955, Vol. 39, No. 8, pp. 2–3.
104. Ibid.
105. Ibid., Apr., 1956, Vol. 40, No. 4, p. 3.
106. Ibid., Mar., 1956, Vol. 40, No. 3, p. 5.
107. Ibid., Apr., 1956, Vol. 40, No. 4, p. 3.
108. "Minutes of the Executive Committee of the N.C.C.C.," Sept. 24, 1932.
109. Parker T. Moon, "Social Work and International Relations," N.C.C.C. Proceedings, 1933, p. 44.

110. Monsignor John O'Grady, "Our Responsibility for Resettlement of Displaced Persons." N.C.C.C. *Proceedings*, 1947, p. 27.
111. Monsignor John O'Grady, "The Conference and Trends in Catholic Social Work," N.C.C.C. *Proceedings*, 1948, p. 14.
112. *Ibid.*, p. 15.
113. Monsignor O'Grady, "Our Responsibility for Resettlement of Displaced Persons," N.C.C.C. *Proceedings*, 1947, p. 30.
114. *Ibid.*
115. Monsignor John O'Grady, "The Conference and Trends in Catholic Social Work," N.C.C.C. *Proceedings*, 1948, p. 11.
116. *Ibid.*
117. *Ibid.*, p. 12.
118. *Catholic Charities Review*, Mar., 1952, Vol. 36, No. 3, p. 58.
119. *Ibid.*, 1957, Vol. 41, No. 10, p. 9.
120. *Ibid.*, Mar., 1956, Vol. 40, No. 3, p. 1.
121. *Ibid.*

CHAPTER IX

Public and Private Agency Relationships

THE NATIONAL CONFERENCE OF CATHOLIC CHARI-TIES in attempting to carry out its avowed interest in social movements could not escape contacts with government and other private agencies. It was the cooperation of the founders of the National Conference prior to 1910 with such agencies that set the pattern for the years to follow. To establish this tradition was not easy. Thomas Mulry relates how and when the New York Charity Organization Society was started in the 1880's he was advised to have nothing to do with it.[1] At the time, Mr. Mulry, a contractor affectionately known as "the cellar-digger," was a member of the Superior Council of the Society of St. Vincent de Paul. Against strong advice he advocated cooperation and practiced it, for which he was known as "the Protestant member of the St. Vincent de Paul Society."[2]

For nearly a year Mr. Mulry kept up his contacts with the New York Charity Organization Society, toward the end of which time Archbishop Corrigan of New York asked him for his impressions. Mr. Mulry's conviction was that many things were done by the organization through ignorance rather than prejudice. About nine hundred Catholic children were found in Protestant Sunday Schools and all of these, according to Mr. Mulry were "reclaimed."[3] There were families neglected by Catholic societies that had been cared for by the organization. Mr. Mulry's conclusion as a result of his experience was, "I believe frankly in cooperation without any surrender of principle."[4]

This type of cooperation has always permeated the operations of the National Conference of Catholic Charities. In 1912, at the annual meeting of the National Conference, Dr. James E. Hagerty, Professor of Economics, Ohio State University, outlined three objectives of this cooperation, the improvement of the community as the responsibility of everyone, to protect the Church's interests, and to influence proper legislation.[5] These objectives clearly envisaged a positive program which carried the concept of charity beyond that of relief. It was Professor Hagerty's contention that "if representatives of our diocesan charities were to attend these State Conferences, the leaders in Catholic Charities would be made familiar with all of our charities, and they could better adapt their work to the present needs of the States."[6]

Cooperation between Catholic Charities and other agencies did not proceed according to any uniform development. The task was for the Catholic agencies to follow the plan of the National Conference and first organize among themselves. This was a slow process. Rev. C. Hubert Le Blond, then diocesan director of Catholic charities in Cleveland, Ohio, and later Bishop of St. Joseph, Missouri, observed that Cleveland had in 1914 "perhaps gone further in that regard than any other city in the Union. . . . We started first by organizing our own charities with one head and a central office. . . . When we had completed our own organization, we began to make use of the organization and agencies already existing to assist us in our own work."[7]

The Cleveland experience was quite successful, and, as Father Le Blond noted, the various other agencies "were not only willing, but anxious to help us, when we went half way and showed them what we wanted."[8] The Associated Charities of Cleveland, a civic organization, did investigating for Catholic charities. Child placement was done by the Cleveland Humane Society, a nonsectarian organization. A central placing bureau for the entire city was later organized with two priests on the committee on placement.

Other areas developing various forms of cooperation were equally convinced of the value and necessity of the action. In Philadelphia in 1915, repeated calls for aid from the Society of St. Vincent de Paul by other organizations eventually brought a request from the Archbishop of Philadelphia to seek some way of joining up the

general relief work of the city. At the quarterly meeting of the
Vincentians in Philadelphia in May, 1915, Edward J. Galbally
pointed out the changing times when he said, "Our Catholic fore-
fathers were glad to be unmolested and thought it impolitic to
rouse unnecessarily the dogs of persecution. But their policy of
aloofness is not for this day and generation. . . . There is no excuse
today for Catholics not taking part in the public movements of
the city, no one is keeping us out of them but ourselves."[9]

It should not be supposed, however, that the idea of cooperation,
relatively new as it was, was accepted wholeheartedly by all Catholic
charitable organizations. At the 1920 annual meeting of the National
Conference, Reverend M. F. McEvoy, diocesan director of Catholic
charities in Milwaukee, called attention to a type of cooperation
that amounted to mere lip service to the idea. He described the
type of person who, when he says he is going to cooperate with
someone, means only that he wants "to get rid of him."[10] There
are others who when they say they are going to cooperate with
anyone "simply want to hang around and watch him and see what
he is going to do."[11] Father McEvoy made it clear that the only
type of cooperation that was worthwhile was the kind where "we
get right down and work with people, and work sympathetically."[12]
It was his experience that "if we are on friendly terms with those
outside agencies, they will turn the beneficiaries over to us, at least
for spiritual direction, and that is what we want."[13]

Monsignor Kerby thought he saw a reason for this lip service to
cooperation in what he called the "dangers of self-sufficiency" from
which it was the mission of the National Conference of Catholic
Charities to protect Catholic agencies.[14] "Whenever you find a
relief agency that is not haunted by the sense of imperfect work,
it would be well to examine its standards of work," warned Monsignor Kerby, and he considered it "the mission of the National
Conference to distill out of all our agencies, the spirit of self-
sufficiency and the attitude of self-complacency."[15] He insisted that
the particularism of the past must give way to a cooperation that
was genuine in its willingness to fight social and economic ills. The
social worker who was content to render service in isolation repre-

sented the type of person who felt that there was nothing to learn from their own organization or any other organization for that matter. There was little room for this attitude in the National Conference.

In the decade between 1920 and 1930 certain obstacles to co-operation frequently arose to hamper the efforts at cooperation. There were clashes on fundamental differences in viewpoint on the purposes of charity. It was a kind of souls vs. citizens argument. Then, too, the issues of divorce and birth control in family counselling were bound to have their effect. Nor did everyone see eye-to-eye on the relation of the state and public charities to private charity. In some communities Catholic agencies were frequently considered inferiors rather than equals and in many others traditional religious antagonisms still remained.

One issue of this period, on which one observer noted that "feelings run high and convictions lie deep," was the use of the resources of other than Catholic agencies in solving problems of the Catholic agencies' clients.[16] The basic of the argument seemed to be the charge of proselytizing placed against the other agencies. Yet there was considerable evidence showing "amazing zeal for, and consideration of, the religious rights of the Catholic case."[17] It was true that in the earlier days the immigrant frequently lost his faith in the hands of some of the so-called nonsectarian agencies. In fact, this was one of the reasons for the development of the Catholic agency. It was only after about 1900 that public welfare agencies took on a real nonsectarian attitude and "came to regard the preservation and development of the faith of its beneficiaries as an integral part of its program."[18] Until around 1915 some public agencies still tended to openly disregard the statutes regarding placement of children in homes of the same religious faith as that of the parents.

It was difficult to convince the descendants of Catholic immigrant parents in the 1920's that "what were really Protestant mission societies twenty-five years ago have become genuinely nonsectarian agencies today."[19] The fact that children's agencies had been slower in developing a nonsectarian character than family agencies made cooperation much more difficult on the child-care level.

Financial cooperation in the Community Chest raised similar questions. There was a tendency, perhaps, in many instances to think only of the monetary aspects of the arrangement, but the safeguarding of the client's faith was still paramount in the mind of the Catholic agency. In the viewpoint of Reverend J. C. Carr, diocesan director of Catholic charities in Buffalo in 1923, while "abuses will arise occasionally . . . this is due to the misguided zeal of some individual rather than the policy of the agency."[20] It was his opinion that "when the faith of our clients is safe-guarded the cooperation with specializing public and non-sectarian agencies should be as frequent as the needs of our dependents demand."[21] Furthermore, he counseled, "cooperation needs to be thought of in terms of what we can give rather than in terms of what we are to receive."[22]

In later years the problems of cooperation attracted more attention to the national than the local scene. Dr. Beverley M. Boyd, executive secretary of the Division of Christian Life and Work of the National Council of Churches of Christ in the United States of America, was invited by Monsignor O'Grady to address the annual meeting of the National Conference of Catholic Charities in 1951. In his address Dr. Boyd gave a picture of how the National Council of Churches works stressing the manner of coordination of activities; he told the members of the National Conference that, while there was cooperation with both federal and state governments on matters affecting social welfare, the National Council of Churches was "as zealous as you to preserve the role of the voluntary agency, in the face of expanding governmental programs due to the defense emergency."[23]

A new problem, provision for safeguarding information in regard to recipients of public assistance made by Congress in 1941, arose when there developed in many communities a tendency to restrict this information in such a way as to make cooperation among agencies difficult. *The Catholic Charities Review* in April, 1952, called attention to the fact that Congress had not intended to disrupt long established practices of communication among social agencies, and regretted that the statement "Private Lives — Public

Funds" prepared by the Social Casework Council of the National Social Welfare Assembly had not called attention to this situation."[24]

In the mid-1950's *The Catholic Charities Review* called attention to what it called "certain new tendencies toward isolation in Catholic Charities and other Catholic activities."[25] The *Review* attributed this development "to fear and to a certain amount of insecurity in our own ranks."[26] This plus a tendency to imitate existing programs raised the question as to whether there was lack of convictions in regard to the Catholic programs, fear that no Catholic program could be developed, or simply lack of interest in "constructive social programs operated on a religious basis."[27] In any case, the *Review* was convinced that Catholic charities should make its own contribution and not permit itself "to be carried away by existing patterns; we ought to stand out as leaders of active, dynamic, voluntary organizations."[28]

Somewhat in the same vein Cecilia G. Kennedy, of the Omaha Catholic Charities, in 1956 thought that Catholic charities had ceased to be a powerhouse of ideas. She regretted that there was difficulty in getting Catholic charities to see itself as "an extension of the pastoral ministry" noting that "we are exhorted by our leadership to do so much more than we know how, while on the other hand secular interests decry our best efforts and seek to wrest our clientele away from us into public or interdenominational hands."[29] Yet Mrs. Kennedy warned that "this does not seem a time to regret our immaturity, or to invoke a currently unpleasant name ('isolationism') upon our agencies. This is instead a time to gird our loins and look to our weapons."[30]

That cooperation with public or other private agencies was becoming more difficult is easier to understand when the criticisms of the lack of cooperation of the Catholic agencies among themselves are considered. Many of these criticisms seem as though they might have been written in 1910 rather than in the 1950's. *The Catholic Charities Review* in April, 1956, singled out "the lack of any close relationship among our agencies" as "one of our greatest weaknesses."[31] Calling attention to the "wide chasm between our central diocesan organizations and the institutions," the *Review* noted that "the relationships are quite strained and in very few places is there a truly close democratic relationship which means continuous communication of ideas and experience."[32] In a number of places the other Catholic organizations were just as isolated from Catholic charities as were the charitable institutions. Catholic Youth Organizations, and in many dioceses the Women's Organizations, had little or no contact with Catholic charities. Much remained to be done before the advantages of cooperation and coordination supported by the National Conference could be realized.

In the area of financial support of charitable enterprises many of the questions of cooperation of the various agencies were inevitably raised. The expansion of social work and the growth by 1900 of charitable institutions and agencies brought forth complaints from those who were asked to support these developments that the donor had no way of knowing the worth of the cause to which he was asked to contribute.

One of the earliest forms of assurance that the charity donor's funds would be put to proper use was the Charities Endorsement Committee. This type of committee was set up in various cities in response to pressure from contributors in order to prevent waste and overlapping of funds. Its merits were debated by the membership of the National Conference especially just before the outbreak of World War I. At the 1914 annual meeting there was a lively debate on the subject with nearly all of the speakers agreeing that in large cities such committees had become indispensable and that no matter what the National Conference thought about them they had come to stay. The appeal to the businessman for funds had brought a counter appeal for information from a trustworthy source.

Cleveland, Ohio, was among the first to experiment with this type of committee. Shortly after the turn of the century the Cleveland Chamber of Commerce established such a committee. Its success in the period prior to 1914 was so great that its foundations were firmly established by that time. Some five hundred fraudulent solicitors had been eliminated, seventy-five undesirable institutions had been prevented from establishing themselves in the city, and some fifteen overlapping organizations had been coordinated.[33]

The speakers at the 1914 meeting, however, divided sharply over the necessity of investigation of the institution or agency prior to qualification for acceptance on the endorsement Committee's lists. Many resented the investigation of Catholic institutions that had long established reputations for good service. The record of these committees, which soon became known because of their fund raising aspects as Community Chests, convinced many of the skeptics that there was much value in them. Archbishop Karl J. Alter, then Director of Catholic Charities in Toledo, Ohio, concluded on the basis of his six years experience with the Community Chest in 1924, that it was a very worthwhile organization. Among its benefits he listed: an increase of available money, more competent personnel and therefore, higher standards, and greater efficiency because a full-time staff becomes possible with the increased funds.[34] He saw no interference with the internal conduct of the institutions of the diocese nor any discrimination in the distribution of funds. However, he did warn that there was a danger of the wrong motive on the part of the donor in this system of contribution.[35]

At least two other diocesan directors of charity were equally impressed with the advantages of the Community Chest. Father Le Blond, director of Catholic Charities in Cleveland in 1924, was willing to admit that local situations could change circumstances so that participation in Chests might not be advisable, but on the whole he felt the question was whether better work could be done with the increased funds available.[36] It was simply a matter, he thought, of "whether we are fulfilling our duty to the communities in which we live more fully and more abundantly when we go in or when we stay out."[37] Reverend Francis A. Gressle, director of the Bureau of Catholic Charities in Cincinnati, held similar views and felt that Catholic work had been brought to the attention of the public in a manner better than that afforded by any advertising.[38]

Not all diocesan directors were so minded; Reverend J. C. Carr, diocesan director of Catholic Charities in Buffalo in 1924, pointed to the success of a recent separate drive conducted by the Catholics and concluded that "no group of Catholic Charities need fear to trust their cause to the generosity of the Catholic community."[39] Among the advantages he saw in separate Catholic drives were the superiority of the motive, the inclusion of rural as well as urban districts, and the better reaction by the Catholic laity.[40] Reverend Edwin L. Leonard, diocesan director of Charities in Baltimore in 1924, also saw great disadvantages in participation in the Community Chest, among them, too much power in the hands of majority in determining how work will be developed, autocratic control of Catholic work by people who do not understand it, undermining of the interest of Catholics in their work, and a sacrifice of the religious ideals of Catholic charity.[41]

Monsignor John J. Butler, secretary of the Central Bureau of Catholic Charities in St. Louis in 1924, was another who felt that, "if we are getting enough money to support our charities by our old, sometimes called old-fashioned, methods, why should we be changing horses in the middle of the stream?"[42] This last point was, perhaps, the key to the discussion of the merits of the Community Chests from the Catholic point of view. There were many areas where long established practices of Catholic contributions provided sufficient funds for Catholic charities without the aid of outside help. Little appeared to be gained by joining a community-wide drive.

Other discussions on this subject at the 1924 annual meeting of the National Conference disclosed a wide variety of views. A number of them supported the Community Chest idea as part of the necessary cooperation between Catholics and others. Some thought that refusal to participate was often tied up with unwillingness to make out reports and prepare budgets. Still others questioned the ability of Catholic charities to support themselves with the additional revenue made possible through the Community Chest.[43]

By the late 1920's it would appear the consideration of the Community Chest placed less emphasis on its usefulness as a financial means, which seemed to be conceded, and stressed more the dangers of secularization of charity and the loss of individual responsibility. The suggestion, however, was made that Catholic charities might have to pass through the same stages as the nonsectarian agencies in their development. Before the advent of the Community Chest joint planning in social work made very little headway. Since the Community Chest, expansion councils of social agencies had sprung up rapidly. For Catholic agencies to experience a similar growth the funds which were necessary for high standards would have to be supplied, presumably by Community Chest methods.

The dangers suggested by this parallel of Catholic charities and the Charity Organization Society which represented the coordination of nonsectarian agencies, were several. In its early stages the Charity Organization Society had been founded, in part at least, as a protest against large centralized relief funds. The Catholic Charities Review noted, however, that by 1930, "The Charity Organization Society has drifted far from its original moorings. At the present the outlook and problems are not of its own making. It has been compelled to surrender to the inevitable demands of time and it finds itself laboring under something of the same conditions today, against which it protested loudly fifty years ago."[44] The implications for Catholic charities if it succumbed to the philosophy that all needs were taken care of by the Community Chest were obvious.

There is a suggestion also that the lessening of the emphasis on volunteer activities in the late 1920's could be traced at least in part to the belief that the Community Chest had made them unnecessary.[45] This was not to be construed as an argument against the Chest for some of the consequences of its introduction were unavoidable. Many, however, could have been avoided, so some felt, "with a little care and a clear understanding of the situation."[46] The real problem was that "the virtue of charity was regarded as fulfilled by a contribution to the Diocesan Charity Campaign or to the Community Chest."[47] Worse than that, "the poor box in most churches was so cunningly hidden as to defy discovery," and, in addition, "the idea of the parish as a congregation of charity taking care of its own poor was dying out generally and in many places already dead."[48] As a result "our Catholic Charities drawn by the light of secular social service were growing away from their roots."[49] Monsignor O'Grady contended in 1933 that, "if the contraction of Chest funds compels Catholic organizations to develop a fuller participation in their own work it will have been a blessing in disguise."[50]

Around 1950 it appeared that the "blessing" might be given. There had been a considerable drop in relief giving under Community Chest auspices as the depression of the 1930's grew and more emphasis was placed on government relief. In the decade of the 1940's there was some agreement among Catholic charities directors that the Community Chests in a great number of cities were approaching their maximum potential.[51] It appeared, therefore, that there was little chance for Catholic expansion unless there was some form of supplementary fund raising.

In all the efforts of Catholic charities at cooperation with other agencies or in participation in Community Chests, it was most frequently the child-care field that occupied the center of the stage. The most rapid growth of these Catholic institutions, however, came at a time when the trend seemed to be away from institutional care of children. Thus cooperation with other agencies and participation in Community Chest financing by Catholic charities frequently brought attacks on the Catholic institutions. The tendency of public agencies to look down on institutional care created added difficulties.

One of the earliest clashes over the question of institutional vs. foster home care for children was the New York charities controversy in 1916. New York had a system of care for dependent children which allowed an annual grant of public money at a fixed per capita rate to private institutions for the maintenance and education of the city's public wards. There was an attack on this system in the Constitutional Convention of New York State in 1894, and a great deal of hostility was shown, particularly toward Catholic institutions. An investigation in 1910 failed to produce any evidence to support the charges against Catholic charities. Another constitutional convention in 1915 renewed the hostilities and produced another investigation. A pamphlet, *Orphans and Pigs fed from the same Bowl* issued anonymously, gives some idea of the tone of the investigation. A Mr. Moree, publicity agent for the State Charities

Aid Association, admitted that the statements in the pamphlet were not true and was quoted as saying that he had a "right to be unfair or not if he liked."[52] Despite the manifest unfairness of the atmosphere of the investigation, the final report of the investigating committee concluded that the dependent children were better off in a good private institution than they were in foster homes.[53]

The controversy tended to bring on some self-examination of institutional care by Catholic institutions, but by 1922 Reverend Edwin L. Leonard, archdiocesan director of Catholic charities in Baltimore, could question why there was a decided decrease in the use of child-care institutions.[54] Two years earlier he had warned that "there are many institutions of long standing which have never changed from the day of their foundation. We cannot afford to stand still; we must adjust ourselves to the spirit of the day."[55] He called attention to the lack of wisdom in mixing dependent and delinquent children and to the necessity of preparing those who leave the institutions to be able to take their place in the world. Brother Barnabas had often spoken on the lack of preparation given the children for the time when they would leave the institution. He felt that this was one of the principal weaknesses of institutional care, and he spent much of his life attempting to remedy it.

Father Leonard attributed the decline of the use of institutions to a number of causes, not the least of which was the failure of the institutions to publicize the good work they were doing. The "inaccessibility" of the heads of some of the institutions and the failure to keep well informed on new developments were other important factors bringing on an eclipse of the child-care institution. Father Le Blond, in the discussion at the annual meeting of the National Conference in 1922 on the subject of institutional child care, declared that "institutions will always have a place. Their scope, however, is changing, and it will continue to change."[56] He admitted, moreover, "we have been too ready to take children out of the natural environment of the home."[57] The development of Parmadale in Cleveland, Ohio, was an effort to meet this type of criticism. Built on the cottage plan and staffed by the Sisters of Charity of St. Augustine, Parmadale, known as the "children's village," was dedicated in 1925. This was an attempt to keep brothers and sisters together and to give the children surroundings as nearly like home as possible.

Concern over the problems of child-caring institutions had prompted the Conference of Religious under the leadership of Sister Miriam Regina in 1920 to appoint a Committee on Standards to study the matter. A preliminary report of this committee was made at the annual meeting of the National Conference in 1922. A final report was published in 1923 under the title *A Program for Catholic Child-Caring Homes*. The report which limited itself to homes caring for children between the ages of two and sixteen covered every phase of the work of the home. The aim, however, was to stimulate the improvement of standards in the existing homes rather than to set up an ideal program. General principles were set down for the admission of children and their care after discharge as well as for their stay in the home. Dietary recommendations for the home and standards for child placing and adoption were included in the appendices of the report.

A report on the study of children's institutions by Reverend John M. Cooper of Catholic University, entitled *Children's Institutions*, was made at the annual meeting of the National Conference in 1929. Dr. Cooper's book was a study of one hundred Catholic child-care homes and some of the best nonsectarian and Protestant homes. The study, which was used as a text for instruction in Catholic child care for a number of years, reached the conclusion that, on the whole, conditions in the institutions were decidedly healthy. Moreover, there was a "wholesome unrest that is bringing about a steady and measured progress each year."[58] Dr. Cooper noted that "as between the two extremes of over-conservatism on the one hand, and unconsidered and radical change on the other, our institutions seem to be following steadily and faithfully the wiser via media."[59] One of the great needs shown by Dr. Cooper's study was that of systematic social work training for members of religious communities staffing such institutions.[60]

The Catholic Charities Review in 1930 took note of what it termed the "peculiar penchant for institutional service" which has been characteristic of Catholic charities in the United States and called it "a part of the legacy of our religious communities."[61] One of the results of this has been the readiness to say that "when a problem arises, let us have a new institution to solve it, and when another problem arises let us have another institution."[62] By the late 1930's, however, it would seem that the debate over institutional vs. foster-home care had taken a new turn. The weak spots in institutional care, such as after care, follow up, lack of cooperation with other institutions, and lack of trained workers, were still present. There was a growing recognition, however, of the proper place of both the foster home and the institution. The net gain from the controversy was that better standards were developed in both areas.

Strangely enough, there were those in 1939 who were still thinking in terms of the 1910 viewpoint. *The Catholic Charities Review* called attention to those child welfare workers who "still have a mania for depopulating institutions" and who, "if they could only get a foster home program in every country they would have attained the millennium."[63] In the late 1940's there was increasing recognition of the unique role of the institution for children, presenting special problems. The ordinary dependent child, it was agreed, should be kept in his own home if possible, or placed in a foster home.[64] The positive values of a sound institutional program were coming into their own again.

Throughout the entire history of the National Conference of Catholic Charities the programs of children's institutions have been greatly influenced by the interest of the government — federal, state, and local — in child welfare. The interest of the Federal Government in child welfare was evidenced by the establishment of a Children's Bureau in the Department of Commerce and Labor in 1912. The establishment of the Bureau culminated a ten-year agitation for some such instrument of investigation of all matters pertaining to children. The first White House Conference on children had been called earlier in 1909 and had pointed up some of the problems in child welfare. The second White House Conference in 1919 had come in the midst of the controversy over institutional care for children and stressed the need for crystallizing standards of child care. The third White House Conference in 1930 noted the progress in state laws governing child care and recommended the expansion of the child-welfare interest to include concern for family problems. The decline in institutional care was also noted at this Conference. This particular Conference issued what it called a "Children's Charter" embodying its recommendations, which were largely statements of principle rather than plans for action. The basic principles of the Charter calling for the protection of spiritual, physical, and mental welfare of children could find no quarrel in the National Conference of Catholic Charities.

The passage of the Social Security Act in 1935 and the impact of World War II on family life tended to bring the government interest in child welfare more directly into the picture. There was a more general acceptance of the principle of government responsibility for public welfare, and in the White House Conference on Children in a Democracy in 1940 there were recommendations for a wide variety of social services for children. There was also a recognition of the obligations of both public and private agencies to develop adequate resources and maintain high standards. The individual states were to provide leadership and the Federal Government was to enlarge its activities in the field.

Catholic child care institutions now found it necessary to re-examine their purposes and endeavor to discover the implications of this government interest in the field of child welfare. One item was clear by 1940: voluntary contributions played only a small part of the total income for institutional care. It was estimated that about ninety-eight per cent of the assistance came from tax funds of one sort or another.[65] In 1939, Miss Mary L. Gibbons, president of the National Conference of Catholic Charities and First Deputy Commissioner of New York City, argued that it might "not be the time for any expansion of private agencies," but that it was most certainly "the time to conserve all that we have acquired as a result of individual and voluntary initiative."[66] Accordingly, she recommended that the Catholic agencies examine themselves to discover whether any were less necessary than when they were founded and whether they were performing services that could just as well be performed by a public agency.

An examination of the picture of child care in Catholic institutions revealed some startling facts. By 1945 there were some communities in which the number of children cared for by Catholic agencies was less than five per cent of those needing care.[67] A demand of Community Chest boards that Catholic charities turn over to public supervision children in foster homes was a threat to those institutions dependent on the Chests since no appropriation would be given the Catholic agency for the care of these children.[68]

Much of the controversy over institutions vs. foster homes was being revived but the basic issue appeared no longer to be one of standards. The voluntary agencies had operated institutions in the early part of the century and they were criticized for low standards. Government agencies were at the time committed to foster homes. By the mid-1940's the government agencies were drifting toward institutional care and the standards of the volunteer agencies were above question. The issue now was how far should the government be permitted to replace the voluntary agency. *The Catholic Charities Review* commented that,

> So far as Catholic agencies are concerned, our principles are clear and our traditions well established. We cannot sit by and turn over our children to government agencies. We have established a pattern and we should fight to maintain it. Most local government authorities are in sympathy with our point of view. . . . But we must keep in mind always the importance of progressive standards. We want to move with the tide of the times.[69]

The great danger in the expansion of government interest in public welfare was that all individuals and institutions would be subservient to a paternalistic state. Voluntary or religious agencies would gradually be supplanted. Child welfare services under the Social Security Act were limited principally to public welfare agencies. At the 1946 annual meeting of the National Conference the diocesan directors of Catholic charities doubted the advisability of a general grants-in-aid program for the care of children in foster homes.[70] The group was divided on whether such a program should be confined to rural areas or perhaps to areas of special need. The directors felt that the voluntary agency should play an expanding role in child welfare since "it is only under agencies of their own faith that children will be assured of proper religious care and upbringing."[71]

The growing tendency to secularize all child-care programs and thus threaten the existence of the voluntary agency became even stronger as the time for the mid-century White House Conference on children approached. Government interest in public welfare was bound to continue in some form or other, and it remained for the National Conference of Catholic Charities to become equally interested and articulate. There was considerable agreement among the members of the Conference that the voluntary agency had the prestige, organization, and tradition to survive but it must fill specific needs. At the annual meeting of the National Conference in 1940, Miss Weltha M. Kelley, Case Work Supervisor of the Family Service Society in Buffalo, contended that,

> it is fallacious to think that the public agencies will push the private agencies out of the picture. With all that the public agencies can do and all that the private agencies can add, there will still remain large areas of unmet needs, larger now than ever before, and destined to grow even greater as problems mount. There is plenty of place for the private agencies, but they must find it and fit into it. . . . It is the task of the private agency to make its own place in the hierarchy of social welfare and then fit into the total community set-up.[72]

Complacency was what had to be attacked and an active interest in public welfare stimulated if the forces of secularization were to be overcome.

The decision of the Federal Security Agency Administration to exclude all clergymen from membership on the Over-All Committee of the 1950 White House Conference offered a clear challenge to those fighting the forces of secularization. After some two weeks of debate over the exclusion, the National Conference was given the opportunity of nominating one priest to the committee.[73] *The Catholic Charities Review* considered that the White House Conference would be a turning point in the history of voluntary child welfare and that if the voluntary groups succeeded in "retaining real leadership in the broad showing of the program it will be due entirely to their own untiring and crusading efforts."[74] Belief was expressed by the *Review* that the "'ivory tower' planners have not yet gained ascendancy."[75]

Evidence that the threat to the voluntary agency was not imaginary could be found in several proposals of legislation in Congress in 1948–49. One bill, H.R. 2892, aimed at giving funds for child care only to the single public agency in a district, and another, H.R. 2430, required the placement of all dependent children under the public agency. Both were defeated. It was clear, however, that the former policy of government not to enter areas already covered by voluntary and religious organizations of child welfare was being abandoned. At the 1949 annual meeting of the National Conference, Monsignor Vincent W. Cooke, archdiocesan supervisor of charities in Chicago, declared that, "now they tell us we must have a public program of child care in every community in the United States."[76] The claim that the public agency would purchase service from the voluntary agency "does not work out once the public agency gets a foothold," observed Monsignor Cooke.[77]

Meanwhile the Child Welfare League of America, Inc., sent a statement of its principles to its member agencies which, if carried out, would eventually eliminate the voluntary child welfare work. Monsignor O'Grady then sent a letter to all the governors of the states and the directors of state departments of public welfare.[78] The basic issue as it emerged from this clash of philosophies on child-welfare services was between the view of many leaders in social work that the government has direct responsibility for each child toward which it is making a contribution and that of the National Conference which held that the Federal Government should enter the field only when the voluntary agency was not doing the job.

The National Conference of Catholic Charities at its annual meeting in 1950 issued a series of resolutions stating its views on child welfare in preparation for the White House Conference. After noting with "pleasure and approbation" the action of the President of the United States in calling the Conference, the resolutions went on to assert some basic principles.[79] Among them were the reiteration of the principle that the government's role was a dual one, promotion and protection, reaffirmation of the principle of intervention of the Federal Government only when the local community fails; and the continuance of the partnership of the government and voluntary agencies as it had been worked out over the years.[80]

The influence of Catholic charities in the 1950 White House Conference was infinitesimal, and this induced the bishops of the United States to appoint a committee to choose someone who would coordinate Catholic activity so far as the 1960 White House Conference was concerned. The committee, consisting of Archbishop Patrick A. O'Boyle of Washington, D. C., Bishop William A. Scully of Albany, N. Y., and Archbishop Leo Binz of Dubuque, Iowa, selected Monsignor Raymond J. Gallagher of Cleveland, Ohio, whose purpose as a coordinator was "to prevent the divide and conquer techniques from prevailing in the 1960 Conference."[81]

Monsignor Gallagher made it clear to the directors of Catholic charities that the White House Conference was not something toward which they could take a "let alone" attitude. It was his understanding that this had been the case with some of them in 1950. Monsignor Gallagher pointed out that this type of rather informal conference "has become a springboard for conclusions that find their way into laws and regulations which often prove embarrassing to voluntary religious agencies."[82] Monsignor Gallagher then presented a plan of preparation which he hoped would better prepare the National Conference for participation in the White House Conference of 1960.

One of the more hopeful signs of some solution of the problem of relation of the government to the private agency was found in the 1958 statement of the Child Welfare League of America. The Board of Directors of the National Conference considered it an improvement over the 1949 statement of the League.[83] The acceptance of the principle of subsidiarity by the League was considered by the diocesan directors as most significant. This principle recognizes a hierarchy of responsibility in social welfare with the family having the basic responsibility, the neighborhood next, and then the community. Noteworthy, too, was that the statement did not propose a fixed formula for child-welfare service. On the whole, Monsignor Joseph P. Springob, diocesan director of Catholic charities in Milwaukee, thought that the statement was "a step forward and that it represents not only a concession to the Catholic point of view from a political standpoint; but also a change in the thinking and convictions on the part of many members of the Committee."[84]

Meanwhile the diocesan directors of Catholic charities were represented by Monsignor Raymond J. Gallagher on the Advisory Council of Child Welfare Services. It was Monsignor Gallagher's task to study the effect of the 1958 amendments to the Social Security Act and report possible effects on Catholic child-welfare services. Of particular concern to the National Conference was the question of planning the expansion of Child-Welfare Services in urban areas where there is a large concentration of Catholic effort. The Advisory Council gave a final report to the diocesan directors in April, 1960. Monsignor Raymond J. Gallagher did not feel that the Advisory Council had discovered anything of startling significance in the amendments but "neither did it countenance any new developments that would be inimical to the development of Catholic Charities service to children."[85] He was convinced, however, that the experience of the last few years gave proof that "our participation from the very inception of legislation and new programs is probably the wisest way in which to avoid the development of programs under public auspices that would be detrimental to our services to children or the principles upon which they are based."[86]

Monsignor Gallagher's report on the White House Conference of 1960 was also encouraging. A little more than ten per cent of the 7602 delegates were known to be Catholics. Of the 135 priests present only 15 were representative of Catholic organizations, the rest were members of state delegations. On the whole, there was a fair opportunity to present the Catholic point of view. It was in a similar manner that Catholic views were presented in the National

Conference of Social Welfare meetings in the late 1930's. The question appeared to be as to how best to accomplish Catholic participation.

The statistics on Catholic child-welfare services for the period 1947 to 1957 indicate the important implications of the government's expanded interest in the field.[87] In 1957 there were eighteen per cent fewer children's homes and thirty-one per cent fewer children in children's homes than in 1947. There was an increase of sixteen per cent in the number of children in foster homes giving an over-all decrease of children cared for of some thirteen per cent. These figures reflected national trends and the decrease was attributed to a combination of circumstances including, more effective family service, greater stability in young families and an increase in available housing.[88] A large number of the children in the institutions were suffering "varying degrees of emotional deprivation" and many of them had come from homes in which one or both parents were under psychiatric treatment.[89] It was this type of special treatment to which some of the institutions had turned.

The renewed emphasis on institutional programs for child welfare found the National Conference well prepared to assess their proper value as a result of the Cecelia McGovern's book on *Services to Children in Institutions*. Published in 1948, the study was "an expression of the thinking of experienced institutional programs."[90] The work was "evidence that the institutions are coming into their own, that they are doing their own planning and thinking, that they are advancing toward an over-all child-caring program which takes into consideration both the child's background and environment and the type of care best suited to the child's needs."[91]

There was one unforeseen result of the government's child-welfare programs on Catholic charities. That was a restoration in some areas of the original role of the Society of St. Vincent de Paul. By 1949 the development of a public child-welfare program had caused the transfer of a portion of the work with dependent and neglected children to the Public Welfare Department from the Catholic Bureau. The tendency of the public social worker to contact the pastor instead of another agency gave the Vincentians a chance, as the pastor's nearest contact, to again play a role in child welfare. Charles A. O'Neill, executive secretary of the Society of St. Vincent de Paul in Milwaukee, said "it was difficult back in 1930, to understand why the Society had been cut off from a work it had fostered and developed," but now it had come back into the picture.[92]

While the general impact of government welfare programs on Catholic charities most frequently involved the clash of philosophies of child care and the respective roles of government and private agencies, there were also involved financial problems which were no less important. At the first meeting of the National Conference in 1920 one of the founders, David F. Tilley of Boston, expressed the view that the "growing tendency to withdraw public support to private institutions" was not to be encouraged.[93] He was convinced that "private institutions supported by contributions of individuals are in a much stronger position than those supported by public funds."[94] Thomas Mulry at the 1912 meeting took issue with those who supported Mr. Tilley's views. Contending that the relationship between the government and private institutions should be a cooperative one looking to the best interests of the work at hand, he held that "there can be no valid argument advanced against the legality and propriety of the State seeking and employing the aid of private institutions in the care of its dependent wards."[95] The private institution would not be supplanted, he thought, because it was economical from the viewpoint of the taxpayer, and in most cases the person in need of help prefers "to come under the care of those who are of his own religious belief and in institutions provided by the generosity of his co-religionists."[96]

Again in 1914 the question of government aid to private agencies was discussed at the meeting of the National Conference. Robert C. Biggs took issue with Mr. Mulry on the wisdom of accepting aid, proving that among the founders of the National Conference there was no complete agreement on the answer to this question. As far as Mr. Biggs was concerned he thought he saw "indications now that an insidious form of material relief having its origin in the State is feeding the disease it was intended to relieve."[97] Mr. Biggs was of the opinion that Rome decayed because the rich were corrupt and the poor fed by the State. He did not want to encourage this condition in the United States. There was something of a paradox in his statement that the "Catholic Church is in this country, as it is everywhere the greatest conservative force in the world," and the objective of social reform of the National Conference.[98] The *Proceedings* record "applause" after the foregoing quotation, indicating that Mr. Biggs had a good many on his side of the argument.

There were forces at work, however, which by 1930 made the argument over whether or not to accept government aid appear academic. Even in 1922 the question was being asked as to how far Catholics should care for their own poor.[99] There were those who would say all should be cared for; others would have used city organizations aided by volunteers; and a third group would have established casework agencies for all cases which involved moral or religious problems.[100] The depression ended much of the argument, for it was clear that private agencies could not only not bear the burden of relief but were also having extreme difficulty in keeping up with the remedial work. Public relief was bound to increase. By 1933 ninety-five per cent of the relief was coming from public funds.

Monsignor O'Grady did not find that the shift of relief to the government was in itself a bad thing. "Generally speaking," he said, "we have been too much inclined to emphasize volume rather than the quality of our service."[101] The "preoccupation with the great volume of industrial hazards," he continued, "tended to make us forget our original objective. . . . It was not our original purpose to carry a large relief load."[102] He thought that now was the time to "articulate the personal services of the church to the people."[103] Others, too, were of the opinion that the "emancipation from the drudgery of relief giving will be a veritable deliverance from bondage," because then, "assured of the provision of life's necessities private social work can minister to the cultural needs of man."[104]

Apart from the government assumption of relief loads, there was also a question as to what extent the government could purchase the services of the private agency in carrying out its program of public welfare. The problems involved in child-care institutions in this area have already been considered. Many of the practical arrangements that had grown up over the years on the local level were being called into question in some twenty of the states in 1956. The National Conference sought to amass evidence of the experience of the courts on the use of the facilities of the voluntary agencies which were religious in character.[105] The sample study, made by the National Probation and Parole Association, showed that "the majority of the courts participating recognized that the work of voluntary agencies operating on a religious basis is an essential part of the program of the courts."[106] The Supreme Court of Pennsylvania in 1956 upheld the long established practice in Allegheny County of child-care payments to voluntary religious agencies. The National Probation and Parole Association had filed a Brief as a Friend of Court in which it used the results of its recent study to support their contention that "existing private sectarian facilities for the care of delinquent, neglected and dependent children are a vital resource for juvenile courts and communities in the care of such children."[107] A second point established in the brief was that "the judge be free to utilize treatment facilities which will best meet the particular needs of the individual child, without regard to sectarian or non-sectarian auspices."[108]

This court decision was an optimistic sign at a time when it appeared that the National Conference had been "oversanguine" in the belief "that the dispute concerning religion in our schools would not overflow into the field of social welfare."[109]

These remarks of Bishop William A. Scully of Albany came in 1956 when a half century of practical solutions to the purchase of the services of voluntary religious agencies had already become a part of the legislation on the local and state level. The placement of children in homes or institutions operating on a religious basis, and recognition of the government's responsibility to make fullest use of the voluntary agency, were all accepted practices and in most instances expressed in legislation. The advocates of the complete secularization of social welfare appeared bent on destroying the cooperative arrangements of earlier years.

Notes — Chapter IX

1. N.C.C.C. Proceedings, 1914, p. 123.
2. Ibid., p. 124.
3. Ibid.
4. Ibid.
5. James E. Hagerty, "Cooperation Among all Charities," N.C.C.C. Proceedings, 1912, p. 97.
6. Ibid.
7. N.C.C.C. Proceedings, 1914, p. 156.
8. Ibid., p. 157.
9. St. Vincent de Paul Quarterly, Feb., 1915, Vol. 20, No. 2, p. 105.
10. N.C.C.C. Proceedings, 1920, p. 81.
11. Ibid.
12. Ibid.
13. Ibid.
14. Monsignor William J. Kerby, "The Mission of the National Conference of Catholic Charities," N.C.C.C. Proceedings, 1921, p. 14.
15. Ibid.
16. Margaret Tucker, "Cross Currents in Catholic Charities," Catholic Charities Review, 1922, Vol. 6, No. 3, p. 79.
17. Ibid.
18. Catholic Charities Review, Jan., 1931, Vol. 15, No. 1, p. 14.
19. Ibid.
20. Reverend John C. Carr, "Cooperation with Non-Sectarian Agencies," N.C.C.C. Proceedings, 1923, p. 93.
21. Ibid., p. 94.
22. Ibid., p. 95.
23. N.C.C.C. Proceedings, 1951, p. 222.
24. Catholic Charities Review, Apr., 1952, Vol. 36, No. 4, pp. 78–79.
25. Ibid., Apr., 1955, Vol. 39, No. 4, p. 2.
26. Ibid.
27. Ibid.
28. Ibid.
29. Ibid., Sept., 1956, Vol. 40, No. 7, p. 7.
30. Ibid.
31. Ibid., Apr., 1956, Vol. 40, No. 4, p. 2.
32. Ibid.
33. Richmond Dean, "Charities Endorsement Committees," N.C.C.C. Proceedings, 1914, p. 36.
34. Most Reverend Karl J. Alter, "What of Community Chests?" Catholic Charities Review, Feb., 1924, Vol. 8, No. 2, p. 44.
35. Ibid., p. 45.
36. Reverend C. Hubert Le Blond, "Charity Organizations and Community Chests," N.C.C.C. Proceedings, 1924, pp. 190–191.
37. Ibid., p. 191.
38. Reverend Francis A. Gressle, "The Advantages of Participating in the Community Chest," N.C.C.C. Proceedings, 1924, p. 193.
39. Reverend John C. Carr, "The Case Against Participation of Catholic Organizations in Community Chests," N.C.C.C. Proceedings, 1924, p. 196.

40. *Ibid.*, p. 198.
41. N.C.C.C. *Proceedings*, p. 207.
42. *Ibid.*
43. *Ibid.*, pp. 209–212.
44. *Catholic Charities Review*, Mar., 1930, Vol. 14, No. 3, p. 76.
45. *Ibid.*
46. *Ibid.*
47. N.C.C.C. *Proceedings*, 1932, pp. 4–5.
48. *Ibid.*, p. 5.
49. *Ibid.*
50. Monsignor John O'Grady, "Catholic Relief Programs," N.C.C.C. *Proceedings*, 1933, p. 130.
51. *Catholic Charities Review*, May, 1949, Vol. 33, No. 5, p. 109.
52. *Ibid.*, Jan., 1917, Vol. 1, No. 1, p. 19.
53. *Ibid.*, p. 23.
54. Reverend Edwin L. Leonard, "The Future of Our Child-Caring Institutions," N.C.C.C. *Proceedings*, 1922, p. 146.
55. Reverend Francis A. Gressle, "The Organization, Character, and Extent of Diocesan Charities of the United States," N.C.C.C. *Proceedings*, 1920, p. 77.
56. N.C.C.C. *Proceedings*, 1920, p. 151.
57. *Ibid.*
58. N.C.C.C. *Proceedings*, 1929, p. 125.
59. *Ibid.*
60. *Ibid.*, pp. 129–130.
61. *Catholic Charities Review*, Mar., 1930, Vol. 14, No. 3, p. 77.
62. *Ibid.*
63. *Ibid.*, Dec., 1939, Vol. 23, No. 10, p. 304.
64. *Ibid.*, Oct., 1944, Vol. 28, No. 8, pp. 197–198.
65. N.C.C.C. *Proceedings*, 1939, p. 11.
66. *Ibid.*
67. *Catholic Charities Review*, May, 1945, Vol. 29, No. 5, p. 114.
68. *Ibid.*, Sept., 1946, Vol. 30, No. 7, p. 169.
69. *Ibid.*, May, 1946, Vol. 30, No. 5, p. 113.
70. Monsignor John O'Grady, "Catholic Agencies and Social Security," N.C.C.C. *Proceedings*, 1946, pp. 64–65.
71. *Ibid.*, p. 65.
72. N.C.C.C. *Proceedings*, 1940, pp. 100–101.
73. "Confidential Bulletin for Directors of Catholic Charities," Aug. 6, 1949.
74. *Catholic Charities Review*, Dec., 1949, Vol. 33, No. 10, p. 248.
75. *Ibid.*, p. 247.
76. Monsignor Vincent W. Cooke, "Catholic Objectives in the Care of Children," N.C.C.C. *Proceedings*, 1949, p. 32.
77. *Catholic Charities Review*, Jan., 1950, Vol. 34, No. 1, p. 8.
78. "Confidential Bulletin for Directors of Catholic Charities," Mar. 10, 1950.
79. N.C.C.C. *Proceedings*, 1950, p. 290.
80. *Ibid.*, pp. 290–291.
81. "Minutes of Meeting of Diocesan Directors of Catholic Charity," Sept. 17, 1957.
82. *Ibid.*
83. *Ibid.*
84. *Ibid.*

85. *Ibid.*, Apr. 27–28, 1960.
86. *Ibid.*
87. *Catholic Charities Review*, Oct., 1957, Vol. 41, No. 8, pp. 6–7.
88. *Ibid.*
89. *Ibid.*
90. Cecelia McGovern, *Services to Children in Institutions* (Washington, 1948), from the foreword by Monsignor John O'Grady.
91. *Ibid.*
92. Charles A. O'Neill, "Catholic Objectives in Child Care," N.C.C.C. Proceedings, 1949, p. 43.
93. David F. Tilley, "The State and Private Institutions," N.C.C.C. Proceedings, 1910, p. 72.
94. *Ibid.*
95. Thomas M. Mulry, "The Government in Charity," N.C.C.C. Proceedings, 1912, p. 45.
96. *Ibid.*, p. 56.
97. N.C.C.C. Proceedings, 1914, p. 280.
98. *Ibid.*, p. 281.
99. *Catholic Charities Review*, Oct., 1922, Vol. 6, No. 8, p. 290.
100. *Ibid.*
101. Monsignor John O'Grady, "Catholic Relief Programs," N.C.C.C. Proceedings, 1933, p. 128.
102. *Ibid.*
103. *Ibid.*
104. N.C.C.C. Proceedings, 1934, p. 20.
105. N.C.C.C. Proceedings, 1956, p. 115.
106. *Ibid.*
107. "Brief on Behalf of National Probation and Parole Association as Amicus Curiae," Supreme Court of Pennsylvania, No. 28, March term, 1956.
108. *Ibid.*
109. Most Reverend William A. Scully, "Are We Going to Remove Religion from its Traditional Place in American Social Welfare?" N.C.C.C. Proceedings, 1956, p. 38.

CHAPTER X

Summary and Evaluation

THE first twenty-five years of the National Conference of Catholic Charities present a remarkable record of achievement. In 1910, "every unpleasant effect of provincialism was in evidence. Relations between our relief work and civic movements were usually remote and without distinction. The units of our Catholic Charities displayed a spirit of offishness that made them to some degree socially ineffective. A defensive attitude on the part of our charitable agencies made criticism unwelcome and they were satisfied at times with ineffective or futile work."[1] This description of the state of affairs at the beginning of the National Conference was given at a National Conference dinner at the annual meeting in 1935, and there is perhaps no better yardstick by which to measure the Conference's progress than to see how well it has improved these conditions over the years.

From 1910 to 1935 there was great advancement in the concept of organized charity. In 1910 many doubted the wisdom of organizing and preferred to find a place in existing organizations where they thought Catholic influence might be more effective. Still others refused to answer letters that sought encouragement and approval, and some steadfastly refused to take part in the movement. By 1925 much of this inertia had been overcome. The office of diocesan director of charities had been recognized and the directors themselves in 1916 came into the National Conference as one of its component parts. In 1920, the Conference of Religious was organized to bring this group into the National Conference as another of its elements. A Catholic directory of charities was published despite considerable difficulty in collecting information. The St.

Vincent de Paul *Quarterly* had expanded into *The Catholic Charities Review,* marking the development of a literature of social work which was badly needed. It was found no longer possible to restrict the meeting of Conference membership to a biennial affair and so the annual meeting was instituted in 1921; the meeting places, moreover, were to be spread over the country as part of the educational mission of the National Conference. The self-complacency of earlier days had begun to break down as a result of personal contacts, consulations, and exchange of ideas provided by the annual meeting. The net gain was the gradual overcoming of a "subtle form of tyranny in low standards."[2] Brother Barnabas was particularly concerned with this aspect of the National Conference, and he had been especially critical of the failure of child-care institutions that had turned out boys and girls unprepared to cope with the outside world. Monsignor John M. Cooper's *Children's Institutions* was a product of the desire to improve standards.

Social work was promoted by the Conference in those early years to a point where it obtained status. Schools of social work were established, and a training program for diocesan directors of charities was inaugurated. The period's emphasis on techniques had its disadvantages, however, and there was a constant struggle to keep Catholic social work from being cast in the same mold as that of the nonsectarian kind. The volunteer suffered at least a partial eclipse in the years down to 1935, and the animosities that developed between the volunteer and the professional worker were a decided hindrance to the movement the National Conference was sponsoring. The role of the layman, or volunteer, was being attacked from another angle, but this attack was more oblique than direct. The appearance in 1916 of the diocesan directors of Catholic charities as a group in the Conference marked a change in the structure of the Conference. The establishment of the Conference of Religious in 1920 further emphasized the change in structure. The layman, and this term is used synonymously with *volunteer,* found not only that his services in social work were of questionable value in many instances but that he occupied also a place of lesser significance in the National Conference. About four fifths of the attendance of the early Conferences was of laymen, particularly members of the Society of St. Vincent de Paul. This proportion shrank substantially in the later years. The violent reaction to the professional worker in the 1930's tended to correct the balance but it was not until a later period that any substantial change could be observed in the role of the layman or volunteer.

In some ways the development of greater clerical influence was unavoidable. The administration of diocesan charities was the obligation of the local Ordinary. The diocesan director of charities was his deputy. Others engaged in charity work had to fit into jurisdictional relationship in such a way as to preserve the hierarchical setup. The problem, however, once organization of Catholic charities was developed as the National Conference intended it to be, was where the layman's place was to be in the new arrangement. Under the old system, the volunteer worked closely with his parish and pastor through the St. Vincent de Paul Society, and, significantly, it was also the pastor who was somewhat lukewarm to the new organization. It is perhaps also significant that not until after World War II did both the layman and the parish seem to be given a new emphasis in the attempt of the National Conference to attain greater impact on the local level.

It may, however, be some time before the quality of the lay leaders of the 1910–1920 period is duplicated. Thomas Mulry, Robert Biggs, Judge Hurley of Chicago, Jack Spaulding of Atlanta formed a nucleus that in Monsignor O'Grady's words was "never again duplicated."[3] The change in 1916 with the introduction of the diocesan directors did not appear to meet with Monsignor Kerby's complete approval and there has been a tendency to blame the decline of the layman's position in Catholic charities on Monsignor O'Grady for sponsoring the changes in 1916 and 1940.[4] This is probably a bit unfair since the clergy and the religious had to be incorporated into the National Conference. Moreover, Monsignor O'Grady's efforts on behalf of the Society of St. Vincent de Paul are testimony of his desire to see the layman or volunteer retain his proper place in the picture.

A spirit of cooperation with other agencies was another characteristic of the first quarter century. Participation in Community Chest activities was probably the most common form of public participation of those years. Government programs had not yet fully developed, but Mr. Mulry, in 1914, had already marked out the lines of cooperation in this area. Obstacles still had to be overcome to bring about complete cooperation among Catholic agencies who were still suspicious of a national organization and wished to preserve their own isolation. There has been close cooperation between the National Conference of Catholic Charities and the National Catholic Welfare Council. At the time of the latter's organization in 1920, the National Conference pledged "its faithful cooperation in all works undertaken by it in the interest of church and country."[5] There was also close cooperation with the National Council of Catholic Women which was the first unit organized in the N.C.W.C. Department of Lay Organizations. The N.C.W.C. was not a new organization entirely since it had developed from the coordination of World War I activities of Catholic Women's Organizations.

In 1921 the executive committee of the National Conference of Catholic Charities, after a conference between its representatives and those of the National Catholic Welfare Council, agreed to a division of labor between the two.[6] The N.C.W.C. was to concentrate on women's activities in social work and settlement work, and the National Conference of Catholic Charities would turn over its work on camping activities to the N.C.WC. and concentrate instead on dependency and family relief. In 1939 the National Conference of Catholic Charities passed a resolution looking toward "closer affiliation with the National Catholic Welfare Conference which, as the official organization of the hierarchy, must be the clearing house for all national Catholic organizations in the United States."[7] The reason expressed was the "desire for the guidance of the hierarchy in its work for the cause of Catholic Charity."[8] Nothing further was done, however, and since that time there would appear to be decidedly advantageous reasons for the traditional position of the National Conference of Catholic Charities. It can speak on its own in the many and varied relationships with the government and other private institutions. While this factor deprives it of a unanimous voice on many issues, there are those who consider that any arrangement which would destroy this advantage would be disastrous.

Probably one of the most significant achievements of the first twenty-five years was the identification of the National Conference of Catholic Charities with the movement for social reform. Despite a strong conservative bent among many of its supporters, the National Conference was true to the intentions of its founders and did not consider charity as relief-giving exclusively. The depression of 1929 tended to accentuate this part of the National Conference's program, and by 1935 the social consciousness had been awakened in many areas by the social and economic facts of the day and the National Conference's educational efforts in their field. Monsignor Marcellus Wagner, president of the National Conference in 1934, and director of Catholic charities in Cincinnati, could point out that "the measured success of the Conference had resulted primarily from a sincere effort to bridge the gap between economic laws and moral principles in response to the Divine commission given to the Church."[9] In 1935 Monsignor Wagner pointed to the achievements in social legislation and the National Conference's part in the achievement, holding that the National Conference should be the advance guard to promote the social and economic betterment which is the expressed desire of every citizen.[10]

The years from 1935 to 1950 saw an even greater emphasis on social legislation. The National Conference participated actively in the hearings on Social Security Act amendments, housing Bills, and child welfare programs. Monsignor O'Grady, one of the pioneers of the housing movement, played a major role in the shaping of legislation to carry out its objectives. Perhaps the greatest interest of the National Conference tended to concentrate on Social Security and child-welfare programs. Legislation in both these areas would profoundly affect the institutions of Catholic charities. Benefits based on rights and not on a needs test was the principle the National Conference supported in discussions on Social Security amendments. The unique role of the voluntary or religious institution or agency was defended vigorously and with much success in all debates on public child-welfare programs. The attempt on the part of those who would have liked to see the public agency absorb the private one was withstood.

In this activity there was a much closer alignment with Labor than there had been. There was a strong "labor tinge" to the Conference in the beginning, due largely to the influence of Monsignor Kerby, who had organized what became known as "Kerby Groups" on behalf of the interests of the workingman. Much of this interest had been secondary, however, to the need for organization and the establishment of social work standards of the early days. It was the common interest in housing on the part of labor and the National Conference that brought about a reunion of the two. Labor participation in the National Conference of Catholic Charities has been much greater since that time.

There was in the years 1935–1950 a swing away from professionalism in social work and a greater emphasis on the volunteer and the Society of St. Vincent de Paul. Part of this was the result of the effort to fight secularism in the field of charity and retain the proper Christian motive. To many it appeared that the pendulum had swung too far in the direction of technique, system, and organization. A new spirit in religious communities helped produce some of the better studies of the period such as Cecelia McGovern's *Services to Children in Institutions*.

This renewed emphasis on the spiritual mission of the Conference brought into focus again the parish and neighborhood organization as key areas of National Conference interest. Perhaps most significant, however, was the realization during this period, aided substantially by the impact of World War II, that the National Conference could not be true to its calling if it refused to enter the field of international charity. The process of self-examination that the National Conference engaged in during the early 1940's helped bring about a better understanding of the role of the Conference. The war had the effect of restoring a better perspective. The annual meeting in Brooklyn in 1944 was described as a " 'down to earth' affair . . . probably the most realistic meeting that has been held since the National Conference of Catholic Charities was organized in 1910."[11] It was the conclusion of *The Catholic Charities Review* that people were talked about as human beings and not as cases.[12] Despite protests in some quarters, Monsignor O'Grady carried the National Conference into the international arena where the problems of displaced persons presented a real challenge and where human needs were of staggering proportions in the post-World-War-II era. In some ways, the conditions of charity activities in the international field in the 1940's was not unlike the conditions in 1910. The International Conference of Catholic Charities established in 1951 had a task before it similar to that of the National Conference in 1910.

One of the problems of the years 1935–1950 arising from the expanding role of the Federal Government in public welfare was that often the responsibility for administration of the various programs rested with the states. There was a tendency to overlook this fact, and Bishop Le Blond called attention to it as early as 1938 when he pointed out that, "if Catholic leaders are to make their full contribution they must have a State-wide viewpoint, understand State-wide needs, and take a constructive and intelligent attitude toward State-wide programs."[13] His hope was that, "such participation will bring a new strength and vitality to public programs of social welfare."[14] By 1948, however, another aspect of this state administration of public welfare was becoming apparent. There were increasing complaints on the state level that it was difficult to deal with Catholic organizations.[15] State officials were complaining that there was no one to whom they could talk on a state-wide level. The diocesan organization of the Church and the local ordinary's authority in his own diocese gave the impression to state officials that Catholic charities had no plans or programs. The need for some solution to this problem remains a significant one.

Although all the major influences of the earlier periods still affected the life of the National Conference in the years from 1950 to 1960, two relatively new approaches to both its internal and external problems were adopted by the National Conference. These approaches were "integration" which militated against the Conference tendency to split into small groups partly as a result of growing specialization; and "subsidiarity" or the recognition of a hierarchy of responsibility for social problems beginning with the family and extending through the neighborhood and community before the government had any right to intervene. Both these approaches were developed largely as a result of the self-analysis of the Conference programs and services which were characteristic of the 1950's.

This self-analysis of the internal problems of the National Conference revealed what many of its members feared was a tendency for the Conference to become "made up principally of specialists dealing with individuals and families on a highly individual basis."[16] At the 1953 annual meeting, Reverend John J. Lennon, then assistant secretary of the National Conference of Catholic Charities, urged that effort should be made to revive "the old spirit of the National Conference of Catholic Charities which was characterized by meetings of priests, Religious and lay people who came together to discuss matters of mutual concern to all."[17] The request for a change, Father Lennon noted, was coming from the specialized groups who had come to realize that all were working toward the same objectives. The proper role of the National Conference was that of a "central thinking and planning organization" a role which it had neglected to an alarming degree.

The Buffalo meeting in 1956 showed a remarkable return to the art of group thinking. There was a recognition in the program of that meeting to give related fields like sociology, psychology, economics, political science, and anthropology their proper place in social work. There was hope that the multi-disciplined approach of the Buffalo Conference would be an example for the broader approach to social work. That such integration would bring certain criticism from those who enjoy a kind of parochialism was recognized by the Conference leaders. Monsignor Raymond J. Gallagher referred to this type of criticism as the kind by which "we are hampered, if not completely hobbled," and labeled the authors of such an attack as "short-sighted individuals" whose "negative approach to the problems of the Conference serves only to complicate the difficulty."[18]

To some extent, the schools of Social Work were blamed for this "splintering." Monsignor Fischer saw what he called a lack of "real organic unity between Catholic schools of social work and the vast variety of agencies and programs under Catholic auspices. We are sort of like good neighbors who will talk over the back-fence, but because of the fence we will not mix in each other's yards."[19] It was his opinion that the schools were "still too elective in their course content" but that by "developing a body of knowledge within the framework of Thomistic philosophy, the schools of social work could make a unique contribution to the entire field of social work education."[20]

The broader approach aimed at by the concept of integration envisioned the development of a "broad program of personal service on a neighborhood and parish basis" as well as a closer working relationship with all educational institutions.[21] One of the best examples of this type of neighborhood activity was the Work Conference on Problems of Juveniles sponsored by the National Conference and the Diocese of Cleveland in Cleveland in 1955. Monsignor Raymond J. Gallagher, who was largely responsible for the success of this Work Conference, hoped that it would result in more community self-help programs in the neighborhood. In this way Catholic charities could be of real service to those caught in shifting population trends in the cities and suburban areas. The development of regional conferences was part of the effort to respond to criticism that there was too much interest in city problems at the expense of the rural areas.

The 1957 annual meeting demonstrated the measure of success that had thus far been attained by the policy of integration. "It demonstrated the ability of all levels of Catholic Charities activity to see the important role of others in a common cause."[22] There was less evidence of isolation of the specialized groups and a common request for more of the same opportunity to exchange ideas.

The development of the idea of integration indicated that what The Catholic Charities Review called the "great pitfalls of Catholic Charities . . . self-sufficiency and pride of achievement" were being avoided in the wake of growing response to constructive criticism.[23]

This fact in addition to a more mature research activity as evidence in the National Conference's studies of the aged which, in addition to those already mentioned, now included a new one, *The Elderly of St. Rose of Lima Parish* (Washington, 1960), indicated the development of a more balanced program. The pendulum seemed to have slowed down considerably in its swing from volunteers to professional workers and back again, or in the oscillations between institutions and foster homes. The Conference seemed to be on its way to a more positive approach to social problems with its component elements finding their proper places.

The second major approach of the 1950's touched the external aspects of the National Conference's relations with public welfare programs sponsored by the government. The problem here was to stem the tide of secularism and make it possible for the voluntary agency to survive. At the 1956 annual meeting of the Conference in Buffalo, Monsignor Gallagher in speaking on this problem said,

> Our ready acceptance of the entrance of government into the area of human need may have created the monster of our own destruction unless we assert ourselves as to the rightful place of individual activity in this same field. . . . We must be vocal about this danger because we have seen in other areas the effect of government's entrance. . . . The tendency to quit when a government agency moves in must be identified for all mankind for what it really is — a naïve surrender. . . . Voluntary welfare service by agency and individually serves to maintain an alert, informed, active citizenry which in itself is a major weapon against social breakdown. . . . Integration — solidarity of thought and pronouncement — this is our great hope.[24]

This last point stressed the connection between integration and subsidiarity, for the forces of secularism could not be met with the specialized approach of many groups.

On his return from Europe in 1952, Monsignor O'Grady was "both impressed and saddened by the extent to which voluntary organizations in those countries have come to depend on the government."[25] This dependence had gone so far that voluntary organizations "are unwilling to undertake anything new without a government grant," and Monsignor O'Grady noted "situations in which church organizations look to government to maintain their cemeteries."[26]

The government threat to voluntary agencies in the United States had been growing since the passage of the Social Security Act in 1935, but in the 1950's it became acute. The fear of the National Conference leadership was that the loss of the original missionary spirit of the Conference might cause its failure in defending the voluntary institution. The voluntary institution's admiration for contemporary principles of social work had allowed it to become entrapped in a secularist approach itself by forgetting that many of the "modern" principles, such as respect for the individual, were Christian in origin.[27]

The emphasis, therefore, was to be on the family as the unit having basic responsibility for social welfare, with the neighborhood and community following in that order. The government's role was to assist, not to monopolize, and to intervene only when all else had failed. The proper working out of the principle of subsidiarity places great faith in the individual at the grass roots level. For this reason the Conference leadership tended to think of its future in terms of mass programs and the lay apostolate.

In 1910 the Conference membership had in a real sense been identified with the operation of the Conference. The 1920's began to mark a cleavage between the two. The 1950's witnessed an effort to return to the 1910 status. Therefore, Monsignor O'Grady declared,

> We must promote our Conference as part of a lay apostolate. The Conference is the spearhead of an apostolate in the United States. We must sell it more and more to the people in these terms. We must think of our Conference on a year-round basis, as a center for the promotion of an apostolate of Catholic Charities. We cannot therefore be satisfied with a small membership. We must enlist the services of people throughout the country who are willing to join with us in promoting our common apostolate. We must constantly remind people that this work cannot be done entirely on a social level.[28]

In this manner the National Conference was coming to recognize its lack of impact on the local level which had been characteristic for a number of years. The interests in children, the family, and the aging would remain the same, but greater importance was being laid on the role of the volunteer and the layman in the demand for a new type of community leadership in Catholic charities. The educational mission of the Conference had its work more clearly defined, and its participation in social movements more fully crystallized.

A pamphlet issued in 1952 by the National Conference of Catholic Charities to explain its function and purposes states in explaining the Conference's participation in social movements that,

> For forty-two years the National Conference of Catholic Charities has promoted the apostolate of the Church to the poor, the weak, the dependent, the distressed, the aged, and the sick. It brings Catholic influence and Catholic thought into the deliberations of national organizations and committees, and now, through membership in the International Conference of Catholic Charities, it will advise international instrumentalities such as the United Nations and will bring our thinking into these sessions. Thus the Conference carries on an important missionary objective which it has had from the beginning. The National Conference of Catholic Charities is a movement rather than an agency.[29]

This perhaps is the most succinct statement of the major role of the National Conference in Catholic Charities.

On the occasion of the Golden Anniversary Meeting of the National Conference of Catholic Charities in New York City, September, 1960, many of the addresses echoed thoughts that seemed reminiscent of the speeches at the first meeting in 1910. There was one major difference, however. In 1910 the call was for organization on the national level; in 1960 it was for more effective operation of Catholic charities on the local or community level.

Commissioner Ralph W. Whelan of the New York City Youth Board gave an address to the New York meeting in which he questioned the wisdom of allowing highly specialized programs of Catholic charities to be emphasized at the expense of broad programs designed for the masses at the neighborhood or community level.[30] Mr. Whelan was in favor of a greater balance in the programs of Catholic charities and reminded his audience that "as an American citizen, it is incumbent that the Catholic social worker understand that the true meaning of his 'charity' is a concern that transcends the limitations of sectarian service, which frees him to serve the total community even while serving his own."[31]

Monsignor O'Grady in his editorial notes in the Catholic Charities Review commented on the satisfaction Mr. Whelan's remarks gave him. They reaffirmed the position Monsignor said he himself had taken in the 1920's when, although criticized for not paying more attention to social work, he had insisted that his own participation in broad community social programs was symbolic of what Catholic leadership generally should be doing.[32] Monsignor O'Grady felt that it was the persistent spirit of the pioneers of the first decade of the Conference's history that enabled the Conference to be prepared to set up the broad social program necessitated by the economic dislocations of the 1930's. The Monsignor considered any departure from this pioneer spirit of social reform a serious problem for Catholic charities in the 1960's.[33]

The Most Reverend Lawrence J. Shehan, then Bishop of Bridgeport, Connecticut, elaborated on this theme of community service pointing out that in most dioceses there had been no real effort to coordinate all of the activities, movements, and organizations that the Catholic Church had developed to meet the problems of the modern age.[34] In fact, Bishop Shehan was convinced that modern developments in social welfare had brought about in many places an isolation of Catholic charities from the Catholic community generally.[35] The Bishop questioned whether the mass of information which Catholic charities had gathered on urban redevelopment, housing projects, unemployment problems, population mobility, new ethnic groupings, and the problems of the aged were being given sufficient consideration at the local level.

The remedies for the situation could not come simply from Catholic charities itself, according to Bishop Shehan. Rather, some formal and official direction was necessary. Accordingly, Bishop Shehan suggested that the bishop in each diocese give attention to the development of an integrated program of community welfare-related services and that knowledge of it be spread through appropriate seminary courses, junior-clergy examinations, and clergy conferences.

In order for the program to relate itself favorably to the local community agencies Bishop Shehan recommended that active participation of the laity be assured. This meant that for the laity, too, provision must be made for adequate knowledge and training. The Bishop warned against thinking that the coordination of all of the Church's activities into a program of community service was something that was achieved "once and for all; it is," he observed, "a continuing process which never ends."[36]

In many ways the personalities and backgrounds of some of the founders of the National Conference in 1910 characterized the history of the fifty years between 1910 and 1960. Bishop Shahan represented the approach of the scholarship and research necessary for the sound foundations of the movement. Monsignor Kerby also represents the scholarly approach but he is much more to be identified with the progress of social reform. In many ways, Monsignor O'Grady has carried on the Kerby tradition. Brother Barnabas and Thomas Mulry were men of action and represented the practical side of the Conference as well as the volunteer and layman's role. Each in his own way contributed to the formation of the character and personality of the National Conference. Monsignor Kerby's words to the members on the occasion of the twenty-fifth anniversary of the Conference looked both forward and backward and seem a fitting conclusion to the story of the first fifty years of the National Conference.

It is your mission now to have a large share in the shaping of Catholic thought, in insisting on the organic unity of the social classes, on the humanizing of industry and the adaptation of Catholic teaching at the low economic level. If you look outward and forward to your task as a whole you might well be dismayed. But if you wish for courage, for the consciousness of strength and the assurance of progress, look back to the timid days of 1910 and you will believe in miracles. Let us hope that 25 years hence, when another jubilee comes, your successors may find equal miracles in the progress that now lies beyond the hills of tomorrow. To that future you are now looking. You have the highest endorsement of the hierarchy and the confidence of the nation. You have ability, scholarship, numbers, experience, competent leadership and splendid organization, all of them sources of great strength.[37]

Notes — Chapter X

1. N.C.C.C. *Proceedings*, 1935, p. 64.
2. Reverend William J. Kerby, "The Mission of the National Conference of Catholic Charities," N.C.C.C. *Proceedings*, 1923, p. 14.
3. Monsignor O'Grady's remark to the author.
4. Conversation of Monsignor O'Grady with the author.
5. N.C.C.C. *Proceedings*, 1920, p. 377.
6. "Minutes of the Executive Committee of the N.C.C.C.," Sept. 26, 1921.
7. N.C.C.C. *Proceedings*, 1939, p. 247.
8. *Ibid.*
9. N.C.C.C. *Proceedings*, 1934, p. 18.
10. N.C.C.C. *Proceedings*, 1934, p. 18.
11. *Catholic Charities Review*, Dec., 1944, Vol. 28, No. 10, p. 261.
12. *Ibid.*
13. Most Reverend C. Hubert Le Blond, "Catholic Charities and Governmental Programs of Child Care," N.C.C.C. *Proceedings*, 1938, p. 45.
14. *Ibid.*
15. "Confidential Bulletin for Directors of Catholic Charities," Feb. 19, 1949.
16. *Catholic Charities Review*, Oct., 1952, Vol. 36, No. 8, p. 175.
17. N.C.C.C. *Proceedings*, 1953, p. 35.
18. Monsignor Raymond J. Gallagher, "A Wider Furrow in the Vineyard of Charity," N.C.C.C. *Proceedings*, 1956, p. 16.
19. *Catholic Charities Review*, Oct., 1957, Vol. 41, No. 8, p. 8.
20. *Ibid.*
21. *Ibid.*, Jan., 1957, Vol. 41, No. 1, p. 2.
22. *Ibid.*, Oct., 1957, Vol. 41, No. 8, p. 12.
23. *Ibid.*, Oct., 1952, Vol. 36, No. 8. p. 177.
24. Monsignor Raymond J. Gallagher, "A Wider Furrow in the Vineyard of Charity," N.C.C.C. *Proceedings*, 1956, p. 47.
25. *Catholic Charities Review*, Mar., 1952, Vol. 36, No. 3, pp. 54–55.
26. *Ibid.*
27. N.C.C.C. *Proceedings*, 1956, pp. 75–77.
28. N.C.C.C. *Proceedings*, 1951, p. 241.
29. "The National Conference of Catholic Charities," p. 5.
30. Ralph W. Whelan, "A New Dimension in Catholic Charities," *Catholic Charities Review*, Vol. 45, No. 1, Jan., 1961, p. 16.
31. *Ibid.*, p. 17.
32. *Catholic Charities Review*, Nov., 1960, Vol. 44, No. 9, p. 2.
33. *Ibid.*, pp. 2–3.
34. Bishop Lawrence J. Shehan, "Coordination of Diocesan Welfare-Related Agencies with Each Other and within the Community," *Catholic Charities Review*, Nov., 1960, Vol. 44, No. 9, p. 18.
35. *Ibid.*
36. *Ibid.*, p. 24.
37. N.C.C.C. *Proceedings*, 1935, p. 67.

Essay on Selected Bibliography

THIS essay on bibliography makes no attempt to list all the works pertaining to the subject of Catholic charities in the United States but rather gives only those which have a direct bearing on the history of the National Conference of Catholic Charities. An indispensable source for the record of the national meetings of the Conference is the *Proceedings* of the National Conference of Catholic Charities, issued biennially until 1920 and annually after that. The bound volumes are published by the Conference itself and contain a record of the addresses, discussions, and business proceedings of the national meetings. Of equal importance are the unpublished "Minutes of the National Conference of Catholic Charities Executive Committee," the title used to designate these minutes from the beginning to 1949. After 1949 the executive committee became the board of directors and the "Minutes" are so entitled after that date. These minutes contain the deliberations that usually preceded the annual meeting and touch all phases of the Conference's interests. Of some use also are the *Proceedings*, 1874–1916, of the National Conference of Charities and Correction.

The establishment of the diocesan directors as an integral part of the National Conference in 1916 made their deliberations important, and so the "Minutes of the Diocesan Directors of Catholic Charities" became a significant source of Conference history as did also the "Confidential Bulletin for Directors of Catholic Charities" issued by the National Conference Office beginning in 1935. The addition of the Conference of Religious in 1920 makes the "Proceedings of the Special Conference of Religious Engaged in Social and Charitable Work" also useful. All these materials are unpublished and available in the National Conference Office.

Other unpublished materials include the papers of Monsignor

Kerby, Bishop Shahan, and Monsignor Ryan available in the Archives of The Catholic University of America. Monsignor O'Grady, whose contact with the National Conference extends back to 1912, has embodied many of his views in the editorial portion of *The Catholic Charities Review*, the hearings before various Congressional committees on legislation on social security, housing, and public welfare, as well as the "Annual Report of the Secretary" of the National Conference of Catholic Charities. He has also published a history of *Catholic Charities* in the United States (Washington, 1930), *Introduction to Social Work* (New York, 1928), *The Catholic Church and the Destitute* (New York, 1929), and contributed Chapter III in F. Ernest Johnson (ed.) *Religion and Social Work* (Harper & Bros., 1956).

Necessary tools for general information are *The Official Catholic Directory, Directory of Diocesan Agencies of Catholic Charities* in the United States and Canada, first published in 1920, the *National Catholic Almanac*, and the *Directory of Catholic Institutions in the United States* first published by the N.C.C.C. in 1953.

The most important periodical literature is the Society of St. Vincent de Paul *Quarterly*, published from 1895–1916 which contains the writings of many of the pioneer leaders of the National Conference such as Thomas Mulry; it also is virtually the only literature of Catholic charities up to 1916. From 1917 on *The Catholic Charities Review* becomes the official organ of the National Conference. Newspapers are of only occasional use, and none is especially useful so far as the National Conference is concerned.

The publications of the National Conference in general pertain directly to the subject matter of Catholic charities rather than Conference history. Exceptions to this would be Monsignor John J. O'Grady, "The Charities Conference Takes Stock" (Washington, 1932), a reprint from *Catholic Action* for March, 1932; "Why the National Conference of Catholic Charities?" (Washington, 1940); "The National Conference of Catholic Charities" (Washington, 1952); "The Conference of Religious 1920–1957" (Washington, 1957).

Secondary works are not especially useful for the history of the

National Conference of Catholic Charities, most of them touching only briefly on related topics. An exception to this, however, is Luke Ebersole's work *Church Lobbying in the Nation's Capitol* (New York: Macmillan, 1951), which deals to some extent with the impact of the National Conference on social legislation. Other works of general interest are Robert H. Bremner, *American Philanthropy* in the Chicago History of American Civilization Series; Marguerite T. Boylan, *Social Welfare and the Catholic Church* (New York, 1941); Rev. Daniel T. McColgan, *A Century of Charity*, 2 vols. (Milwaukee: Bruce, 1951); William Norton, *The Cooperative Movement in Social Work* (New York: Macmillan, 1927); Frank D. Watson, *Charity Organization Movement in the United States* (New York: Macmillan, 1927); Arthur C. Millspaugh, *Public Welfare Organizations* (Brookings Institution, 1935); A. G. Warner, S. A. Queen, E. B. Harper, *American Charities and Social Work* (New York: Thomas Y. Crowell, 1942).

CONSTITUTION AND BYLAWS

OF THE

NATIONAL CONFERENCE OF CATHOLIC CHARITIES

Incorporated under the Laws of the District of Columbia

NATIONAL CONFERENCE OF CATHOLIC CHARITIES
Washington, D. C.

CONSTITUTION AND BYLAWS

OF THE

NATIONAL CONFERENCE OF CATHOLIC CHARITIES

PREAMBLE

Penetrated with the belief that each human being reflects the image of God, is something rare and unique, and is the focus of Christ's redemptive sacrifice, the National Conference of Catholic Charities strives to foster among Catholic workers, volunteer and professional, a supernatural motivation and inspiration, and a thoughtful and discriminating utilization of modern as well as traditional ways of exemplifying the charity of God toward our neighbor.

CONSTITUTION

ARTICLE I — Name

The name of this Conference shall be the National Conference of Catholic Charities.

ARTICLE II — Objects

This Conference shall provide a forum for discussing the application of Catholic thought in the general field of social welfare and shall stimulate action, research, and the publication of material in this field.

ARTICLE III — Eligibility for Membership

Any individual, organization, agency, or institution interested in the field of activity of the Conference is eligible for membership upon payment of dues.

ARTICLE IV — Officers and Organization

SECTION 1. The officers of the Conference shall be a president, five vice-presidents — one of whom shall be designated as first vice-president, a secretary, a treasurer, and an assistant treasurer. All of the officers shall be elected annually by the members of the Conference at its regular business meeting. They shall assume office immediately after the close of the public sessions of the Conference.

SECTION 2. Government of the Conference shall be vested in a board of directors (formerly the executive committee) which shall consist of the president, the vice-presidents, the treasurer, the secretary, and fifteen members, five of whom shall be elected by the members of the Conference each year, for a term of three years. Provided, that members serving on the executive committee at the time of the adoption of this section shall be members of the board of directors for the remainder of the terms for which elected for service on the executive committee.

SECTION 3. The board of directors shall meet at least twice a year and at other times upon the call of the president.

SECTION 4. A majority of the board of directors is necessary to constitute a quorum at any meeting of the Board.

SECTION 5. The board of directors shall exercise all of the power of the Conference not otherwise reserved.

ARTICLE V — Amendments

This Constitution and the Bylaws under it may be amended at the annual business meeting of the Conference by two thirds of the members voting, providing written notice of the proposed amendments be sent to the secretary at least two months prior to said meeting. The proposed amendment shall be published in the Catholic Charities Review or notification shall be sent, to all members of the Conference, at least one month before said meeting.

ARTICLE VI — Public Meetings

The Conference shall annually hold a public meeting.

BYLAWS

ARTICLE I — Permanent Headquarters

The Conference shall maintain permanent headquarters in Washington, D. C.

ARTICLE II — Duties of Officers

SECTION 1. The president shall be chairman of the board of directors and shall preside over the general sessions of the Conference.

SECTION 2. The president shall appoint, in consultation with the board of directors, persons to fill vacancies which may occur in any office or committee.

SECTION 3. In the event of the death of the president or his inability for any other reason to carry out his duties, the first vice-president shall discharge the regular duties of the president.

SECTION 4. The secretary shall be ex-officio member and secretary of the board of directors. He shall have charge of the office and records of the Conference and shall conduct all of its business subject to the general policies formulated by the board. Subject to these policies the secretary is authorized to incur all expenses necessary for the discharge of his duties. He is empowered to appoint such employees as he may deem necessary and to fix their compensation.

SECTION 5. The treasurer shall receive all monies of the Conference and disburse the same upon vouchers duly certified by the secretary. The accounts of the treasurer shall be audited annually.

ARTICLE III — Appointment of Committees

SECTION 1. The president, in consultation with the board of directors, shall appoint the following committees:

a) A Committee on Nominations to consist of seven members none of whom shall be members of the board of directors, whose duty it shall be to submit to the Conference at its next regular annual meeting nominations to all elective offices. Four members of the Committee on Nominations shall constitute a quorum. Members of the Conference may submit by mail suggestions for nominations to all offices. Notice to this effect shall be sent by the secretary to all members of the Conference immediately after the Committee on Nominations is appointed. Such recommendations shall be signed and shall in all cases state the experience and qualifications of the persons proposed.

b) A Program Committee to consist of such members of the Conference as will be representative of the several groups and activities of the Conference. The board of directors shall be empowered to draw up such rules and regulations concerning the number of members of which the Program Committee shall consist and tenure, as it decides is advisable and circumstances warrant, provided no member shall serve for more than three consecutive years. This Committee, subject to the approval of the board of directors shall be responsible for the program of the annual meeting. The Program Committee is empowered to enlist such assistance as in its judgment is appropriate. Five members shall constitute a quorum.

c) A Committee on Time and Place to consist of five members whose duty it shall be to make recommendations to the Conference at its annual meeting relative to the time and place of the meeting of the Conference for the ensuing year. Three members shall constitute a quorum.

d) A Committee on Resolutions to consist of five members, to which all resolutions shall be referred without debate. It shall submit its report at the closing session of the Conference. Three members shall constitute a quorum.

e) Only individual or supporting members of the Conference shall be eligible for elective offices and membership on committees.

SECTION 2. The president may appoint special and temporary committees as and when needed.

ARTICLE IV — Term of Office

The term of office of all officers shall be for one year, to begin immediately after the close of the public sessions during which they were elected.

ARTICLE V — Official Organ

The official organ of the Conference shall be the *Catholic Charities Review*.

ARTICLE VI — Membership

SECTION 1. There shall be five classes of membership — Individual, Institutional, Organization, Supporting, and Sustaining membership.

SECTION 2. Individual Membership. Any person contributing five dollars is classified as an individual member for one year.

SECTION 3. Institutional Membership. Any institution contributing twenty dollars is classified as an institutional member for one year.

SECTION 4. Organization Membership. Any organization contributing ten dollars is classified as an organization member for one year.

SECTION 5. Supporting Membership. Any individual contributing ten dollars or more shall be classified as a supporting member for one year.

SECTION 6. Sustaining Membership. Any Diocesan Bureau, Agency, or subdivision of a Diocesan Bureau or Agency, contributing a sum fixed equitably on a quota basis approved by the board of directors for a given year is classified as a sustaining member for that year.

SECTION 7. Any member institution or organization may designate a representative from its staff as an individual voting member of the Conference.

SECTION 8. An individual member shall receive a copy of the *proceedings* of the annual meeting of the Conference or a subscription to the *Catholic Charities Review*. All other members shall receive a copy of the *proceedings* of the annual meeting of the Conference and a subscription to the *Catholic Charities Review*.

October, 1957.

PRESIDENTS OF THE NATIONAL CONFERENCE OF CATHOLIC CHARITIES

1910–1928 Bishop Thomas J. Shahan
1929   Thomas J. Farrell, K.S.G., New York
1930   Thomas J. Farrell, K.S.G., New York
1931   Honorable William L. Igoe, St. Louis
1932   James F. Murphy, Detroit
1933   Monsignor Robert F. Keegan, New York
1934   Monsignor R. Marcellus Wagner, Cincinnati
1935   Monsignor R. Marcellus Wagner, Cincinnati
1936   Monsignor John J. Butler, St. Louis
1937   James F. Fitzgerald, Detroit
1938   Monsignor Thomas J. O'Dwyer, Los Angeles
1939   Miss Mary L. Gibbons, New York
1940   Monsignor John R. Mulroy, Denver
1941   Most Reverend Bryan J. McEntegart, New York
1942   Honorable G. Howland Shaw, Washington, D. C.
1943   Honorable G. Howland Shaw, Washington, D. C.
1944   Reverend William A. O'Connor, Chicago
1945   George J. Gillespie, New York
1946   Monsignor J. Jerome Reddy, Brooklyn
1947   Miss Florence M. Mason, Cleveland
1948   Reverend Joseph B. Toomey, Syracuse
1949   Monsignor J. Joseph Jacobi, New Orleans
1950   Edmond B. Butler, New York
1951   Monsignor Vincent W. Cooke, Chicago
1952   Monsignor Eugene A. Loftus
1953   Joseph P. Glaser, Detroit
1954   Joseph P. Glaser, Detroit
1955   George E. Heneghan, K.S.G., St. Louis
1956   Monsignor Floyd F. Fischer
1957   Monsignor Floyd F. Fischer
1958   Monsignor William L. Wozniak, Buffalo
1959   Monsignor William L. Wozniak, Buffalo
1960   Monsignor George H. Guilfoyle, New York

Index

Addams, Jane, 4

Aged, growing concern for, 137; and social security, 131; and Social Security Act, 137; studies of, 121, 190

Agencies, Catholic, lack of cooperation among, 159–160; Catholic, multiplication of institutions, 167; government welfare, 169; nonsectarian, cooperation with, 155; private, care for aged under social security, 137; private, defense of, 131; private, government aid to, 175; private, government purchase of service, 176–177; private, government threat to, 191; private, need for, 170; private, and relief problem, 131; private, stimulated by federal government, 134; public and institutional care, 164; public, nonsectarianism, 157

Agency, the private: defense of, 136; and health legislation, 141; threats to, 171

Alter, Archbishop Karl J., on Community Chests, 161

Associated Charities of Cleveland, 155

Barnabas, Brother, 182, 194; and Mulry, Thomas, 16; sponsorship of a National Catholic Conference, 16–17; on weaknesses of institutional care, 165

Biggs, Robert, 175, 176; advocates trained social workers, 55; opposes government aid, 175; and organized charity, 7

Binz, Archbishop Leo, 172

Bower, Janet, 121

Boyd, Dr. Beverley M., 158

Boylan, Marguerite, 97

Brace, Charles Loring, and foster-home placement, 5

Burke, Rev. John J., C.S.P., on Catholic group consciousness, 8

Butler, Edmond J., and organized Catholic charity, 7

Butler, Monsignor John J., on Community Chests, 162

Carr, Rev. John C., 100, 156, 161

Carter, Mrs. Thomas, 18

Case work, lack of discussion in parish conferences, 70; volunteer's understanding of, 69

Catholic Charities, cooperation with other agencies, 155; coordination of, 194; first meeting of, 20 ff; government control of, 135; institutional studies, 119–120; international scope of, 147; isolation in programs, 159; lack of contact with other charities, 15; need for full-time service, 48; and non-Catholic agencies, 19; obstacles to coordination, 43; secularizing influences on, 163

Catholic Charities, Diocesan: agencies of, 146; bureau of, 85, 88–92, 99, 146; bureau of, relations with volunteers, 71–72; bureau of, role of the pastor, 98; bureaus of, new problems in 1930's, 93–94; bureaus of, role in training volunteers, 69; director of, extent of authority, 87; director of, and laity, 43; directors of, 37, 38, 86, 136–137; directors of, and child welfare, 170; directors of, on immigration, 148; directors of, link between national and local levels, 86; directors of, and rugged individualism, 130; need for organization in, 35–36; opposition to centralization by, 36

Catholic Charities Review, 50 ff; controversy over content, 52–54; estab-